Guide to Law Enforcement Careers

Second Edition

by
Donald B. Hutton and
Anna Mydlarz

BARRON'S

For
Victoria Haley Hutton &
John Bradley Hutton

And in Memory of

Frank C. Hutton
Philadelphia Police Department

Ronald Donahue
New York State Police

In the Line of Duty

© Copyright 2001 by Barron's Educational Series, Inc.

Prior edition © copyright 1997 by Barron's Educational Series, Inc.

All inquiries should be addressed to:
Barron's Educational Series, Inc.
250 Wireless Boulevard
Hauppauge, New York 11788
www.barronseduc.com

Library of Congress Catalog Card No. 00-056452

International Standard Book No. 0-7641-1551-0

Library of Congress Cataloging-in-Publication Data

Hutton, Donald B.
   Guide to law enforcement careers / by Donald B. Hutton & Anna Mydlarz.—2nd ed.
      p.   cm.
   ISBN 0-7641-1551-0
   1. Police—Vocational guidance—United States.   2. Law enforcement—United States   I. Mydlarz, Anna.   II. Title.
HV8143.H87 2001
363.2'023'73—dc21   00-056452
                                                    CIP

PRINTED IN THE UNITED STATES OF AMERICA
9 8 7 6 5 4 3 2 1

CONTENTS

⬡ SECTION 1

CHAPTER 1

CHAPTER 2

CHAPTER 3

CHAPTER 4

⬡ SECTION 2

CHAPTER 5

CHAPTER 6

CHAPTER 7

⬡ SECTION 3

CHAPTER 8

CHAPTER 9

⬡ SECTION 4

CHAPTER 10

APPENDICES

DISCLAIMER

Every effort has been made to provide accurate and complete information in this guide, however, there may be mistakes made in the content due to changes in law enforcement policy or anticipated budgets, which may change without notice. Therefore, this book should be used only as a general guide to law enforcement careers, and not as the final and permanent information source.

PREFACE

THE NATURE OF LAW ENFORCEMENT EMPLOYMENT

In the first edition we made the following statement.

The United States needs law enforcement officers and always will; however, hiring trends vary from time to time. The current trend in law enforcement is exciting. It is anticipated that within the next five years thousands of municipal, state, and federal law enforcement officers will be hired at a record pace.

Guess what? It's still true—but the future has finally caught up with law enforcement hiring. That means that candidates have to embrace it. You must become computer friendly to enter into the search for a position and to be successful in a law enforcement career. In this edition, we have listed Internet sites for agencies. Some web sites have on-line hiring applications. Others allow you to send e-mail and ask the important questions. Law enforcement hiring is expected to continue at a moderate pace over the next four years.

However, the very nature of law enforcement employment is problematic. There is no national police force but there is a multitude of municipal, county, and state law enforcement agencies. Historically, all jurisdictions like the idea of having their own individual law enforcement entity to maintain law and order. Even the federal government maintains a separate law enforcement agency for each component or department. With all these separate entities, there are separate application processes, hiring procedures, and requirements. It is an admitted self-imposed maze of law enforcement networks. Not only do the agencies differ in appearance, but the hiring trends and requirements vary as well. In some agencies, education is the key to employment; in others, being a veteran or having real-world experience is the deciding factor. Depending on where you apply, your age and vision may bar you from employment; in other agencies and departments, these are not major factors. Some places have a high turnover; some do not. The main point is that the uniqueness and individuality of America's law enforcement agencies have made searching for a position an investigative process in which candidates not only have to make themselves desirable and qualified, but also have to find the actual agencies. To add to the complex situation is the fact that many agencies do not hire directly, but rely on civil service or federal employment centers to screen candidates.

The southern and western parts of the country, spurred by their economy, will continue to add law enforcement officers at a quick pace. In response to the overcrowding of our nation's jails and prisons, there has been increased funding to build new facilities, which will require hiring more corrections officers. On the federal side, agencies like the U.S. Border Patrol, the Federal Bureau of Investigation, and U.S. Customs, among a few, are expected to increase their ranks in response to federal mandates.

In the past, there has been binge hiring by law enforcement agencies, which has had disastrous results. During the 1970s and 1980s many large police departments lowered their admission standards, completed improper background checks on candidates, and shortened training in order to allow unprepared officers to fill the ranks. Certain cities were particularly embarrassed after numerous scandals and corruption investigations resulted from improper hiring practices. The general philosophy was: We have permission to hire. Let's not waste time—let's grab some bodies.

With these lessons in mind, police commissioners and administrators have learned that hiring law enforcement officers is a process involving time and increased standards. Now, larger departments are following the suburban departments in requiring college education for police officers. Cities like New York, Chicago, Dallas, and Los Angeles are now requiring at least two years of college or 60 credits to even apply. More than ever, individuals seeking law enforcement positions must be prepared and qualified for the selection process and know how and where to apply.

There is no official master list of law enforcement positions available or where to apply. This publication is intended to be used by anyone interested in law enforcement as a career, as well as those in the field who are looking for a change. We studied the research material, then we realistically compiled a guide of law enforcement agencies that are most likely to hire now or in the near future. Not all agencies are listed; some are too small or are, in fact, downsizing.

This guide was prepared to make candidates aware of the real possibilities that exist in the field of law enforcement.

Anna Mydlarz
Donald B. Hutton
September 2000

SECTION

Chapter 1

INTRODUCTION

HOW TO USE THIS BOOK

This book is designed to be a *user-friendly* guide to law enforcement positions. It is segmented into groupings that fit, such as municipal agencies, military agencies, state and federal agencies, etc. Part of the research for this book came from an information questionnaire that was sent to a multitude of agencies in which specific questions were asked in order to obtain a general picture of the information about the agencies. Many agencies participated and have personnel in active recruitment and public information offices who were more than willing to shed some light on their agencies. Whenever possible, a helpful hint or comment has been carefully included; however, readers are strongly encouraged to conduct follow-up research into the law enforcement agency or department in which they are interested. This book is divided into four sections:

SECTION 1 *Introduction*

This section examines law enforcement choices, common requirements, and opportunities to enhance one's background and résumé. In addition, opportunities involving college, internships, and the U.S. military are highlighted.

SECTION 2 *Police Officer and Deputy Sheriff Opportunities*

Large municipal police and sheriff departments are identified and opportunities are outlined. The departments' addresses, profiles, officer benefits, and department requirements are outlined.

State Law Enforcement Opportunities

The second part of this section profiles opportunities and information for state law enforcement agencies, including state police, highway patrol, environmental conservation, corrections, college campus, probation, parole, and attorney general agencies offices. Agencies that can assist law enforcement officers with specific lateral transfer information and requirements are also identified.

How to Apply for Municipal Police, Deputy Sheriff, and State Law Enforcement Positions

This part of the section outlines the general application process at the city, county, and state levels. It further identifies state civil and personnel departments that may act both as recruiters and hiring agents for various law enforcement agencies. Sample law enforcement résumés and cover letters are presented as examples.

SECTION 3 *Federal Law Enforcement Opportunities*

An extensive listing of federal law enforcement agencies and numerous positions are provided here. The mission of the agencies, anticipated positions, requirements, and where to apply are outlined.

How to Apply for Federal Law Enforcement

This part of the section describes the federal application process and includes the new Optional Form 612 (known as the OF-612), the SF-171, and federal résumé. Federal pay scales and federal employment information centers (FEIC) are listed.

SECTION 4 *Special Law Enforcement Listings*

This section profiles special law enforcement agencies: Airport, Authority, Harbor, Railroad, and Transit Police Departments. Also listed are: law enforcement publications, associations, and research organizations.

Throughout this book, organizational charts of law enforcement agencies and departments have been included to provide the reader with a description of how the agency looks and operates. In the federal chapters the organizational charts also show the interconnectedness of the agencies to one another.

AGENCY LISTINGS All law enforcement agencies in this book are highlighted in a special listing format that displays the key information of the agency so that the reader can determine the agency's profile, its requirements, where to apply, and the actual opportunities that exist.

Throughout this book, agencies that have the best opportunities will be highlighted by a star ✪. Lateral transfers for nonresidents will be indicated by ➤.

SAMPLE AGENCY LISTING

NEW YORK

**New York City
Police Department**
One Police Plaza
New York, NY 10038
(212) 374-5000

Anticipated Positions ✪ Up to 3,000

Profile of Department
Sworn Officers: 38,328
Population: 7,380,906

Officer Benefits
Starting Salary: $34,970
Retirement: 20 years
Medical/Dental: Yes
Educational: Yes

Department Requirements
Age: 22 (minimum)
Education: 60 college credits
Vision: 20/30 corrected
20/100 uncorrected

Nonresidents ✔ Yes
Lateral Transfers No
Comments Veterans receive credit in place of college requirement.

Where to Apply
New York City
Police Department
Recruitment Section
4 Auburn Place
Brooklyn, NY 11205
(212) RECRUIT

Web *www.nyc.ny.us*

SPECIAL NOTE ON EMPLOYMENT OPPORTUNITY BLOCK		
Nonresidents:	YES	means candidates may take the test but must move to the jurisdiction before appointment.
	NO	means only residents of the jurisdiction may take the exam.
Lateral Transfers:		Agency will consider a transfer of an experienced law enforcement officer from another agency. Several factors are involved: 1. Age, vision, and medical requirements. 2. Previous training. Officer training must meet the specific agency's requirements and the state certification board's level. 3. Law enforcement record. The officer must have a solid law enforcement career with good service time.

ANTICIPATED POSITIONS: PLANNING FOR THE FUTURE

Law enforcement hires in waves. For instance, in the 1960s a large group of law enforcement officers started their careers. In the 1980s, many of them retired, and a new group replaced them. Now, 20 years later, a new group is about to enter. Will you be with them? Throughout this book you will note agencies that have relayed their "anticipated positions." The agencies' planners have a formula of factors that have given them an anticipated amount of new personnel to be hired for their department or agency. The rationale is to keep the agency at a certain level of manpower in order to handle the mission. Planners have to consider the number of officers retiring each year and the time it will take to test, process, hire, and train new personnel to fill the ranks. Finally, and most important, is the budget for the new personnel. To help plan, agencies were asked to provide a number of anticipated positions for the next four years. Therefore, you, as a possible candidate, can begin the process now, targeting agencies that are looking to hire many new officers over the next four years. Remember, it takes time to go through the hiring maze at some agencies, also it allows you time to enhance your background to be better qualified for consideration.

ANTICIPATED POSITIONS FIGURES FOR ALL AGENCY LISTINGS IN THIS BOOK ARE FOR THE YEARS 2000–2004. ALL ARE BASED ON AGENCY RESPONSES.

✪ BEST OPPORTUNITIES: A FEW SELECTED AGENCIES

Some agencies are downsizing due to economic factors and will not be filling the departing ranks. Some agencies cannot predict when and if they will be hiring due to budget factors. Many agencies, however, have received special funding and will be hiring in huge groups in the near future. Below are a few selected agencies with outstanding career opportunities:

Agency	Anticipated Positions (2000–2004)
New York City Police Department	✪ Over 3,000 Police Officers
Chicago Police Department	✪ Over 2,000 Police Officers
Los Angeles Police Department	✪ Over 1,000 Police Officers
California Corrections Department	✪ Over 3,000 Corrections Officers
U.S. Border Patrol	✪ Over 3,000 Border Patrol Agents
Federal Bureau of Investigation (F.B.I.)	✪ Over 1,000 Agents
U.S. Customs	✪ Over 1,000 Inspectors

LAW ENFORCEMENT CHOICES

What Type of Law Enforcement Career Do You Want?

Your interest in seeking a law enforcement position can be a complex investigation that you may find thrilling and time consuming at the same time. You will find clues on where and how to obtain a law enforcement position throughout this book; first however, you have to make a choice.

According to the U.S. Department of Justice there are over 12,500 general purpose local police departments, 3,086 sheriff's departments, 49 primary state police departments, and 1,721 special police agencies in the United States, as well as over 70 federal law enforcement agencies.

Which agency or department do you want to work for? While you may only think you want to work for one particular agency, you should consider other options. There are thousands of law enforcement officers who applied at one place and were finally hired at another. Being a police officer is only one entry position in law enforcement. How about being a Border Patrol Agent, or a Conservation Officer? If becoming a uniformed officer does not interest you, there are many entry-level investigator positions in several federal agencies and departments.

Years ago, we both chose to enter law enforcement; however, our decision and actually becoming a law enforcement officer did not happen at the same time. First, we had to gain experience and education so that we could become attractive candidates to the law enforcement administrators who do the actual hiring. You have to decide one thing first: What type of law enforcement job do you want to do? The following table gives you a picture of each possible selection.

MUNICIPAL AND COUNTY LAW ENFORCEMENT	
Positions	**Basic Mission**
Police Officer (municipal)	The uniform officer on patrol is a "generalist" who maintains law and order and arrests violators.
Deputy Sheriff	Performs the same duties as municipal police officers with the added responsibility of maintaining a county jail.
County District Attorney Investigator	Conducts case and background investigations for the county district attorney.

STATE LAW ENFORCEMENT POSITIONS	
Positions	**Basic Mission**
State Trooper	Conducts statewide patrol; maintains law and order.
Highway Patrol Officer	Patrols state highways, conducting traffic and performing general law enforcement duties.
University Police Officer College Public Safety	Maintains law and order on state university or college campuses or properties.
Conservation and Wildlife Officer	Patrols the outdoors for violations of wildlife and natural resources.
Park Police	Patrols state parks and reservations.
Corrections Officer	Maintains the custody, security, and well-being of inmates in state correctional facilities.
Parole Officer	Provides supervision and guidance to an assigned case load of releasees from state and local correctional facilities.
Attorney General Investigator	Conducts specialized case background and criminal investigation for the state attorney general's office.

FEDERAL LAW ENFORCEMENT POSITIONS	
Positions	**Basic Mission**
Border Patrol Agent	Protects the U.S. border from illegal entry by aliens.
Federal Police Officer	Maintains protection of employees and property of designated federal agency.
Federal Corrections Officer	Maintains safekeeping, care, and protection of federal inmates.
Federal Parole Officer	Maintains supervision and guidance of federal releasees.
Federal Protection Officer	Maintains protection of federal buildings nationwide.
Postal Inspector	Conducts investigations of postal crimes.
DEA Special Agent	Enforces laws and regulations involving narcotic and controlled substances.
Deputy U.S. Marshall	Provides protection for U.S. courts and judges; apprehends federal fugitives; transports federal prisoners.

FEDERAL LAW ENFORCEMENT POSITIONS (continued)	
Positions	**Basic Mission**
Postal Police Officer	Protects postal employees and property.
IRS Agent	Conducts criminal investigations involving tax laws.
Customs Inspector	Enforces laws governing the importation of merchandise, including the inspection of persons and carriers.
Immigration Inspector	Prevents ineligible people from entering the United States.
FBI Special Agent	Investigates violations of federal criminal law; protects the United States from foreign intelligence activities.
Secret Service Agent	Protects the president and other dignitaries; investigates threats against them; investigates counterfeiting crimes.
U.S. Park Police Officer	Patrols and protects U.S. parks; maintains law and order in parks.
U.S. Park Ranger	Patrols and protects U.S. parks and reservations from harm.
ATF Special Agent	Investigates criminal use of firearms and explosives; enforces federal alcohol and tobacco regulations.
Intelligence Officer	Gathers and analyzes intelligence; engages in covert and overt operations.
Inspector General Investigator	Conducts investigations into allegations of waste fraud and abuse of government resources.
Inspector General Auditor	Conducts audits involving allegations of waste fraud and abuse of government resources.

MILITARY LAW ENFORCEMENT POSITIONS	
Positions	**Basic Mission**
Military Police Officer	Patrols and polices assigned military facilities, ships, and bases.
Law Enforcement Officer	Administrative position; supervises and conducts investigations involving military personnel.
Intelligence Officer	Gathers intelligence and conducts analysis; conducts covert and overt operations.

SPECIAL LAW ENFORCEMENT AGENCIES	
Positions	**Basic Mission**
Airport Police Officer	Polices and maintains order on airport property and grounds.
Authority Police Officer	Polices specific authority jurisdiction.
Harbor Police Officer	Conducts land and water patrols of harbor for illegal activities.
Railroad Police Officer	Patrols and protects railroad property; prevents trespassing.
Transit Police Officer	Patrols and protects property and public use of the transit system.

SPECIAL CONSIDERATIONS IN CHOOSING A LAW ENFORCEMENT POSITION

Deciding what position you want is setting only one part of your parameter; you should also ask yourself several questions before you accept a position with a law enforcement agency that is not near your present home.

1. *Where do you want to work?*
   Where are you willing to work? Not everyone can simply pick up and move. If you have a family, it must be a family decision. Anyone considering a position in a distant location with which they are not familiar should conduct their own research into the prospective area before accepting a position there.

2. *What is the cost of living?*
   Can you afford the position? Some law enforcement positions pay very little on entry in high-cost areas such as California or New York. Take a trip to visit the area first and check out the real estate prices, rentals, and prices on everyday items. Can you afford to live there on the salary being offered?

3. *If you have children, are there good schools in the new location? Are there adequate health services?*
   A U.S. border patrol agent's first duty station is along the Texas-Mexico border in remote areas where schools, community services, and hospitals are sometimes less than standard (no offense intended to the areas). Be aware of these conditions before making your decision to move there.

4. *Are you ready for travel and reassignments?*

Military law enforcement officers may be transferred throughout the world several times during their careers, which means there may be a possibility of living on military bases until retirement. Unlike municipal and county law enforcement officers, who basically work and live within their jurisdiction, federal law enforcement officers may be in a position where they have to travel extensively. And, like military law enforcement officers, they are often subject to reassignment.

5. *Are you ready for the responsibility?*

Being a law enforcement officer means more than carrying a badge and gun. For the most part, the duties and responsibilities are a significant burden that individuals must accept for their conduct both on and off duty, 24 hours a day. It is a job that changes people for better or worse. Some positions are very trying in law enforcement; others are less difficult. For that reason, the decision to pursue a particular position must be well thought out and planned in advance.

6. *Is this an agency with a future?*

Smaller agencies usually remain that way—small, meaning the opportunity for advancement may also be very small. Larger agencies have special units or squads that allow officers the opportunity to gather specialized experience as well as the possibility of promotion at a higher rate. However, some large cities are on a decline, especially in the Northeast. Is it possible the city you are applying to may actually lay off officers? Currently, the southwestern part of the nation is prospering; therefore, departments in that region may actually double their personnel in the next four years. Is it possible that the advance track is quicker in those agencies? While this guide has conducted the primary research for you, before you make your final decision, check out the agency's history, status, and local news articles to give you a clearer picture of the situation in various parts of the country.

7. *What are the benefits?*

I am reminded of an old New York City PBA advertisement that depicted a dark, scary alleyway and had the following caption: "You won't go in there for a million bucks . . . a cop does for a lot less . . . ." While the overall pay standards have improved over the years, be aware that you will not get rich in a law enforcement position. For the most part, however, law enforcement officers do have a wide range of benefits. They vary from agency to agency, but most offer some or all of the following:

- Health and dental insurance
- Life insurance
- Paid holidays
- Paid vacations

- Sick leave
- Family illness leave
- Bereavement leave
- Uniform allowance (if applicable)
- Educational assistance programs
- Retirements from 20 to 30 years

OPTIONS FOR CURRENT
LAW ENFORCEMENT OFFICERS

Many of you reading this book—if you are not already law enforcement officers—may not fully understand why anyone who is currently working in law enforcement may be looking for a new job. There are a wide variety of good reasons why a current law enforcement officer may and should consider a change of assignment and employment, such as:

- Poor salary base
- Little or no medical or dental benefits
- No educational benefits
- Limited promotion range; poor career-ladder opportunities
- High cost areas that eat away hard-earned dollars
- Too high housing costs
- High taxes
- Poor quality of life in the area of current employment
- High crime areas in the currently employed location
- Poor school systems in the current location
- Poor retirement plan
- Poor position satisfaction

As we compiled this guide, we made sure to consider that current law enforcement officers may wish to consider new positions for many of the reasons outlined above. The two main options officers may wish to consider are:

Lateral Transfers

These are moves from one municipal or state department to another that allow an experienced/trained law enforcement officer to join with service toward retirement or other incentives. We compiled several opportunities in this guide for officers to consider.

Transfer From a Municipal Agency
to a State or Federal Agency

Officers should note that most federal law enforcement agencies require education or experience in order to qualify for various positions.

The experience that you have acquired will give you a tactical edge in a multitude of state and federal positions in law enforcement; however, one word of caution: Officers should avoid being tagged with a transient officer stigma. If your law enforcement résumé is filled with short-term placements, you will give the impression that you can't hold a job, or there must be a reason for your constant movement.

RETIRED OFFICERS:
SECOND RETIREMENT OPPORTUNITIES

Retired law enforcement officers should consider a second career in a different retirement system. The "double dip" cannot only allow you continued enjoyment in a career you are trained for, but may also provide you with an outstanding total retirement package. Many officers retire from the municipal, state, or federal law enforcement position after 20 years and are still young enough to enter another department or agency and receive a dual retirement. Municipal law enforcement officers are usually in the state system, so going to a state law enforcement agency may affect the retirement you have already earned. With that in mind officers may wish to consider the following options:

Scenario 1

Officer O'Brien retires from a Municipal Police Department with a 20-year retirement and lands a position as a special agent with a Railroad Police Department. After ten years he has secured a federal retirement, as railroad retirements are administered by the U.S. Railroad Retirement Board.

Scenario 2

U.S. Border Patrol Agent Smith retired from her federal law enforcement position. She joined a state police agency and was able to secure a state retirement.

Scenario 3

U.S. Coast Guard Chief Petty Officer Thompson took a series of local law enforcement exams in the south Florida area during his last year of duty before retiring with 20 years of service. One of the departments hired him two weeks after his U.S. Coast Guard retirement.

Scenario 4

A State Corrections Officer decides that the opportunities may be better with the Federal Bureau of Prisons. After he was vested in the state system, he began the application process for the federal position and was able to enter service with the federal prison system.

Chapter 2

GENERAL LAW ENFORCEMENT

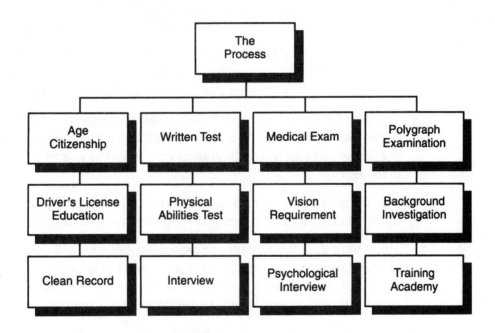

COMMON THREADS

Law enforcement is paramilitary in nature regarding operation and function so it should be no surprise that the selection process is strict, rigid, and complex, leaving many candidates stymied. Typically, candidates must successfully complete several steps of the selection process before they can be considered for appointment as law enforcement officers. These steps include a written test, interview, medical examination to include vision testing and urinalysis, written psychological test, extensive background investigation, physical abilities test, and a psychological interview.

The completed selection process could take several weeks or months, depending on the agency's procedures, needs, and urgency. Candidates must satisfactorily complete each step in the selection process before being scheduled for the next step.

When openings occur, law enforcement agencies try to fill each job with a person who is well qualified, has an interest in the job, and who will be committed to a career with them. It is a large investment for a law enforcement agency to train candidates. Law enforcement officers are required to perform a wide range of duties. While their past learned skills and background may help in handling these duties, law enforcement officers must be trained to handle specific duties.

GENERAL LAW ENFORCEMENT DUTIES

The general duties of law enforcement officers are universal. They require the dynamics of communication, knowledge, understanding, and maturity. Some of the general duties of law enforcement officers are:

- Filling out forms, logs, and reports; which requires good written skills. The ability to write legibly and clearly and have a good working knowledge of English grammar, vocabulary, and spelling is mandatory.

- Testifying accurately and credibly in court regarding arrests, reports taken, evidence recovered, and victims' statements.

- Employing excellent listening skills—in person and on the telephone. The officers must listen closely to what is being said and retain that information, identifying needs and emotions being expressed and demonstrating interest and involvement.

- Dealing with all segments of society. Some members of the general public may be hostile toward law enforcement officers and may express that hostility. A law enforcement officer must always behave professionally in the face of provocation.

- Evaluating situations, determining whether a crime has taken place, and making an independent decision about what action is appropriate. In doing so, the officer must consider numerous factors, recognize patterns, and develop theories based on available information and evidence.

- Paying attention to detail, noticing minute elements or components of a particular person or crime scene. Officers must also be able to visualize and recall an event after the fact in order to reconstruct documentation of the event, for possible future court testimony. Officers must also recognize and gather evidence at the scene of a crime, and are responsible for the safe storage and transportation of the evidence.

- Learning and remaining current with large quantities of complex and detailed material, including penal codes, legal terms, procedures and policies, and laws of arrest, search and seizure, evidence, and the like.

- Developing problem-solving and reasoning skills in order to initiate innovative solutions to difficult and unique problems they must face while on duty.

- Resolving citizen conflicts such as business, neighbor, family, and traffic-related disputes. Officers must separate the parties involved, interview them, try to calm them, and mediate a solution to the problem. These disputes can be loud, emotionally charged, combative, and time consuming.

- Monitoring and controlling crowds at scenes where tensions may run high, such as picket lines and demonstrations.

- Observing crowd behavior and communicating with group leaders to keep peace and order.

- Exhibiting leadership by taking control of situations, inspiring confidence, delegating tasks, and providing a positive example for others.

- Using their interpersonal skills to calm distraught persons, subdue angry or combative persons, and coax uncooperative persons into cooperating and providing information.

CONDITIONS OF LAW ENFORCEMENT EMPLOYMENT

Law enforcement officers must be able to work under a great deal of pressure, while maintaining a clear head and a positive work ethic. They deal with a multitude of people under a wide variety of situations. They must be open-minded, fair, unbiased, and sensitive in order to deal with people of diverse backgrounds, cultures, and lifestyles. Depending on the agency operation, they may or may not work with a partner.

Officers may work any hour of the day, all days of the week, including holidays. Schedules are subject to change, and often overtime is required. They must be adaptable and willing to adjust to frequent compulsory changes in work shifts, travel, work locations, and other factors. They are also symbols of stability and trust and are expected to behave ethically and resolve moral conflicts appropriately, both on and off the job.

Law enforcement officers may be involved in numerous physically demanding activities throughout the work shift. These may include the pursuit of suspects in a vehicle or on foot, walking foot patrol for up to eight hours, physically subduing, detaining, and arresting sometimes combative suspects, physically searching suspects, performing rescues by dragging or carrying victims, first aid procedures, and controlling crowds. They must be able to use firearms in a proficient manner. Officers are required to prove their proficiency with firearms by qualifying periodically. They also must:

- Be able to respond to calls for help by using directional information such as north-south, left-right, etc.

- Work in all locations, under all types of conditions, with all types of people. Officers may be required to search and/or touch suspects who are dirty, neglected, injured, or bleeding. They may also be required to enter buildings or establishments that are unsanitary or structurally unsound.

- After establishing probable cause, detain and/or take suspects into custody. This involves using approved techniques and equipment such as verbalization, control holds, batons, guns, and handcuffs to physically subdue suspects while treating them with as much dignity as possible and using the minimum force necessary.

GENERAL LAW ENFORCEMENT REQUIREMENTS

With the above general duties in mind, the rationale for certain requirements from candidates becomes clear. Listed below are a somewhat universal list of law enforcement requirements, however, every agency has its own set of qualification standards. Candidates should use the following only as a guideline and contact each agency directly for exact requirements, which vary and change with time.

AGE   For most law enforcement positions, you must be at least 21 years of age at the time of appointment, the most notable exception being the military (age 18) and the Federal Bureau of Investigation (age 23). Many, however, will allow you to take the exam and begin the application process between the ages of 18 and 21 years of age. Most agencies realize that candidates have an age window of opportunity and allow them to participate as early as possible. If you are currently in the military or in college, take the exams now for the agencies or departments in which you are interested. You will be on the list for years and may cut down on the waiting time for the rest of the process. Remember, many agencies allow you to take the exam before you are old enough to be appointed to the law enforcement position. In addition, many agencies have a narrow window of time for consideration. For example, if you wish to join some police departments, you have to be hired between the ages of 20 and 29 years of age. The NYPD, however, allows candidates to take the test at the age of 19 so they have additional time to experience the process. The same situation exists with federal law enforcement agencies, with their window usually being between 21 to 37 years in age. It is important to note that challenges to the age rule continue every year so many agencies vary their requirement.

CITIZENSHIP For the most part, U.S. citizenship is required prior to employment, however, some law enforcement agencies have made provisions for noncitizens. Generally, noncitizens must have applied for citizenship before they apply for law enforcement employment. Proof of citizenship is required during the selection process. Failure to provide such proof may lead to disqualification from the process.

DRIVER'S LICENSE Most law enforcement agencies require a valid driver's license and, more notably, a clean driving record. A poor driving record can reflect on your suitability for law enforcement work.

EDUCATION Most law enforcement agencies require a high school education from a U.S. high school or GED equivalent from a U.S. institution, however, the new trend is the requirement of at least 60 credits of college from an accredited U.S. college or university.

RESIDENCY The general rule for most municipal and state law enforcement agencies is that you must legally reside in the jurisdiction in which you are going to serve before you are appointed. Further, many municipal and state law enforcement agencies give credit with extra hiring points for being a resident. Larger municipal and state agencies allow for out-of-towners to take part in their selection process in order to increase their pool of qualified candidates. Smaller municipal agencies and state agencies are more selective due to the low number of possible openings, and are more sensitive to the resident-first rule. Federal agencies do not maintain a residency requirement, but there are some rare situations due to station assignments.

WRITTEN TESTS Most law enforcement agencies require candidates to pass a written test, and they are rated on their ability to pass these exams. The written test is usually a multiple-choice test designed to measure reading comprehension, English usage, and possibly an essay that can measure candidates' writing and communication skills. Only a few candidates will be picked for the remainder of the hiring process based on the test scores. You must at least overcome this first hurdle. The bottom line is simple, *you must become an expert test taker.*

How do you become an expert test taker? Practice, practice, and more practice. Study how to take these type of exams. There are a wide variety of study guides and books on how to take law enforcement exams. If you are serious, locate a testing instruction course either at a local college or educational center. There are also several private agencies that will teach you to take exams. When you are comfortable with taking exams, apply to take several tests for a variety of positions (whether you want the job or not). But make sure that they are similar in style or content to the law enforcement exam that you might eventually take.

We recommend that you study *How to Prepare for the Police Officer Examination* by Donald Schroeder and Frank Lombardo (NYPD), Barron's Educational Series, Inc., 250 Wireless Blvd, Hauppauge, NY 11788, telephone: (631) 434-3311.

PHYSICAL ABILITIES TEST

One of the toughest challenges for law enforcement candidates is the physical requirement of the Physical Abilities Test. Because of the physical demands of law enforcement work in the field, there is a great deal of importance placed on physical conditioning. As part of the general requirement process to obtain law enforcement positions, candidates are required to pass the Physical Abilities Test, which typically and currently consists of five areas designed to measure endurance, strength, and agility. The Physical Abilities Test rates candidates according to their quickness or ability to accomplish several of the following measures:

- *Cardiovascular Test*
  Endurance Run: Candidates must run as many laps as possible within a set time on a mile track for points. This is related to a law enforcement officer running after a suspect for four or five minutes.

- *Agility Test*
  Wall Scale: Candidates must run several yards, then scale a smooth six-foot wall, scoring points for the time elapsed. Other versions may include climbing a wooden or chainlink fence, or sidesteps.

- *Speed Test*
  90-yard run: Candidates must run the 90-yard dash within a specified time.

- *Endurance Test*
  Grip: Candidates must maintain an overhand grip on a chinning bar for a specified length of time.

- *Strength Test*
  Weight Drag: Candidates must be able to drag a dead weight over 100 pounds for a specified distance.

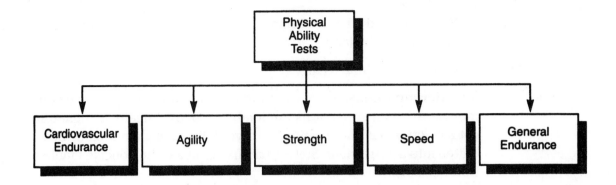

It is important to note that passing these tests indicates only the *minimum* level of fitness usually required to begin law enforcement academy training. If you are unable to perform any one of these exercises, you should initiate a regular physical fitness program to prepare yourself for the academy. Before beginning, it is recommended that you receive a medical examination from your own physician. Remember, you do not achieve excellent physical fitness overnight and it does take physical and mental effort.

Physical Abilities Classes

Many large law enforcement agencies maintain physical abilities classes to assist candidates in preparing for the Physical Abilities Test. Female candidates are especially encouraged to participate in this program since physical tests are historically designed by men for men. Physical training classes should be of special interest to all candidates who need help to prepare. If you are unsure of your ability, test it before it counts against you. If you need to practice, it is obviously beneficial to practice with those people who are going to give you the test.

THE INTERVIEW The interview process usually involves a panel of veteran law enforcement officers and possibly a personnel representative who ask the candidates several questions designed to test problem-solving skills, respect for diversity, role adaptability, and personal accomplishments.

Hints for the Interview

- Practice with others. Have a family member or friend conduct a mock interview.

- If possible, videotape your practice interview. Note any behavior that reflects nervousness, such as foot tapping, arm crossing, fidgeting, etc.

- Men should wear a business suit, white shirt and tie, and polished shoes.

- Women should wear a business suit, and polished flat shoes; they should leave the large purse at home and avoid flashy jewelry.

- Arrive a few minutes early.

Interview questions are designed to put you to the test, so use common sense. Some questions are loaded and specifically designed to get a reaction out of the candidate. Avoid displaying emotion or being baited into an argument. State your answer in a clear, concise manner. Don't be surprised if you hear:

- Why do you want to be a law enforcement officer? (To help people.)

- Would you give your mother or brother a ticket for running a stop sign? (Be realistic. You would not, but you would politely ask them to obey the law and not put you on the spot.)

VISION Next to the maximum age limits set, no other requirement causes more heartache than the vision requirement. You have a great deal of control over other requirements such as education and experience, but you are born with a certain vision. For the most part, law enforcement officers must have distance visual acuity no worse than 20/200 uncorrected, and corrected to 20/20. Vision requirements may vary depending on the corrective measures used, the position sought, and what part of the country is involved. Waivers may be granted if you have worn soft contact lenses for at least six months by the date of the physical examination. You must have normal functional color vision. Candidates who have had refractive surgery (surgery on the cornea), also called radial keratotomy, may be subject to denial from consideration for a period of time from the date of surgery or they may be disqualified. Candidates with functional monocular vision due to vision loss or strabismus (inability to focus both eyes on the same subject) may be subject to medical disqualification.

MEDICAL EXAMINATION Law enforcement officers must be in excellent health with no physical conditions that would restrict the ability to perform all the functions of the position. A designated physician usually conducts the medical examination to determine whether the candidate meets the medical standards of the agency.

PSYCHOLOGICAL INTERVIEW Candidates are interviewed and evaluated by a psychologist using psychological parameters related to successful performance to determine if the candidate is currently suited for the difficult and stressful job of a law enforcement officer.

POLYGRAPH   The polygraph examination is a process in which the candidate is physically connected to a polygraph machine (lie detector) while answering a series of questions about such things as:

- the application information
- prior employment
- possible alcohol and drug abuse
- the candidate's economic situation
- possible criminal activities

The polygraph is not without controversy; many in law enforcement doubt its effectiveness in determining a candidate's background, but it is currently in use at many levels of law enforcement for employment and investigative applications.

BACKGROUND INVESTIGATION   Felony convictions or any misdemeanor conviction that would preclude the candidate's carrying a gun can bar that candidate from law enforcement employment. In addition, a history of criminal or improper conduct, poor employment or poor military record, or a poor driving record that may affect the candidate's suitability for law enforcement work can also affect possible employment. Candidates must also have a responsible financial history and a pattern of respect and honesty in dealings with individuals and organizations.

All law enforcement candidates are fingerprinted and photographed. The investigative phase of the background process requires a thorough check of police records and personal, military, and employment histories, as well as field reference checks. Candidates are evaluated by: respect for the law, honesty, mature judgment, respect for others, employment record, military record, financial record, driving record, and use of drugs and intoxicants. All candidates are required to submit comprehensive biographical information prior to their background investigation interview. Failure to provide complete and accurate information could result in disqualification.

ACADEMY/ TRAINING   After being appointed, all local, state, and federal agencies require their law enforcement officers to successfully attend and graduate from their designated training academy. Law enforcement officers are usually certified following their academy graduation and then given their assignment in the field of duty. In most agencies, officers are given a probationary period in which to prove their worthiness to the agency.

Chapter 3

ENHANCING YOUR OPTIONS

○ **Law Enforcement College Education**
○ **Law Enforcement Internships**

OVERVIEW

Plan Your Course of Action

One does not accidentally walk into a law enforcement position. Most successful candidates had planned a course of action that guided them to finally obtain their desired position. Make a list of several positions you are interested in. The more positions you apply for, the better your chances for obtaining a law enforcement position. Check the qualifications for the positions. Do you qualify? If not, continue to enhance your background by obtaining more qualifying education and experience.

Ask Yourself Some Important Questions

- What am I willing to do for a law enforcement position?
- Am I willing to move?
- Should I attend college?
- Should I gain experience as an intern?
- Should I join the military?
- Should I obtain employment experience?
- Should I apply for every position possible?

Enhancing Your Options

You need to set the parameters of what you are willing to do to obtain a law enforcement position. If you answered Yes to the above questions, you are on the right path toward your goal. Remember, you must not be just a qualified candidate; you must be a desirable candidate! A candidate who has a well-rounded package of experience, education, and willingness to relocate has the tactical edge.

Mapping a Path

In the next chapters we will explore three avenues that will enhance your background package for law enforcement positions: college, law enforcement internships, and the military. They not only offer education opportunities, but also have law enforcement-type positions that provide real experience. Avenues to pursue to enhance your background include the following:

College
  Education
  College Law Enforcement Positions

Law Enforcement Internships
  Local Agencies
  State Agencies
  Federal Agencies

Military
  General Experience and Training
  Military Law Enforcement Positions

Civic and Community Involvement
  Community Policing Assistance
  Neighborhood Watch
  Law Enforcement Explorers

Work Experience
  Private Security Employment
  Responsible Work Experience

LAW ENFORCEMENT COLLEGE EDUCATION

THE COLLEGE DECISION Over the past three decades, criminal justice education has increased as a degree program at a record pace in colleges throughout the nation. There are thousands of junior or community colleges that have Criminal Justice programs. The definition of a Criminal Justice or law enforcement degree varies from institution to institution, but the basic premise remains the same.

Criminal Justice as a college program is broad in scope and design. The Criminal Justice field requires students to adopt a general approach in learning at the undergraduate level in order to enable students to apply their knowledge to a wide range of vocations. This means, in a sense, that once they have the education, they can apply for positions as law enforcement officers, in corrections, parole, police, etc. Graduate Criminal Justice students direct their studies toward a specialization such as white collar crime, parole and probation issues, forensic science management, and a host of others.

SAMPLE CRIMINAL JUSTICE ASSOCIATE DEGREE PROGRAM		
	Required Core Courses	**Credit Hours**
CRJ 101	Introduction to Criminal Justice	3
CRJ 103	Criminology	3
CRJ 105	Juvenile Delinquency	3
CRJ 107	Law Enforcement Ethics	3
CRJ 109	Deviant Behavior and Public Safety	3
ENG 215	Writing and Composition	3
SOC 101	Introduction to Sociology	3
CRJ 202	Police Administration	4
CRJ 204	Criminal Investigations I	3
CRJ 206	Criminal Investigations II	3
COM 201	Computer Literacy	4
CRJ 320	Law and Social Control	4
CRJ 340	Seminar in Judicial Process	4
CRJ 330	Corrections	4
GOV 234	American Government	3
ELECTIVES		14
	Degree Total	64

Law enforcement officers must face the reality that advancement or transfer to a better position will only occur if they invest in a college education. While experience is valuable, the reality is that the promotion tracks clearly recognize the importance of education. Therefore the candidate should:

- Choose a college with outstanding placement or internship programs in law enforcement. Research and check out the programs with past students.

- Choose a program that is tailor made for the law enforcement career the candidate is looking for.

- Check to see if the college is a "link" facility to area law enforcement agencies. Many agencies use college campuses on which to conduct and house their law enforcement academies. By attending this type of college you could be increasing your chances with these agencies.

Recommended Electives

Criminal Justice majors can enhance their education by taking some of the following recommended courses as electives or as a minor degree:

- *Accounting:*
Many agencies such as the IRS, DEA, FBI, and Inspector General Offices hire investigators with an accounting background to conduct investigative audits. In addition, many police departments are hiring officers with an accounting background for white collar crime and narcotics investigations.

- *Foreign Language:*
All agencies need personnel with foreign language skills.

- *Computer:*
All agencies need personnel with computer skills.

Traditional Colleges and Universities

Major universities or colleges with Criminal Justice programs are a key source for law enforcement employment information or intern opportunities. Many also have a record of career placement with certain agencies. Make sure that the college or university is accredited and not a diploma mill. Visit or contact them directly by letter or telephone.

Selection Considerations

Before deciding on what college or university you attend, find out the answers to the following questions:

- Are there full-time studies?
- Are there part-time studies?
- What are the costs?
- What are the day course offerings?
- What are the evening course offerings?
- Is there flexible scheduling?
- Are there internship programs?

Nontraditional Colleges

For those who, for whatever reason, do not wish to go to a traditional college there are several nontraditional college degree programs; many people opt to attend these nontraditional colleges to obtain a degree. Working parents or older students, in particular, find this more fitting to their lifestyle and situation; for example, New York State has an extensive state university system. One such college in the state system is Empire State College, which offers nontraditional forms of college education and is authorized and certified to issue Criminal Justice degrees. Students work with a mentor in a one-on-one relationship instead of in a large class. They conduct research and studies at home and independently away from the college.

State Universities/Colleges with Criminal Justice Degree Programs

Write or contact any of the following colleges or universities for a catalog and/or application, as well as any upcoming information session.

CJ Degree Offered: A = Associates (two-year degree)
B = Bachelors (four-year degree)
M = Masters (graduate degree)
D = Doctorate (postgraduate degree)

ALABAMA

Alabama State University
Criminal Justice Department
Montgomery, AL 36195
(215) 293-4291
CJ Degree Offered: B
www.ua.edu

ALASKA

University of Alaska at Anchorage
Criminal Justice Department
Anchorage, AK 99508
(907) 786-1529
CJ Degrees Offered: A, B, M
www.alaska.edu

ARIZONA

Arizona State University
Criminal Justice Department
Tempe, AZ 85287
(602) 965-7788
CJ Degrees Offered: B, M
www.asu.edu

ARKANSAS

Arkansas State University at Fayetteville
Criminal Justice Department
Fayetteville, AR 72701
(501) 575-5346
CJ Degrees Offered: A, B, M
www.uark.edu

CALIFORNIA

CSU = California State University

CSU at Los Angeles
Criminal Justice Department
Los Angeles, CA 90032
(213) 343-2752
CJ Degrees Offered: B, M
www.ucla.edu

CSU at Sacramento
Criminal Justice Department
Sacramento, CA 95819
(916) 278-3901
CJ Degrees Offered: B, M
www.csus.edu

CSU at San Bernadino
Criminal Justice Department
San Bernadino, CA 92407
(909) 880-5190
CJ Degrees Offered: B, M
www.csusb.edu

COLORADO

University of Southern Colorado
Criminal Justice Department
Pueblo, CO 81001
(719) 549-2461
CJ Degrees Offered: B, M
www.colorado.edu

CONNECTICUT

University of Hartford
Criminal Justice Department
Hartford, CT 06117
(203) 768-4296
CJ Degrees Offered: B, M
www.hartford.edu

DELAWARE

University of Delaware
Criminal Justice Department
Newark, DE 19716
(302) 831-8123
CJ Degrees Offered: A, B, M
www.udel.edu

DISTRICT OF COLUMBIA

American University
Criminal Justice Department
4400 Washington Avenue
Washington, DC 20016
(202) 885-6000
CJ Degrees Offered: B, M, D
www.american.edu

George Washington University
Criminal Justice Department
Washington, DC 20052
(202) 994-6040
CJ Degrees Offered: B, M, D
www.circ.gwu.edu

FLORIDA

University of Miami
Criminal Justice Department
Coral Gables, FL 33124
(305) 284-4323
CJ Degrees Offered: B, M
www.ir.miami.edu

University of Florida
Criminal Justice Department
Gainesville, FL 32611
(904) 392-1365
CJ Degrees Offered: B, M, D
www.ufl.edu

GEORGIA

University of Georgia
Criminal Justice Department
Athens, GA 30602
(404) 542-8776
CJ Degrees Offered: A, B, M, D
www.uga.edu

HAWAII

Hawaii Pacific University
Criminal Justice Department
Honolulu, HI 96813
(808) 544-0238
CJ Degrees Offered: A, B, M
www.hawaii.edu

IDAHO

University of Idaho
Criminal Justice Department
Moscow, ID 83844
(208) 885-6326
CJ Degrees Offered: B, M
www.uidaho.edu

ILLINOIS

Loyola University Chicago
Criminal Justice Department
820 North Michigan Avenue
Chicago, IL 60611
(312) 915-6500
CJ Degrees Offered: B, M
www.loyola. edu

Southern Illinois University
at Carbondale
Criminal Justice Department
Carbondale, IL 62901
(618) 536-4405
CJ Degrees Offered: B, M
www.siu.edu

INDIANA

University of Indianapolis
Criminal Justice Department
Indianapolis, IN 46227
(317) 788-3216
CJ Degrees Offered: A, B, M
www.uindy.edu

Indiana State University
Criminal Justice Department
Terre Haute, IN 47809
(812) 237-2121
CJ Degrees Offered: A, B, M, D
www.indstate.edu

IOWA

St. Ambrose University
Criminal Justice Department
Davenport, IA 52803
(319) 383-8888
CJ Degrees Offered: B, M
www.sau.edu

KANSAS

Kansas Wesleyan University
Criminal Justice Department
Salina, KS 67401
(913) 827-5541
CJ Degrees Offered: A, B
www.kwu.edu

KENTUCKY

Kentucky State University
Criminal Justice Department
Frankfort, KY 40601
(502) 227-6813
CJ Degrees Offered: A, B, M
www.kysu.edu

LOUISIANA

Northeast Louisiana University
Criminal Justice Department
Monroe, LA 71209
(318) 342-5252
CJ Degrees Offered: A, B, M
www.nlu.edu

MAINE

University of Southern Maine
Criminal Justice Department
Gorham, ME 04038
(207) 780-5670
CJ Degrees Offered: A, B, M
www.maine.edu

MARYLAND

University of Maryland
Criminal Justice Department
College Park, MD 20742
(301) 314-8385
CJ Degrees Offered: B, M, D
www.umd.edu

MASSACHUSETTS

University of Massachusetts
at Boston
Criminal Justice Department
Boston, MA 02125
(617) 287-6000
CJ Degrees Offered: B, M, D
www.umb.edu

University of Massachusetts
at Lowell
Criminal Justice Department
Lowell, MA 01854
(508) 934-3939
CJ Degrees Offered: A, B, M
www.uml.edu

MICHIGAN

University of Michigan
Criminal Justice Department
Flint, MI 48502
(313) 762-3300
CJ Degrees Offered: B, M
www.umich.edu

MINNESOTA

University of Minnesota
Criminal Justice Department
Duluth, MN 55182
(218) 726-7171
CJ Degrees Offered: B, M
www.d.umn.edu

MISSISSIPPI

Mississippi Valley State University
Criminal Justice Department
Itta Bena, MS 38941
(601) 254-9041
CJ Degrees Offered: B, M
www.mvsu.edu

MISSOURI

UM = University of Missouri

UM at Kansas City
Criminal Justice Department
Kansas City, MO 64110
(816) 235-1111
CJ Degrees Offered: B, M
www.umkc.edu

UM at St. Louis
Criminal Justice Department
St. Louis, MO 63121
(314) 553-5451
CJ Degrees Offered: B, M, D
www.umsl.edu

MONTANA

College of Great Falls
Criminal Justice Department
Great Falls, MT 59405
(406) 761-8210
CJ Degrees Offered: A, B, M
www.ugf.edu

NEBRASKA

University of Nebraska at Omaha
Department of Criminal Justice
Omaha, NE 68182
(402) 554-2393
CJ Degrees Offered: A, B, M, D
www.unomaha.edu

NEVADA

UN = University of Nevada

UN at Las Vegas
Criminal Justice Department
Las Vegas, NV 89154
(702) 895-3443
CJ Degrees Offered: B, M, D
www.nscee.edu

UN at Reno
Criminal Justice Department
Reno, NV 89577
(702) 784-6865
CJ Degrees Offered: B, M
www.scs.unr.edu

NEW JERSEY

Rutgers University
School of Criminal Justice
15 University Street
Newark, NJ 07102
CJ Degrees Offered: B, M, D
www.rutgers.edu

NEW MEXICO

New Mexico State University
Criminal Justice Department
Las Cruces, NM 88003
(505) 646-3121
CJ Degrees Offered: A, B, M
www.nmsu.edu

NEW YORK

John Jay College of Criminal Justice
City University of New York (CUNY)
New York, NY 10019
(212) 237-8873
CJ Degrees Offered: A, B, M, D
✪ *Special Opportunity:* John Jay
College has an outstanding reputation
as a criminal justice institution and
an excellent relationship with several
law enforcement agencies, NYPD
being one of them.
www.cuny.edu

SUNY = State University of New York

SUNY at Albany
Criminal Justice Department
Albany, NY 12222
(518) 442-5435
CJ Degrees Offered: B, M, D
www.albany.edu

SUNY College at Brockport
Criminal Justice Department
Brockport, NY 14420
(716) 395-2751
CJ Degrees Offered: B, M
www.acs.brockport.edu

SUNY College at Buffalo
Criminal Justice Department
Buffalo, NY 14222
(716) 878-4017
CJ Degrees Offered: B, M
www.buffalo.edu

SUNY College at Oswego
Criminal Justice Department
Oswego, NY 13126
(315) 341-2250
CJ Degrees Offered: B, M
www.oswego.edu

SUNY College at Plattsburg
Criminal Justice Department
Plattsburg, NY 12901
(518) 564-2040
CJ Degrees Offered: B, M
www.plattsburg.edu

SUNY Empire State College
Two Union Avenue
Saratoga Springs, NY 12866
(518) 587-2100
CJ Degrees Offered: B, M
www.esc.edu

NORTH CAROLINA

University of North Carolina
Criminal Justice Department
Chapel Hill, NC 27599
(919) 966-3621
CJ Degrees Offered: B, M
www.unc.edu

NORTH DAKOTA

University of North Dakota
Criminal Justice Department
Grand Forks, ND 58202
(701) 777-3367
CJ Degrees Offered: B, M, D
www.und.nodak.edu

OHIO

Ohio State University
Department of Criminal Justice
Cincinnati, OH 45219
CJ Degrees Offered: B, M, D
www.ohiou.edu

Union Institute
440 East McMillan Street
Cincinnati, OH 45206
(513) 861-6400
CJ Degrees Offered: B, D
www.tui.edu

OKLAHOMA

Southern Nazarene University
Criminal Justice Department
Bethany, OK 73008
(405) 789-6400
CJ Degrees Offered: A, B, M
www.snu.edu

OREGON

Portland State University
Criminal Justice Department
Portland, OR 97207
(503) 725-3511
CJ Degrees Offered: B, M
www.pdx.edu

PENNSYLVANIA

Pennsylvania State University
Criminal Justice Department
University Park, PA 16802
(814) 865-5471
CJ Degrees Offered: A, B, M, D
www.psu.edu

RHODE ISLAND

Salve Regina University
Criminal Justice Department
Newport, RI 02840
(401) 847-6650
CJ Degrees Offered: A, B, M
www.salve.edu

SOUTH CAROLINA

University of South Carolina
Criminal Justice Department
Spartanburg, SC 29303
(803) 599-2280
CJ Degrees Offered: A, B
www.csd.scarolina.edu

SOUTH DAKOTA

University of South Dakota
Criminal Justice Department
Vermillion, SD 57069
(605) 677-5434
CJ Degrees Offered: A, B, M, D
www.usd.edu

TENNESSEE

University of Tennessee
Criminal Justice Department
Martin, TN 38238
(901) 587-7020
CJ Degrees Offered: B, M
www.utm.edu

TEXAS

Sam Houston State University
College of Criminal Justice
Huntsville, TX 77341
(409) 294-1056
CJ Degrees Offered: B, M, D
✪ *Special Opportunity:* Sam Houston
University has a national reputation
as a criminal justice institution and an
outstanding relationship with several
law enforcement agencies.
www.shsu.edu

UT = University of Texas

UT at Arlington
Criminal Justice Department
Arlington, TX 76019
(817) 273-2199
CJ Degrees Offered: B, M
www.uta.edu

UT at El Paso
Criminal Justice Department
El Paso, TX 79968
(915) 747-5576
CJ Degrees Offered: B, M
www.utep.edu

UT at San Antonio
Criminal Justice Department
San Antonio, TX 78249
(512) 691-4530
CJ Degrees Offered: B, M
www.utsa.edu

UTAH

Weber State University
Criminal Justice Department
Ogden, UT 84408
(801) 626-6046
CJ Degrees Offered: A, B, M
www.weber.edu

VERMONT

Southern Vermont College
Criminal Justice Department
Bennington, VT 05201
(802) 442-5427
CJ Degrees Offered: A, B
www.svc.edu

VIRGINIA

Virginia Commonwealth University
Criminal Justice Department
Richmond, VA 23284
(804) 367-1190
CJ Degrees Offered: A, B, M, D
www.vcu.edu

WASHINGTON

Washington State University
Criminal Justice Department
Pullman, WA 99164
(509) 335-5586
CJ Degrees Offered: B, M
www.wsu.edu

WEST VIRGINIA

West Virginia State College
Criminal Justice Department
Institute, WV 25112
(304) 766-3221
CJ Degrees Offered: A, B
www.wvu.edu

WISCONSIN

University of Wisconsin
Criminal Justice Department
Eau Claire, WI 54701
(715) 836-5415
CJ Degrees Offered: A, B, M
www.uwec.edu

WYOMING

University of Wyoming
Criminal Justice Department
Laramie, WY 82071
(307) 766-5160
CJ Degrees Offered: B, M
www.uwyo.edu

RECOMMENDED COLLEGE DIRECTORIES A more descriptive assessment of colleges and universities that have criminal justice programs can be obtained by consulting the following publications:

Barron's Profiles of American Colleges
Barron's Educational Series, Inc.
250 Wireless Blvd.
Hauppauge, NY 11788
(631) 434-3311

Bears' *Guide to Earning College Degrees Nontraditionally*
Ten Speed Press
P.O. Box 7123
Berkeley, CA 94707
(800) 841-BOOK

LAW ENFORCEMENT INTERNSHIPS

THE BASIC PROCESS Search, locate, and identify law enforcement intern opportunities. Follow these steps:

- Contact the agency.
- Send a résumé and cover letter.
- Secure an agency interview.
- Do an internship to obtain experience.
- Receive a rating and recommendation.

OVERVIEW Law enforcement internships exist, but they have to be found. Your investigatory skills will be tested in finding and obtaining the right internship for you. In this section we will identify avenues, hints, and methods to use to find and obtain internships in law enforcement. Some internships pay a salary but, for the most part, they present an opportunity for experience and college course credit. While college students do use internships, one does not have to be a college student to obtain one; however, most law enforcement agencies have to deal with the issue of liability. Colleges and universities have special place liability coverage for students while they are doing an approved internship. Many law enforcement agencies allow interns to obtain valuable experience learning the inner workings of that particular agency's function, and often, interns gain the inside track toward employment opportunities. To begin, let's ask some logical questions:

1. Who should consider obtaining experience through a law enforcement internship?

Anyone interested in obtaining a law enforcement position. Law enforcement internships offer one of the best real world opportunities to not only receive résumé-building experience, but also to put one in contact with a possible law enforcement position.

2. Should I settle only for a law enforcement internship?

No. While there is no limit to law enforcement internship opportunities, location and time schedules may conflict with personal schedules. Many opportunities exist in other fields, such as government and public affairs, which are related and which will enhance your background. Remember, experience is counted as a plus by an evaluation board.

3. How do I obtain an internship?

By looking in and applying to the right places (see below), then sending a cover letter and résumé.

WHERE TO LOOK FOR THE RIGHT INTERNSHIP

Internships exist everywhere; you just have to find them. Try contacting college placement offices, libraries, and law enforcement agencies directly. Then telephone them and, if they can help you with the information you are looking for, write a formal letter of request.

Sources:
- College placement offices
- Libraries
- Guides and publications
- Police departments
- Sheriff departments
- State agencies
- Federal agencies
- District attorney offices
- State attorney general offices
- U.S. attorney offices
- Government offices

If you are not able to find the internship opportunity that you desire, try to make your own. Contact law enforcement agencies directly by writing a cover letter asking them to consider you for an internship. Many agencies will consider the situation an opportunity to have extra help. There always appears to be a special project or item that has been shelved because of lack of help. Many times that project is waiting for an intern to come along and complete it. Remember, any experience is valuable!

Interns are usually added to an organization with a contract of learning and understanding. The contract of learning is a description of what you expect your internship to teach you and whether you are to receive credit or not. It also reminds the host agency that you are there to learn a function of the agency and not to act simply as a file clerk or minimal help. It should also be established that a particular individual is designated as your field supervisor and is, in a sense, responsible for you. This person will monitor you and evaluate your work. Interns in law enforcement are not evaluated only for their work ability; they are also viewed for their trustworthiness, as interns will be in and around sensitive situations. It is important that you receive a rating and a letter of recommendation. Remember, you are not only documenting your experience for educational learning and college credit, you are also expanding your résumé by real experience in a law enforcement setting that could make the difference between you and another candidate. In addition, many interns make such an impression on the law enforcement staff and the agency head that they are encouraged to apply and take the next agency exam. This is the very contact that could lead toward a permanent position.

THE COVER LETTER
After making initial contact to establish the existence or possibility of an internship with an agency, follow it up with a formal letter of introduction and request. The cover letter is critical as it reflects a portrait of you and your background. As such, the letter should be neat and typed and include several key elements:

1. Your address
2. The address of the agency
3. Your purpose for contacting the agency
4. Related background connected to the internship
5. Closing remarks

SAMPLE COVER LETTER

Your Name
Your Address
Your City, State, Zip Code
Your Phone Number

Chief of Police
City Police Department
Address
City, State, Zip Code

Date

Dear Chief Smith:

I am currently a student at State College majoring in Criminal Justice. Dr. Jones of the Criminal Justice Department has recommended that I contact you for placement as an intern. In particular, I was advised that you are interested in a summer intern to assist your department in compiling the department's statistics. I believe my studies in statistics, computer information systems, and responsible work experience background qualifies me for this opportunity.

I am interested in a career in law enforcement and believe that an internship with the City Police Department could assist me in that goal. I have enclosed my résumé and a letter of recommendation from the State College's Criminal Justice internship program director. As my résumé indicates, my studies and employment background are interconnected to a career in law enforcement. I have worked as a security guard for experience and currently serve on the Criminal Justice Newsletter staff at the college. In addition, I have served as a citizen patrol officer for my neighborhood watch association.

Please contact me if you need more information or wish to interview me for the internship. Thank you for your time and consideration.

Respectfully,

Your Name

Chapter 4

THE MILITARY

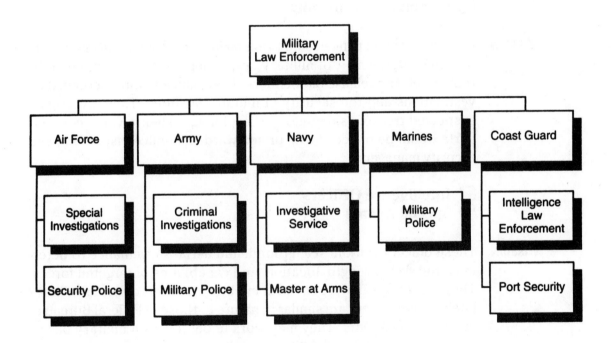

MILITARY LAW ENFORCEMENT

◯ **Military Police Officers**

MISSION   Like their civilian counterparts, they maintain law and order, prevent crime, and arrest violators. They conduct patrol on foot, in vehicles, boats, and other military modes of transportation to guard military bases, ships, planes, and installations. Military Police Officers may be assigned undercover. Many train and work with police dogs. They could be assigned to guard prisoners during wartime. The military branches recruit thousands of new Military Police Officers yearly.

◯ **Law Enforcement Officers**
◯ **Criminal Investigators**

MISSION   Law Enforcement Officers and Criminal Investigators in the military direct the enforcement of military law, supervise the arrest, custody, transfer of, and release of offenders. They plan and direct criminal investigations and the security of military facilities. They investigate suspected treason, sabotage, and espionage. Their civilian counterparts would be police chiefs, prison wardens, police inspectors, and security managers.

◯ **Intelligence Officers**
◯ **Special Agents**

MISSION   These officers work in sea, ground, and aerial surveillance to determine the size, strength, location, and capabilities of targeted forces. They gather and analyze complex intelligence. Their duties as military Intelligence Officers are similar in nature to those of Federal Bureau of Investigation Agents. They may work undercover on military bases, ships, planes, and other military installations.

Opportunities

UNITED STATES AIR FORCE

MISSION The mission of the Air Force is to defend the United States through the control and exploitation of air and space. The Air Force flies and maintains aircraft, and maintains the bases that house them. Air Force personnel are stationed worldwide.

Profile
Combined: 400,000

Requirements
Age: 17 to 29
Enlistment: 3-, 4-, 5-, 6-year terms

Training
Recruit: San Antonio, TX

Contact   Local recruiter
Web   *www.af.mil*

LAW ENFORCEMENT COMPONENTS

Air Force Intelligence

⬡ **Intelligence Officers**

Office of Special Investigations

⬡ **Criminal Investigators**
The office provides criminal, counterintelligence, personnel security, and special investigative services to Air Force activities. It collects, analyzes, and reports significant information about these matters.

Office of Security Police

⬡ **Military Police Officers**
This office conducts the program of security for Air Force resources and information and the delivery of law enforcement services. The Office of Security Police also maintains industrial security programs, law and order, prisoner rehabilitation and corrections, and traffic management.

UNITED STATES ARMY

MISSION   The U.S. Army protects the security of the United States and its vital resources. The Army stands ready to defend American interests and the interests of our allies through land-based operations anywhere in the world.

Profile	
Officers:	69,000
Enlisted:	450,000
Opportunities	
Enlistments:	90,000 each year
Requirements	
Age:	17 to 35
Enlistment:	3-, 4-, 5-, 6-year terms
Training	
Recruit:	South Carolina, Georgia, Kentucky, Alabama, Oklahoma, Missouri
Contact	Local recruiter or 1-800-USA-ARMY
Web	*www.army.net*

LAW ENFORCEMENT COMPONENTS

U.S. Army Intelligence

⬡ **Intelligence Officers**

Criminal Investigation Division

⬡ **Criminal Investigators**
CID conducts worldwide investigations of serious crime, provides investigative services to Army elements, conducts sensitive and special interest investigations, and provides personal security for selected Army and Department of Defense officials.

Military Police

⬡ **Military Police Officer**

UNITED STATES NAVY

MISSION   The Navy maintains freedom on the seas. It defends the rights of our country and its allies to travel and trade freely on the world's oceans and helps protect our country during times of international conflict. Navy sea and air power make it possible for our country to use the oceans when and where our national interests require it. Navy personnel serve on ships, on submarines under the sea, in aviation positions on land, and at shore bases around the world.

Profile	
Combined:	550,000
Requirements	
Age:	17 to 34
Enlistment:	2-, 3-, 4-, 5-, 6-year terms
Training	
Recruit:	Orlando, Great Lakes, or San Diego
Contact	Local recruiter
	or 1-800-327-Navy
Web	*www.navy.mil*

LAW ENFORCEMENT COMPONENTS

U.S. Navy Intelligence

◌ **Intelligence Officers**

Navy Criminal Investigative Service (Civilian/Military)

◌ **Special Agents**
Provides criminal investigations, law enforcement and physical security, counterintelligence, and personnel security to the Navy and Marine Corps, both ashore and afloat.

Masters-at-Arms
The Master-at-Arms is a rating that enlisted members of the Navy are eligible to apply for on the petty officer level. The Master-at-Arms personnel perform the duties and responsibilities of Military Police in the Navy.

UNITED STATES MARINE CORPS

MISSION   The Marines are an elite fighting force that are part of the Department of the Navy and operate in close cooperation with U.S. naval forces at sea. Marines serve on U.S. Navy ships, protect naval bases, guard U.S. embassies, and provide a quick, ever-ready strike force to protect U.S. interests anywhere in the world.

Requirements

Age:	17 to 29
Enlistment:	3-, 4-, 5-, 6-year terms

Training

Basic Recruit:	Paris Island, SC
	or San Diego, CA
Contact	Local recruiter
	or 1-800-Marine
Web	*www.usmc.mil*

LAW ENFORCEMENT COMPONENTS

U.S. Marine Corps Intelligence

☐ **Intelligence Officers**

Law Enforcement

☐ **Law Enforcement Specialist**

Military Police

☐ **Military Police Officer**

UNITED STATES COAST GUARD

MISSION The U.S. Coast Guard is a branch of the Armed Forces at all times and is a service within the U.S. Department of Transportation except operating as part of the U.S. Navy during a time of war or when the president directs. The Coast Guard is the primary maritime law enforcement agency for the United States.

Profile	
Officers:	6,000
Enlisted:	29,000
Requirements	
Age:	17 to 28
Enlistment:	3-, 4-, 5-, 6-year terms
Training	
Basic Recruit:	Cape May, NJ
Contact	Local recruiter or 1-800-424-8883
Web	*www.uscg.mil*

LAW ENFORCEMENT COMPONENTS

Coast Guard Investigative Service (Civilian/Military) Office of Intelligence and Law Enforcement

◯ Special Agent

Coast Guard Intelligence uses civilian agents and both regular and reserve members to act as internal and external law enforcement officers. Special Agents investigate criminal matters to include the interdiction of narcotics and conduct background investigations for personnel. Special Agents are primarily enlisted members of the Coast Guard. Intelligence Officers are Commissioned Officers in the Coast Guard. Coast Guard personnel interested in pursuing a career in the Office of Intelligence and Law Enforcement should contact directly the district office to which they are assigned.

Port Security

◯ Port Securityman

The Port Security program is largely a reserve specialty, but is related to the Port Safety and Security mission. Port Security Specialists enforce rules and regulations governing the safety and security of ports, vessels, and harbors. They also conduct inspection of facilities and investigate pollution of U.S. waters. Civilian candidates can apply directly for this program through Coast Guard recruiting offices or by contacting (202) 267-1240.

GENERAL MILITARY INFORMATION AND HINTS

OVERVIEW The military provides some outstanding opportunities. There are hundreds of career occupational specialties for a candidate to choose from, law enforcement being one of them. Most civilian law enforcement agencies give credit or consideration to an applicant who is a veteran. If the veteran served in military law enforcement, he or she receives special consideration from a wide variety of civilian agencies because, as noted earlier, law enforcement in general is a paramilitary field in nature with ranks, chain of command, etc. Law enforcement officials recognize that a veteran has already received military training and may have a level of military bearing, which makes law enforcement training and duty easier. Military personnel still on active duty or in the reserves may wish to switch or transfer to a law enforcement specialty or rating if they are not in one. Further, the military allows candidates to become law enforcement officers at the earliest possible age—18. Many people make military law enforcement a career, and retire early enough after 20 years to begin another law enforcement career. There are opportunities for education, travel, and gaining personnel and management experience in the U.S. military.

Of course, the military life is not for everyone. The pay is usually low, a majority of personnel are stationed on overseas bases, personnel is subject to transfer on short notice, and, most important, the members of the military have signed a commitment, meaning they cannot simply quit if they do not like the service.

GENERAL MILITARY OPPORTUNITIES DEFINED

Enlisted Personnel

Enlisted personnel begin at the lowest rank in the military. The military prefers candidates with a high school education. While beginning at a low rank, with time, good service and education, advancement can be a steady path upward.

Officers

Officers begin at a supervisory rank. They must have a four-year college degree from an accredited institution. Pathways to becoming a commissioned officer include:

- Service Academies
- Officer Candidate School
- Reserve Officer Training Corps (ROTC)
- Direct Appointments

Regular Service

Personnel serve on a full-time basis. After enlisting in the service, they are sent to basic training, and after graduation to a specialty job training school. Upon completion, they are assigned to a station or unit for duty.

Reserve Service

Personnel serve an initial period of active duty after attending basic training and job training. After the training period, which usually lasts several months, the reservists return to civilian life. For the remainder of the service obligation, they attend training sessions and perform work in the job specialty one or two days a month with their local unit. Once a year, reservists participate in an active duty training session for 14 days.

Benefits

- Health
- Education
- Leave/vacation
- Insurance
- Retirement after 20 years

Enlisting in the Military

Step 1: Meet with a recruiter.

Step 2: Qualify for enlistment.

Step 3: Select a law enforcement specialty for your Military Occupation Specialty (MSO). Make sure that you receive a guaranteed agreement for the specialty training program after basic training.

Step 4: Agree on the number of years of your service obligation. Enlist in the service.

Hints

- On recruiters: Be careful, and sign nothing on your first meeting. Recruiters are geared for high-pressure dealings and will try to have you sign up on the first meeting.

- Meet with recruiters or representatives from all of the services you are interested in.

- Obtain all the publications that will clearly explain the programs that you are interested in.

Military Academies

The military services maintain educational institutions that offer specialized academic education opportunities similar to those of major colleges and universities. The differences are that graduates not only receive a baccalaureate degree after four years, but also receive regular commissions as officers. It should be noted that military academies are strict learning institutions. The selection process is rigid. For further information regarding particular requirements and admission procedures, contact the following academies:

U.S. Air Force Academy
Admissions Office
Colorado Springs, CO 80840
www.af.mil

U.S. Coast Guard Academy
Director of Admissions
New London, CT 06320
www.uscg.mil

U.S. Naval Academy
Candidate Guidance Office
Annapolis, MD 21402
www.navy.mil

U.S. Military Academy
Admissions Office
West Point, NY 10996
www.army.net

Reserve Officer Training Corps (ROTC)

Numerous universities and colleges maintain active ROTC programs to include military police or military law enforcement units. After four years the candidate receives a baccalaureate degree and a reserve commission. Typically, candidates perform weekend drills and summer military service activity toward their enlistment commitment. Check with individual colleges and universities or the military units in the areas you are interested in for a military ROTC and law enforcement unit.

Promotions in the Military

The military offers a wide area of advancement if you are willing to be motivated. A military person can start as a lowly Private (E-1 pay grade) and retire as a full Colonel (O-6). Promotions in the military are based on several factors that include:

- Length of time served
- Time in present pay grade
- Job performance
- Leadership ability
- Awards or commendations
- Job specialty
- Educational achievement through technical, on-the-job, or civilian instruction

UNITED STATES ARMED FORCES
RANKS AND PAY GRADES

Pay Grade	Army	Air Force	Navy	Marine	Coast Guard
O-10	General	General	Admiral	General	Admiral
O-9	Lieutenant General	Lieutenant General	Vice Admiral	Lieutenant General	Vice Admiral
O-8	Major General	Major General	Rear Admiral	Major General	Rear Admiral
O-7	Brigadier General	Brigadier General	Rear Admiral Lower Half	Brigadier General	Rear Admiral Lower Half
O-6	Colonel	Colonel	Captain	Colonel	Captain
O-5	Lieutenant Colonel	Lieutenant Colonel	Commander	Lieutenant Colonel	Commander
O-4	Major	Major	Lieutenant Commander	Major	Lieutenant Commander
O-3	Captain	Captain	Lieutenant	Captain	Lieutenant
O-2	First Lieutenant	First Lieutenant	Lieutenant Junior Grade	First Lieutenant	Lieutenant Junior Grade
O-1	Second Lieutenant	Second Lieutenant	Ensign	Second Lieutenant	Ensign
W-4	Chief Warrant	Chief Warrant	Chief Warrant	Chief Warrant	Chief Warrant
W-3	Chief Warrant	Chief Warrant	Chief Warrant	Chief Warrant	Chief Warrant
W-2	Chief Warrant	Chief Warrant	Chief Warrant	Chief Warrant	Chief Warrant
W-1	Warrant Officer	Warrant Officer	Warrant Officer	Warrant Officer	Warrant Officer
E-9	Sergeant Major	Chief Major Sergeant	Master Chief Petty Officer	Sergeant Major	Master Chief Petty Officer
E-8	Master Sergeant	Senior Master Sergeant	Senior Chief Petty Officer	Master Sergeant	Senior Chief Petty Officer
E-7	Sergeant First Class	Master Sergeant	Chief Petty Officer	Gunnery Sergeant	Chief Petty Officer
E-6	Staff Sergeant	Technical Sergeant	Petty Officer First Class	Staff Sergeant	Petty Officer First Class
E-5	Sergeant	Sergeant	Petty Officer Second Class	Sergeant	Petty Officer Second Class
E-4	Corporal	Senior Airman	Petty Officer Third Class	Corporal	Petty Officer Third Class
E-3	Private First Class	Airman First Class	Seaman	Lance Corporal	Seaman
E-2	Private	Airman	Seaman Apprentice	Private First Class	Seaman Apprentice
E-1	Private	Airman Basic	Seaman Recruit	Private	Seaman Recruit

O = Officer Ranks   W = Warrant Officer Ranks   E = Enlisted Ranks

2000 MILITARY PAY CHART

(Monthly pay rates for military personnel)
Effective January 1, 2000
YEARS OF SERVICE

	<2	2	3	4	6	8	10	12	14	16	18	20	22	24	26
COMMISSIONED OFFICERS															
O-10	8214.90	8503.80	8503.80	8503.80	8503.80	8830.20	8830.20	9319.50	9319.50	9986.40	9986.40	10655.10	10655.10	10655.10	11318.40
O-9	7280.70	7471.50	7630.50	7630.50	7630.50	7824.60	7824.60	8150.10	8150.10	8830.20	8830.20	9319.50	9319.50	9319.50	9986.40
O-8	6594.30	6792.30	6953.10	6953.10	6953.10	7471.50	7471.50	7824.60	7824.60	8150.10	8503.80	8830.20	9048.00	9048.00	9048.00
O-7	5479.50	5851.80	5851.80	5851.80	6114.60	6114.60	6468.90	6468.90	6792.30	7471.50	7985.40	7985.40	7985.40	7985.40	7985.40
O-6	4061.10	4461.60	4754.40	4754.40	4754.40	4754.40	4754.40	4754.40	4916.10	5693.10	5983.80	6114.60	6468.90	6687.30	7015.50
O-5	3248.40	3813.90	4077.90	4077.90	4077.90	4077.90	4200.30	4427.10	4723.80	5077.50	5368.20	5531.10	5724.60	5724.60	5724.60
O-4	2737.80	3333.90	3556.20	3556.20	3622.20	3781.80	4040.40	4267.50	4461.60	4658.10	4785.90	4785.90	4785.90	4785.90	4785.90
O-3	2544.00	2844.30	3041.10	3364.80	3525.90	3652.20	3850.20	4040.40	4139.10	4139.10	4139.10	4139.10	4139.10	4139.10	4139.10
O-2	2218.80	2423.10	2910.90	3009.00	3071.10	3071.10	3071.10	3071.10	3071.10	3071.10	3071.10	3071.10	3071.10	3071.10	3071.10
O-1	1926.30	2004.90	2423.10	2423.10	2423.10	2423.10	2423.10	2423.10	2423.10	2423.10	2423.10	2423.10	2423.10	2423.10	2423.10
COMMISSIONED OFFICERS WITH OVER 4 YEARS ACTIVE DUTY SERVICE AS AN ENLISTED MEMBER OR WARRANT OFFICER															
O-3E				3364.80	3525.90	3652.20	3850.20	4040.40	4200.30	4200.30	4200.30	4200.30	4200.30	4200.30	4200.30
O-2E				3009.00	3071.10	3168.60	3333.90	3461.40	3556.20	3556.20	3556.20	3556.20	3556.20	3556.20	3556.20
O-1E				2423.10	2588.40	2683.80	2781.30	2877.60	3009.00	3009.00	3009.00	3009.00	3009.00	3009.00	3009.00
WARRANT OFFICERS															
W-5												4423.80	4591.20	4724.10	4923.30
W-4	2592.00	2781.30	2781.30	2844.30	2974.20	3105.00	3235.50	3461.40	3622.20	3749.40	3850.20	3974.10	4107.00	4235.10	4427.10
W-3	2355.90	2555.40	2555.40	2588.40	2618.70	2810.40	2974.20	3071.10	3168.60	3263.40	3364.80	3495.90	3622.20	3622.20	3749.40
W-2	2063.40	2232.60	2232.60	2297.40	2423.10	2555.40	2652.60	2749.80	2844.30	2944.50	3041.10	3136.80	3263.40	3263.40	3263.40
W-1	1719.00	1971.00	1971.00	2135.70	2232.60	2328.00	2423.10	2522.70	2618.70	2716.20	2810.40	2910.90	2910.90	2910.90	2910.90
ENLISTED MEMBERS															
E-9							3015.30	3083.40	3152.70	3225.60	3298.20	3361.50	3537.90	3675.60	3882.60
E-8						2528.40	2601.60	2669.70	2739.00	2811.60	2875.50	2946.30	3119.40	3258.00	3467.10
E-7	1765.80	1906.20	1976.10	2045.70	2115.60	2182.80	2252.70	2323.20	2427.90	2496.90	2566.20	2599.50	2774.40	2912.40	3119.40
E-6	1518.90	1655.70	1724.40	1797.60	1865.40	1932.60	2003.40	2106.60	2172.90	2242.80	2277.00	2277.00	2277.00	2277.00	2277.00
E-5	1332.60	1450.50	1521.00	1587.30	1691.70	1761.00	1830.00	1898.10	1932.60	1932.60	1932.60	1932.60	1932.60	1932.60	1932.60
E-4	1242.90	1312.80	1390.20	1497.30	1556.70	1556.70	1556.70	1556.70	1556.70	1556.70	1556.70	1556.70	1556.70	1556.70	1556.70
E-3	1171.50	1235.70	1284.60	1335.90	1335.90	1335.90	1335.90	1335.90	1335.90	1335.90	1335.90	1335.90	1335.90	1335.90	1335.90
E-2	1127.40	1127.40	1127.40	1127.40	1127.40	1127.40	1127.40	1127.40	1127.40	1127.40	1127.40	1127.40	1127.40	1127.40	1127.40
E-1>4	1005.60	1005.60	1005.60	1005.60	1005.60	1005.60	1005.60	1005.60	1005.60	1005.60	1005.60	1005.60	1005.60	1005.60	1005.60
E-1<4	930.30														

C/S $12,488.70	M/S $4,719.00

Recommended Reading

Barron's Guide to Military Careers
by Donald B. Hutton
Barron's Educational Series, Inc.
250 Wireless Blvd.
Hauppauge, NY 11788
(631) 434-3311

SECTION

Chapter 5

POLICE AND SHERIFF DEPARTMENTS

MUNICIPAL POLICE DEPARTMENTS

⬡ Police Officer

MISSION Uniform Police Officers are the backbone of America's law enforcement system. They are the public's clearest understanding of law enforcement. Uniform officers on patrol are "generalists." They maintain vehicle patrol in diverse weather and traffic conditions for extended periods of time; they may utilize speed control devices such as radar and aid disabled motorists. They are required to be proficient in the use of firearms and may be required to use physical force. They investigate accidents, aid the injured, and handle fatal crime scenes. They need to be dependable, able to work without supervision, and make decisions under pressure. They interrogate suspects, execute search warrants, and testify in court. They are required to maintain a good personal appearance, keep equipment and uniforms in proper condition, perform strenuous physical activities, and take action in physically dangerous situations.

PROFILE There are over 400,000 Police Officers nationwide.

COMMENTS *Employment Outlook:* The future outlook is excellent. Currently, the country is on a pro-law enforcement bandwagon and almost every municipality in the country is looking for ways to increase its police department's ranks. In addition, the Crime Bill has added special funds for hiring Police Officers in many cities and towns.

Employment Conditions: Conditions vary from city to city and county to county nationwide, however, there is a trend for city law enforcement agencies to increase their educational requirement from high school to at least 60 college credits. Military service still counts in assisting candidates in meeting this requirement.

WHERE TO APPLY   Directly to the agencies listed below.

LARGE POLICE DEPARTMENT STRUCTURE

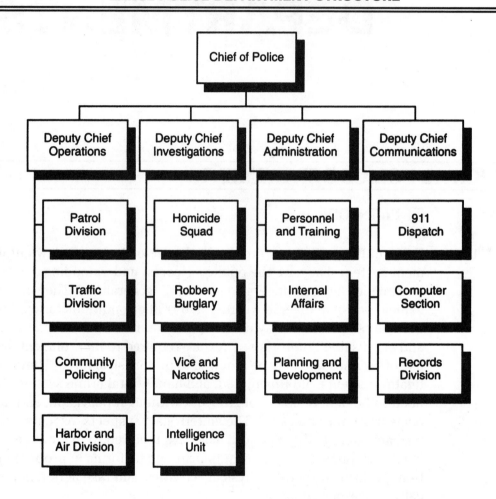

Larger departments range from over a hundred to thousands of officers. They have special units or squads that assign officers on a full-time basis to specialized units such as narcotics, vice, burglary, or homicide. Since large departments are usually located in densely populated areas with high crime rates, opportunities for employment and promotion are usually greater in those departments.

SMALL POLICE DEPARTMENT STRUCTURE

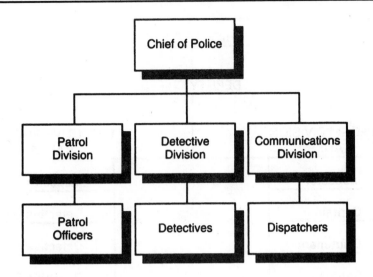

America has more small police departments than large ones. They range in size from one officer to under 100. The crime rates and population of these jurisdictions are usually low, which correlates with their limited employment and promotion opportunities.

There exists a yearly *Directory of Police Departments* that includes small police departments. The directory gives the current phone numbers and addresses of those police departments, as well as the name of the chief or administrator. It does *not* give employment information, and it is somewhat costly ($99.00). Write to:

National Directory of Law Enforcement Administrators
P.O. Box 365
1308 Main Street
Stevens Point, WI 54481
Telephone: (800) 647-7579

POLICE OFFICER CAREER LADDER

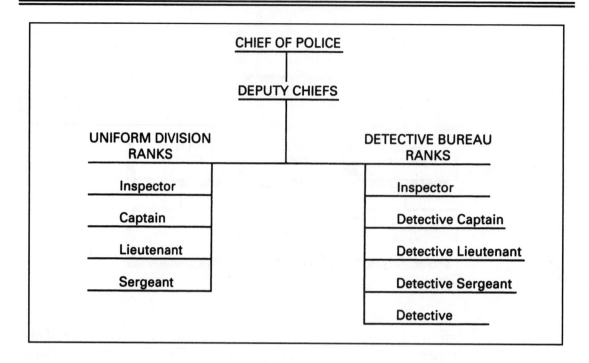

CHIEF OF POLICE

DEPUTY CHIEFS

UNIFORM DIVISION RANKS	DETECTIVE BUREAU RANKS
Inspector	Inspector
Captain	Detective Captain
Lieutenant	Detective Lieutenant
Sergeant	Detective Sergeant
	Detective

Opportunities

See page 5 for explanations of the entries in the following listings:

ALABAMA

Birmingham Police Department
417 South 6th Avenue
Birmingham, AL 35205
(205) 254-6356

Anticipated Positions	✪ Over 50
Profile of Department	
Sworn Officers:	914
Population:	258,543
Officer Benefits	
Starting Salary:	$22,859
Retirement:	20 years
Medical/Dental:	Yes
Educational:	Yes
Department Requirements	
Age:	21 minimum
Education:	High school
Vision:	20/20 corrected
Nonresidents	✔ Yes
Lateral Transfers	➤Yes
Where to Apply	City Hall 710 20th Street North Birmingham, AL 36101 (205) 254-2000
Web	*www.ci.bham.us*

Montgomery Police Department
P.O. Drawer 159
Montgomery, AL 36101
(334) 241-2816

Anticipated Positions	Under 50
Profile of Department	
Sworn Officers:	454
Population:	196,363
Officer Benefits	
Starting Salary:	$24,008
Retirement:	20 years
Medical/Dental:	Yes
Educational:	No
Department Requirements	
Age:	21 minimum
Education:	High school
Vision:	20/20 corrected
Nonresidents	✔ Yes
Lateral Transfers	No
Where to Apply	Montgomery Personnel Department
	P.O. Box 1111
	City Hall
	Montgomery, AL 36101
	(334) 241-2676
Web	*www.montgomery.al.us*

ALASKA

Anchorage Police Department
4501 South Bragaw Street
Anchorage, AK 99507
(907) 786-8500

Anticipated Positions	Over 50
Profile of Department	
Sworn Officers:	311
Population:	250,505
Officer Benefits	
Starting Salary:	$45,064
Retirement:	20 years
Medical/Dental:	Yes
Educational:	Yes
Department Requirements	
Age:	21 minimum
Education:	High school
Vision:	20/30 corrected
Nonresidents	✔ Yes
Lateral Transfers	No
Where to Apply	Above address
Web	*www.anchorage.net*

ARIZONA

Phoenix Police Department
620 West Washington Street
Phoenix, AZ 85003
(602) 262-6925

Anticipated Positions	✪ Over 300
Profile of Department	
Sworn Officers:	2,428
Population:	1,159,014
Officer Benefits	
Starting Salary:	$30,129
Retirement:	20 years
Medical/Dental:	Yes
Educational:	No
Department Requirements	
Age:	20 minimum
Education:	High school
Vision:	20/20 corrected
	20/200 uncorrected
Nonresidents	✔ Yes
Lateral Transfers	No
Where to Apply	Above address
Web	*www.ci.phoenix.az.us*

Tucson Police Department
270 South Stone Avenue
Tucson, AZ 86701
(520) 791-4499

Anticipated Positions	✪ Over 100
Profile of Department	
Sworn Officers:	802
Population:	449,002
Officer Benefits	
Starting Salary:	$29,400
Retirement:	20 years/age 55
Medical/Dental:	Yes
Educational:	No
Department Requirements	
Age:	21 minimum
Education:	High school
Vision:	20/20 corrected
	20/80 uncorrected
Nonresidents	✔ Yes
Lateral Transfers	➤Yes
Where to Apply	Above address
Web	*www.ci.tucson.az.us*

ARKANSAS

Little Rock Police Department
700 West Markham Street
Little Rock, AR 72201
(501) 371-4621

Anticipated Positions	Under 50
Profile of Department	
Sworn Officers:	549
Population:	175,752
Officer Benefits	
Starting Salary:	$23,053
Retirement:	30 years/age 55
Medical/Dental:	Yes
Educational:	No
Department Requirements	
Age:	21 minimum
Education:	High school
Vision:	20/20 corrected
	20/100 uncorrected
Nonresidents	✔ Yes
Lateral Transfers	No
Where to Apply	Above address
	(501) 371-4862 only
Web	*www.littlerock.org*

CALIFORNIA

Los Angeles Police Department
150 North Los Angeles Street
Los Angeles, CA 90012
(213) 485-2504

Anticipated Positions	✪ Over 1,000
Profile of Department	
Sworn Officers:	9,423
Population:	3,553,638
Officer Benefits	
Starting Salary:	$35,000
Retirement:	20 years/age 55
Medical/Dental:	Yes
Educational:	No
Department Requirements	
Age:	18 minimum
Education:	High school
Vision:	20/30 corrected
Nonresidents	✔ Yes
Lateral Transfers	No
Where to Apply	Above address
Web	*www.lapd.org*

San Diego Police Department
1401 Broadway
San Diego, CA 92101
(619) 531-2126

Anticipated Positions	✪ Over 100

Profile of Department

Sworn Officers:	1,960
Population:	1,171,100

Officer Benefits

Starting Salary:	$29,196
Retirement:	20 years/age 50
Medical/Dental:	Yes
Educational:	Yes

Department Requirements

Age:	21 minimum
Education:	High school
Vision:	20/20 corrected
	20/70 uncorrected

Nonresidents	✔ Yes
Lateral Transfers	➤Yes
Where to Apply	Above address
Web	*www.sandag.co.ca.us*

San Francisco Police Department
850 Bryant Street
San Francisco, CA 94103
(415) 553-1999

Anticipated Positions	✪ Over 100

Profile of Department

Sworn Officers:	2,009
Population:	735,315

Officer Benefits

Starting Salary:	$43,952
Retirement:	25 years/age 50
Medical/Dental:	Yes
Educational:	Yes

Department Requirements

Age:	21 minimum
Education:	High school
Vision:	20/30 corrected
	20/100 uncorrected

Nonresidents	No
Lateral Transfers	No
Where to Apply	Above address
Web	*www.ci.sf.ca.us*

COLORADO

Denver Police Department
1331 Cherokee Street
Denver, CO 80204
(303) 640-3623

Anticipated Positions	Over 50
Profile of Department	
Sworn Officers:	1,400
Population:	500,000
Officer Benefits	
Starting Salary:	$34,488
Retirement:	20 years
Medical/Dental:	Yes
Educational:	Yes
Department Requirements	
Age:	$20\frac{1}{2}$ minimum
Education:	High school
Vision:	20/20 corrected
Nonresidents	✔ Yes
Lateral Transfers	➤Yes
Where to Apply	Above address or (303) 640-2575
Web	*www.denver.org*

CONNECTICUT

Hartford Police Department
50 Jennings Road
Hartford, CT 06112
(860) 527-6300

Anticipated Positions	Under 50
Profile of Department	
Sworn Officers:	470
Population:	133,000
Officer Benefits	
Starting Salary:	$37,102
Retirement:	20 years/age 55
Medical/Dental:	Yes
Educational:	Yes
Department Requirements	
Age:	21 minimum
Education:	High school
Vision:	20/20 corrected 20/40 uncorrected

Nonresidents	✔ Yes
Lateral Transfers	No
Where to Apply	City of Hartford
	550 Main Street
	Hartford, CT 06103
	(860) 543-8590
Web	*www.hartfordpolice.com*

DELAWARE

New Castle County Police Department
3601 North Dupont Highway
New Castle, DE 19720
(302) 571-7900

Anticipated Positions	50 to 100
Profile of Department	
Sworn Officers:	300
Population:	471,000
Officer Benefits	
Starting Salary:	$31,432
Retirement:	25 years/age 55
Medical/Dental:	Yes
Educational:	Yes
Department Requirements	
Age:	18 minimum
Education:	60 college credits
Vision:	20/20 corrected
	20/200 uncorrected
Nonresidents	✔ Yes
Lateral Transfers	No
Where to Apply	New Castle County
	Department of Personnel
	800 North French Street
	Wilmington, DE 19801
	(302) 571-7980
Web	*www.nccpd.com*

Wilmington Police Department
300 North Walnut Street
Wilmington, DE 19801
(302) 571-4435

Anticipated Positions	Under 50
Profile of Department	
Sworn Officers:	250
Population:	69,000
Officer Benefits	
Starting Salary:	$27,652
Retirement:	25 years
Medical/Dental:	Yes
Educational:	No
Department Requirements	
Age:	21 minimum
Education:	High school
Vision:	20/25 corrected
	20/100 uncorrected
Nonresidents	✔ Yes
Lateral Transfers	No
Where to Apply	Above address
Web	*www.ci.wilmington.de.us*

DISTRICT OF COLUMBIA

Washington Metropolitan Police Department
300 Indiana Avenue NW
Washington, DC 20001
(202) 727-4383

Anticipated Positions	✪ 300
Profile of Department	
Sworn Officers:	3,600
Population:	543,600
Officer Benefits	
Starting Salary:	$23,258
Retirement:	25 years/age 50
Medical/Dental:	Yes
Educational:	Yes
Department Requirements	
Age:	20½ minimum
Education:	High school
Vision:	20/20 corrected
Nonresidents	✔ Yes
Lateral Transfers	No
Where to Apply	Above address
	Recruitment (202) 645-0083
Web	*www.mpdc.org*

FLORIDA

Fort Lauderdale Police Department
1300 West Broward Blvd.
Fort Lauderdale, FL 33312
(305) 761-5700

Anticipated Positions	Under 50
Profile of Department	
Sworn Officers:	460
Population:	151,800
Officer Benefits	
Starting Salary:	$30,534
Retirement:	20 years/age 47
Medical/Dental:	Yes
Educational:	Yes
Department Requirements	
Age:	19 minimum
Education:	High school
Vision:	20/20 corrected
	20/50 uncorrected
Nonresidents	✔ Yes
Lateral Transfers	No
Where to Apply	City of Fort Lauderdale
	Personnel Division
	100 North Andrews Avenue
	Fort Lauderdale, FL 33301
	(954) 761-5300
Web	*www.ci.ftlaud.fl.us*

Miami Police Department
300 South Biscayne Way Blvd
Miami, FL 33131
(3050 579-2411

Anticipated Positions	✪ Over 200
Profile of Department	
Sworn Officers:	1,014
Population:	360,000
Officer Benefits	
Starting Salary:	$29,111
Retirement:	20 years
Medical/Dental:	Yes
Educational:	Yes
Department Requirements	
Age:	19 minimum
Education:	High school
Vision:	20/30 corrected
	20/50 uncorrected

Nonresidents	✔ Yes
Lateral Transfers	➤Yes
Where to Apply	Human Resources Department
	Above address
	(305) 579-6111

Metro-Dade Police Department
9105 NW 25th Street
Miami, FL 33172
(305) 471-2565

Anticipated Positions	✪ 800
Profile of Department	
Sworn Officers:	2,860
Population:	1,900,000
Officer Benefits	
Starting Salary:	$25,427
Retirement:	25 years
Medical/Dental:	Yes
Educational:	Yes
Department Requirements	
Age:	19 minimum
Education:	High school
Vision:	20/30 corrected
	20/100 uncorrected
Nonresidents	✔ Yes
Lateral Transfers	➤Yes
Where to Apply	Above address
Web	*www.mdpd.com*

Tampa Police Department
1710 North Tampa Street
Tampa, FL 33602
(813) 274-5896

Anticipated Positions	Under 50
Profile of Department	
Sworn Officers:	910
Population:	285,000
Officer Benefits	
Starting Salary:	$23,053
Retirement:	20 years
Medical/Dental:	Yes
Educational:	Yes

Department Requirements

Age:	21 minimum
Education:	High school
Vision:	20/20 corrected
	20/100 uncorrected

Nonresidents	No
Lateral Transfers	No
Where to Apply	Above address
Web	*www.ci.tampa.fl.us*

GEORGIA

Atlanta Police Department
175 Decatur Street SE
Atlanta, GA 30335
(404) 658-6042

Anticipated Positions	✪ Over 100

Profile of Department

Sworn Officers:	1,700
Population:	401,000

Officer Benefits

Starting Salary:	$23,053
Retirement:	20 years
Medical/Dental:	Yes
Educational:	No

Department Requirements

Age:	21 minimum
Education:	High school
Vision:	20/20 corrected
	20/50 uncorrected

Nonresidents	✔ Yes
Lateral Transfers	No
Where to Apply	Above address
Web	*www.atlantapd.org*

Savannah Police Department
201 Habersham Street
Savannah, GA 31401
(912) 651-4226

Anticipated Positions	Under 50

Profile of Department

Sworn Officers:	423
Population:	137,000

Officer Benefits

Starting Salary:	$21,178
Retirement:	10 years/age 58
Medical/Dental:	Yes
Educational:	No

Department Requirements

Age:	21 minimum
Education:	High school
Vision:	20/20 corrected
Nonresidents	✔ Yes
Lateral Transfers	➤Yes
Where to Apply	Savannah Human Resources
	132 East Broughton Street
	Savannah, GA 31401
	(912) 651-6484
Web	*www.savannahpd.org*

HAWAII

Honolulu Police Department
801 South Beretania Street
Honolulu, HI 96813
(808) 529-3336

Anticipated Positions	✪ Over 100
Profile of Department	
Sworn Officers:	1,646
Population:	875,000
Officer Benefits	
Starting Salary:	$29,000
Retirement:	25 years
Medical/Dental:	Yes
Educational:	No
Department Requirements	
Age:	20 minimum
Education:	High school
Vision:	20/20 corrected
	20/40 uncorrected
Nonresidents	✔ Yes
Lateral Transfers	No
Comments	Internet address
	http://www.maui.com/hpd/
Where to Apply	Honolulu Department of Personnel
	550 South King Street
	Honolulu, HI 96813
	(808) 523-4301
Web	*www.co.honolulu.hi.us*

ILLINOIS

Chicago Police Department
1121 South State Street
Chicago, IL 60605
(312) 747-5544

Anticipated Positions	✪ Over 2,000
Profile of Department	
Sworn Officers:	13,282
Population:	2,731,743
Officer Benefits	
Starting Salary:	$33,580
Retirement:	20 years/age 50
Medical/Dental:	Yes
Educational:	Yes
Department Requirements	
Age:	21 minimum
Education:	60 college credits
Vision:	20/25 corrected
	20/200 uncorrected
Nonresidents	✔ Yes
Lateral Transfers	No
Comments	Veterans receive extra credit.
Where to Apply	Above address
Web	*www.ci.chi.ill.us*

INDIANA

Indianapolis Police Department
50 North Alabama Street
Indianapolis, IN 46204
(317) 327-3722

Anticipated Positions	Over 50
Profile of Department	
Sworn Officers:	970
Population:	746,737
Officer Benefits	
Starting Salary:	$25,695
Retirement:	20 years/age 55
Medical/Dental:	Yes
Educational:	Yes
Department Requirements	
Age:	21 minimum
Education:	High school
Vision:	20/30 corrected
Nonresidents	No
Lateral Transfers	►Yes
Where to Apply	Above address
Web	*www.ci.indianapolis.in.us/ipd*

KANSAS

Kansas City Police Department
701 North 7th Street
Kansas City, KS 66101
(913) 573-6010

Anticipated Positions	Under 50
Profile of Department	
Sworn Officers:	360
Population:	142,650
Officer Benefits	
Starting Salary:	$25,000
Retirement:	10 years/age 62
Medical/Dental:	Yes
Educational:	Yes
Department Requirements	
Age:	21 minimum
Education:	High school
Vision:	20/20 corrected
	20/100 uncorrected
Nonresidents	No
Lateral Transfers	No
Where to Apply	Above address
Web	*www.kansascity.com*

Wichita Police Department
455 North Main Street
Wichita, KS 67202
(316) 268-4111

Anticipated Positions	Under 50
Profile of Department	
Sworn Officers:	590
Population:	320,390
Officer Benefits	
Starting Salary:	$22,670
Retirement:	20 years/age 55
Medical/Dental:	Yes
Educational:	No
Department Requirements	
Age:	21 minimum
Education:	High school
Vision:	20/30 corrected
	20/100 uncorrected
Nonresidents	✔ Yes
Lateral Transfers	No
Where to Apply	Above address
Web	*www.wichitapolice.com*

KENTUCKY

Lexington-Fayette County Police Department
150 Main Street
Lexington, KY 40507
(606) 258-3600

Anticipated Positions	50 to 100
Profile of Department	
Sworn Officers:	430
Population:	239,900
Officer Benefits	
Starting Salary:	$20,000
Retirement:	20 years/age 46
Medical/Dental:	Yes
Educational:	Yes
Department Requirements	
Age:	21 minimum
Education:	High school
Vision:	20/20 corrected
Nonresidents	✔ Yes
Lateral Transfers	No
Where to Apply	Lexington-Fayette County Government
	200 East Main Street
	Lexington, KY 40507
	(606) 258-3030
Web	*www.lexingtonpolice.com*

Louisville Police Department
633 West Jefferson Street
Louisville, KY 40202
(502) 574-3565

Anticipated Positions	Under 50
Profile of Department	
Sworn Officers:	650
Population:	260,600
Officer Benefits	
Starting Salary:	$23,396
Retirement:	20 years
Medical/Dental:	Yes
Educational:	Yes
Department Requirements	
Age:	21 minimum
Education:	High school
Vision:	20/20 corrected
Nonresidents	✔ Yes
Lateral Transfers	No

Where to Apply	LPD Civil Service 609 West Jefferson Street Louisville, KY 40202
Web	*www.loupolice.org*

LOUISIANA

New Orleans Police Department
715 South Broad Avenue
New Orleans, LA 70119
(504) 821-2222

Anticipated Positions	✪ Over 100
Profile of Department	
Sworn Officers:	1,570
Population:	476,650
Officer Benefits	
Starting Salary:	$17,124
Retirement:	20 years/age 55
Medical/Dental:	Yes
Educational:	Yes
Department Requirements	
Age:	20 minimum
Education:	High school
Vision:	No requirement stated
Nonresidents	✔ Yes
Lateral Transfers	No
Comments	The city has allocated special federal funds to assist officers in purchasing new homes.
Where to Apply	Department of Civil Service 1300 Perdido Street New Orleans, LA 70118 (504) 565-6800
Web	*www.neworleans.com*

Shreveport Police Department
1234 Texas Avenue
Shreveport, LA 71161
(318) 673-7300

Anticipated Positions	50 to 100
Profile of Department	
Sworn Officers:	500
Population:	191,550
Officer Benefits	
Starting Salary:	$20,000
Retirement:	20 years/age 50
Medical/Dental:	Yes
Educational:	Yes

Department Requirements

Age:	21 minimum
Education:	High school
Vision:	20/20 corrected

Nonresidents   ✔ Yes

Lateral Transfers   No

Comments   New officers must complete 30 college credits within 5 years.

Where to Apply   Above address

Web   *www.ci.shreveport.la.us*

MARYLAND

Baltimore Police Department
601 East Fayette Street
Baltimore, MD 21202
(410) 396-2080

Anticipated Positions   ✪ Over 100

Profile of Department

Sworn Officers:	3,039
Population:	680,400

Officer Benefits

Starting Salary:	$25,496
Retirement:	20 years/age 55
Medical/Dental:	Yes
Educational:	No

Department Requirements

Age:	21 minimum
Education:	High school
Vision:	20/20 corrected
	20/40 uncorrected

Nonresidents   ✔ Yes

Lateral Transfers   No

Where to Apply   Above address

Web   *www.ci.baltimore.md.us*

Montgomery County Police Department
2350 Research Blvd.
Rockville, MD 20850
(301) 217-4090

Anticipated Positions   Undetermined

Profile of Department

Sworn Officers:	977
Population:	800,000

Officer Benefits

Starting Salary:	$27,581
Retirement:	20 years/age 46
Medical/Dental:	Yes
Educational:	No

Department Requirements

Age:	21 minimum
Education:	60 college credits
Vision:	20/20 corrected
	20/40 uncorrected
Nonresidents	✔ Yes
Lateral Transfers	No
Where to Apply	Above address
	(301) 217-4230
Web	*www.co.mo.md.us*

MICHIGAN

Detroit Police Department
2110 Park Avenue
Detroit, MI 48201
(313) 596-2660

Anticipated Positions	✪ Over 1,000
Profile of Department	
Sworn Officers:	4,000
Population:	1,200,974
Officer Benefits	
Starting Salary:	$27,856
Retirement:	20 years
Medical/Dental:	Yes
Educational:	Yes
Department Requirements	
Age:	18 minimum
Education:	60 college credits
Vision:	20/20 corrected
Nonresidents	✔ Yes
Lateral Transfers	No
Where to Apply	Above address
	or (301) 217-4230
Web	*www.ci.detroit.mi.us*

Grand Rapids Police Department
333 Monroe Avenue
Grand Rapids, MI 49503
(616) 456-3400

Anticipated Positions	50 to 100
Profile of Department	
Sworn Officers:	340
Population:	1,045,268

Officer Benefits

Starting Salary:	$28,000
Retirement:	age 50
Medical/Dental:	Yes
Educational:	No

Department Requirements

Age:	18 minimum
Education:	High school
Vision:	20/20 corrected

Nonresidents   ✔ Yes

Lateral Transfers   No

Where to Apply   Above address
(616) 456-3176

Web   *www.grpolice.grand-rapids.mi.us*

MINNESOTA

Minneapolis Police Department
350 South 5th Street
Minneapolis, MN 55415
(612) 673-3428

Anticipated Positions   Under 50

Profile of Department

Sworn Officers:	890
Population:	358,780

Officer Benefits

Starting Salary:	$29,065
Retirement:	20 years/age 55
Medical/Dental:	Yes
Educational:	Yes

Department Requirements

Age:	19 minimum
Education:	Two-year college degree
Vision:	20/20 corrected
	20/120 uncorrected

Nonresidents   No

Lateral Transfers   No

Where to Apply   Minneapolis Civil Service
Commission
312 3rd Avenue
Minneapolis, MN 55415
(612) 763-2282

Web   *www.ci.mpls.mn.us*

St. Paul Police Department
101 East 11th Street
St. Paul, MN 55101
(612) 291-1111

Anticipated Positions	Under 50
Profile of Department	
Sworn Officers:	581
Population:	259,600
Officer Benefits	
Starting Salary:	$34,400
Retirement:	Age 55
Medical/Dental:	Yes
Educational:	Yes
Department Requirements	
Age:	21 minimum
Education:	Two-year college degree
Vision:	20/20 corrected
	20/100 uncorrected
Nonresidents	✔ Yes
Lateral Transfers	➤Yes
Where to Apply	Human Resources
	400 City Hall Annex
	St. Paul, MN 55102
	(612) 266-6500
Web	*www.stpaul.gov*

MISSISSIPPI

Jackson Police Department
219 South President Street
Jackson, MS 39201
(601) 960-1389

Anticipated Positions	Over 50
Profile of Department	
Sworn Officers:	410
Population:	196,000
Officer Benefits	
Starting Salary:	$17,042
Retirement:	20 years
Medical/Dental:	Yes
Educational:	No
Department Requirements	
Age:	21 minimum
Education:	60 college credits
Vision:	20/20 uncorrected
Nonresidents	✔ Yes
Lateral Transfers	No
Where to Apply	Above address
Web	*www.city.jackson.ms.us/police*

MISSOURI

Kansas City Police Department
1125 Locust Street
Kansas City, MO 64106
(816) 234-5000

Anticipated Positions	✪ Over 100
Profile of Department	
Sworn Officers:	1,196
Population:	435,146
Officer Benefits	
Starting Salary:	$26,104
Retirement:	25 years/age 55
Medical/Dental:	Yes
Educational:	No
Department Requirements	
Age:	21 minimum
Education:	High school
Vision:	20/20 corrected
	20/200 uncorrected
Nonresidents	✔ Yes
Lateral Transfers	No
Where to Apply	Above address
	(816) 234-KCPD
Web	*www.kcpd.org*

St. Louis Police Department
1200 Clark Avenue
St. Louis, MO 63103
(314) 444-5617

Anticipated Positions	✪ 200
Profile of Department	
Sworn Officers:	1,611
Population:	355,000
Officer Benefits	
Starting Salary:	$27,963
Retirement:	20 years
Medical/Dental:	Yes
Educational:	Yes
Department Requirements	
Age:	21 minimum
Education:	60 college credits
Vision:	20/20 corrected
	20/200 uncorrected
Nonresidents	✔ Yes
Lateral Transfers	➤Yes
Where to Apply	Above address
Web	*www.st-louis.mo.us*

St. Louis County Police
7900 Forsyth
Clayton, MO 63105
(314) 889-2273

Anticipated Positions	✪ Over 50
Profile of Department	
Sworn Officers:	600
Population:	1,000,000
Officer Benefits	
Starting Salary:	$26,634
Retirement:	20 years
Medical/Dental:	Yes
Educational:	Yes
Department Requirements	
Age:	21 minimum
Education:	60 college credits
Vision:	20/20 corrected
	20/200 uncorrected
Nonresidents	✔ Yes
Lateral Transfers	No
Comments	Candidates with military or police experience receive credit.
Where to Apply	Above address
Web	*www.co.st-louis.mo.us*

NEBRASKA

Omaha Police Department
505 South 15th Street
Omaha, NE 68102
(402) 444-5600

Anticipated Positions	18
Profile of Department	
Sworn Officers:	690
Population:	364,000
Officer Benefits	
Starting Salary:	$28,310
Retirement:	20 years
Medical/Dental:	Yes
Educational:	Yes
Department Requirements	
Age:	21 minimum
Education:	High school
Vision:	20/20 corrected
	20/200 uncorrected
Nonresidents	✔ Yes

Lateral Transfers	➤Yes
Where to Apply	Omaha City Personnel
	1819 Farnam Street
	Omaha, NE 68183
	(402) 444-5300
Web	*www.opd.ci.omaha.ne.us*

NEVADA

Las Vegas Metropolitan Police Department
400 East Stewart Avenue
Las Vegas, NV 89101
(702) 229-3497

Anticipated Positions	✪ Over 400
Profile of Department	
Sworn Officers:	1,700
Population:	1,048,000
Officer Benefits	
Starting Salary:	$35,000
Retirement:	Age 50
Medical/Dental:	Yes
Educational:	Yes
Department Requirements	
Age:	21 minimum
Education:	High school
Vision:	20/20 corrected
	20/200 uncorrected
Nonresidents	✔ Yes
Lateral Transfers	No
Where to Apply	Above address
Web	*www.ci.las-vegas.nv.us*

NEW HAMPSHIRE

Manchester Police Department
351 Chestnut Street
Manchester, NH 03101
(603) 658-8711

Anticipated Positions	Under 50
Profile of Department	
Sworn Officers:	195
Population:	103,659
Officer Benefits	
Starting Salary:	$28,000
Retirement:	20 years/age 45
Medical/Dental:	Yes
Educational:	Yes

Department Requirements

Age:	21 minimum
Education:	High school
Vision:	20/25 corrected
	20/200 uncorrected
Nonresidents	✔ Yes
Lateral Transfers	No
Where to Apply	Above address
	(603) 624-6543
Web	*www.manchesterpd.com*

NEW JERSEY

Atlantic City Police Department
3200 Fairmount Avenue
Atlantic City, NJ 08401
(609) 347-5252

Anticipated Positions	Under 50
Profile of Department	
Sworn Officers:	403
Population:	38,000
Officer Benefits	
Starting Salary:	$30,400
Retirement:	25 years
Medical/Dental:	Yes
Educational:	No
Department Requirements	
Age:	18 minimum
Education:	High school
Vision:	20/30 corrected
Nonresidents	No
Lateral Transfers	No
Where to Apply	Above address
Web	*www.atlanticcity.nj.com*

Jersey City Police Department
8 Erie Street
Jersey City, NJ 07302
(201) 547-5477

Anticipated Positions	Undetermined
Profile of Department	
Sworn Officers:	840
Population:	228,539
Officer Benefits	
Starting Salary:	$30,159
Retirement:	25 years
Medical/Dental:	Yes
Educational:	No

Department Requirements

Age:	18 minimum
Education:	High school
Vision:	20/20 corrected

Nonresidents	No
Lateral Transfers	No
Where to Apply	Above address
Web	*www.ci.jersey-city.nj.us*

Newark Police Department
31 Green Street
Newark, NJ 07102

Anticipated Positions	Undetermined

Profile of Department

Sworn Officers:	1,400
Population:	268,000

Officer Benefits

Starting Salary:	$30,000
Retirement:	25 years
Medical/Dental:	Yes
Educational:	No

Department Requirements

Age:	19 minimum
Education:	High school
Vision:	20/20 corrected

Nonresidents	No
Lateral Transfers	No
Where to Apply	Above address
Web	*www.newarkpd.org*

NEW MEXICO

Albuquerque Police Department
400 Roma Avenue NW
Albuquerque, NM 87102
(505) 768-2200

Anticipated Positions	✪ Over 100

Profile of Department

Sworn Officers:	869
Population:	419,000

Officer Benefits

Starting Salary:	$18,720
Retirement:	20 years/age 46
Medical/Dental:	Yes
Educational:	Yes

Department Requirements

Age:	21 minimum
Education:	60 college credits
Vision:	20/20 corrected
	20/40 uncorrected

Nonresidents	✔ Yes
Lateral Transfers	No
Comments	Candidates with military or police experience receive credit.
Where to Apply	Above address
Web	*www.abqpoa.org*

NEW YORK

Buffalo Police Department
74 Franklin Street
Buffalo, NY 14202
(716) 851-4444

Anticipated Positions	Under 50

Profile of Department

Sworn Officers:	920
Population:	310,500

Officer Benefits

Starting Salary:	$28,814
Retirement:	20 years
Medical/Dental:	Yes
Educational:	Yes

Department Requirements

Age:	20 minimum
Education:	High school
Vision:	20/20 corrected
	20/40 uncorrected

Nonresidents	No
Lateral Transfers	No
Where to Apply	Department of Civil Service City Hall Buffalo, NY 14202 (716) 851-5407
Web	*www.ci.buffalo.ny.us*

New York City Police Department
One Police Plaza
New York, NY 10038
(212) 374-5000

Anticipated Positions	✪ Up to 3,000

Profile of Department

Sworn Officers:	38,328
Population:	7,380,900

Officer Benefits
Starting Salary: $34,970
Retirement: 20 years
Medical/Dental: Yes
Educational: Yes

Department Requirements
Age: 22 minimum
Education: 60 college credits
Vision: 20/30 corrected
20/100 uncorrected

Nonresidents   ✔ Yes
Lateral Transfers   No
Comments   Veterans receive credit in place of college requirement.

Where to Apply   New York City
Police Department
Recruitment Section
4 Auburn Place
Brooklyn, NY 11205
(212) RECRUIT

Web   *www.nyc.ny.us*

Nassau County Police Department
1490 Franklin Avenue
Mineola, NY 11501
(516) 573-7000

Anticipated Positions   ✪ Over 100
Profile of Department
Sworn Officers: 2,935
Population: 1,303,389

Officer Benefits
Starting Salary: $30,336
Retirement: 20 years
Medical/Dental: Yes
Educational: No

Department Requirements
Age: 21 minimum
Education: 32 college credits
Vision: 20/20 corrected
20/40 uncorrected

Nonresidents   ✔ Yes
Lateral Transfers   No
Where to Apply   Nassau County Police Department
140 Old Country Road
Mineola, NY 11501
(516) 571-2139

Web   *www.co.nassau.ny.us*

Rochester Police Department
150 South Plymouth Avenue
Rochester, NY 14612
(716) 428-6716

Anticipated Positions	50 to 100
Profile of Department Jurisdiction	
Sworn Officers:	693
Population:	221,590
Officer Benefits	
Starting Salary:	$26,000
Retirement:	20 years
Medical/Dental:	Yes
Educational:	Yes
Department Requirements	
Age:	20 minimum
Education:	High school
Vision:	20/30 corrected
	20/100 uncorrected
Nonresidents	✔ Yes
Lateral Transfers	No
Where to Apply	Above address
Web	*www.ci.rochester.ny.us*

Suffolk County Police Department
30 Yaphank Avenue
Yaphank, NY 11980
(631) 852-6000

Anticipated Positions	✪ Over 100
Profile of Department	
Sworn Officers:	2,710
Population:	1,350,000
Officer Benefits	
Starting Salary:	$34,616
Retirement:	20 years
Medical/Dental:	Yes
Educational:	Yes
Department Requirements	
Age:	20 minimum
Education:	High school
Vision:	20/30 corrected
	20/100 uncorrected
Nonresidents	✔ Yes
Lateral Transfers	No
Where to Apply	Suffolk County Civil Service
	Rabro Drive
	Hauppauge, NY 11788
	(631) 853-5500
Web	*www.co.suffolk.ny.us*

NORTH CAROLINA

Charlotte Police Department
825 East 4th Street
Charlotte, NC 28202
(704) 525-6145

Anticipated Positions	Undetermined
Profile of Department	
Sworn Officers:	1,280
Population:	441,000
Officer Benefits	
Starting Salary:	$22,000
Retirement:	Age 50
Medical/Dental:	Yes
Educational:	No
Department Requirements	
Age:	21 minimum
Education:	High school
Vision:	20/20 uncorrected
Nonresidents	✔ Yes
Lateral Transfers	➤Yes
Where to Apply	Above address
Web	*www.charmeck.nc.us*

OHIO

Cincinnati Police Department
310 Ezzard Charles Drive
Cincinnati, OH 45214
(513) 352-3536

Anticipated Positions	✪ Over 100
Profile of Department	
Sworn Officers:	978
Population:	360,000
Officer Benefits	
Starting Salary:	$33,616
Retirement:	25 years/age 48
Medical/Dental:	Yes
Educational:	Yes
Department Requirements	
Age:	21 minimum
Education:	High school
Vision:	20/30 corrected
	20/100 uncorrected
Nonresidents	✔ Yes
Lateral Transfers	No

Where to Apply	City of Cincinnati
	Personnel Department
	801 Plum Street
	Cincinnati, OH 45202
	(513) 352-2400
Web	*www.cincinnatipolice.org*

Cleveland Police Department
1300 Ontario Street
Cleveland, OH 44113
(216) 623-5153

Anticipated Positions	Under 100
Profile of Department	
Sworn Officers:	1,700
Population:	498,000
Officer Benefits	
Starting Salary:	$30,000
Retirement:	Age 50
Medical/Dental:	Yes
Educational:	No
Department Requirements	
Age:	21 minimum
Education:	High school
Vision:	20/20 corrected
Nonresidents	✔ Yes
Lateral Transfers	No
Where to Apply	Civil Service
	(216) 664-2467
Web	*www.cleveland.oh.us*

Columbus Police Department
Columbus, OH 43215
(614) 645-4642

Anticipated Positions	✪ Over 100
Profile of Department	
Sworn Officers:	1,726
Population:	650,902
Officer Benefits	
Starting Salary:	$27,601
Retirement:	25 years
Medical/Dental:	Yes
Educational:	No

Department Requirements

Age:	18 minimum
Education:	High school
Vision:	No requirement stated

Nonresidents ✔ Yes

Lateral Transfers No

Where to Apply Above address

Web *www.ci.columbus.oh.us*

OKLAHOMA

Oklahoma City Police Department
701 Colcord Drive
Oklahoma City, OK 73102
(405) 297-1216

Anticipated Positions Under 100

Profile of Department

Sworn Officers:	988
Population:	469,000

Officer Benefits

Starting Salary:	$25,000
Retirement:	20 years/age 45
Medical/Dental:	Yes
Educational:	Yes

Department Requirements

Age:	21 minimum
Education:	High school
Vision:	20/30 corrected

Nonresidents ✔ Yes

Lateral Transfers No

Where to Apply Above address
(405) 297-3438

Web *www.okc-cityhall.org*

Tulsa Police Department
600 Civic Center
Tulsa, OK 74103
(918) 596-9316

Anticipated Positions Under 50

Profile of Department

Sworn Officers:	800
Population:	379,587

Officer Benefits

Starting Salary:	$23,904
Retirement:	20 years/age 55
Medical/Dental:	Yes
Educational:	Yes

Department Requirements

Age:	21 minimum
Education:	108 college credits
Vision:	20/20 corrected
Nonresidents	✔ Yes
Lateral Transfers	No
Where to Apply	City of Tulsa Personnel 200 Civic Center Tulsa, OK 74103
Web	*www.tulsapolice.org*

OREGON

Portland Police Department
111 SW 2nd Avenue
Portland, OR 97204
(503) 823-0333

Anticipated Positions	Under 50

Profile of Department

Sworn Officers:	960
Population:	480,800

Officer Benefits

Starting Salary:	$30,680
Retirement:	25 years/age 50
Medical/Dental:	Yes
Educational:	Yes

Department Requirements

Age:	21 minimum
Education:	Four-year college degree
Vision:	20/30 corrected 20/200 uncorrected
Nonresidents	✔ Yes
Lateral Transfers	No
Where to Apply	Portland Bureau of Personnel 1400 SW 5th Portland, OR 97204
Web	*www.ci.portland.or.us*

PENNSYLVANIA

Philadelphia Police Department
1328 Race Street
Philadelphia, PA 19106
(215) 686-1475

Anticipated Positions	✪ Over 500
Profile of Department	
Sworn Officers:	6,700
Population:	1,478,002
Officer Benefits	
Starting Salary:	$26,246
Retirement:	20 years/age 55
Medical/Dental:	Yes
Educational:	No
Department Requirements	
Age:	19 minimum
Education:	High school
Vision:	20/20 corrected
Nonresidents	No
Lateral Transfers	No
Where to Apply	Above address
Web	*www.phi.org*

Pittsburgh Police Department
100 Grant Street
Pittsburgh, PA 15219
(412) 255-2814

Anticipated Positions	Under 50
Profile of Department	
Sworn Officers:	1,175
Population:	350,700
Officer Benefits	
Starting Salary:	$28,680
Retirement:	25 years/age 65
Medical/Dental:	Yes
Educational:	No
Department Requirements	
Age:	18 minimum
Education:	High school
Vision:	20/30 corrected
Nonresidents	✔ Yes
Lateral Transfers	No
Where to Apply	Civil Service Commission
	440 Grant Street
	Pittsburgh, PA 15219
	(412) 255-2710
Web	*www.city.pittsburgh.pa.us*

RHODE ISLAND

Providence Police Department
209 Fountain Street
Providence, RI 02903
(401) 272-3121

Anticipated Positions	50
Profile of Department	
Sworn Officers:	468
Population:	152,558
Officer Benefits	
Starting Salary:	$30,987
Retirement:	20 years
Medical/Dental:	Yes
Educational:	Yes
Department Requirements	
Age:	21 minimum
Education:	High school
Vision:	No requirement stated
Nonresidents	✔ Yes
Lateral Transfers	No
Where to Apply	Above address (401) 272-3121
Web	*www.providencepolice.com*

SOUTH CAROLINA

Columbia Police Department
1409 Lincoln Street
Columbia, SC 29201
(803) 733-8415

Anticipated Positions	Under 50
Profile of Department	
Sworn Officers:	288
Population:	110,000
Officer Benefits	
Starting Salary:	$23,953
Retirement:	25 years/age 65
Medical/Dental:	Yes
Educational:	Yes
Department Requirements	
Age:	21 minimum
Education:	High school
Vision:	No requirement stated
Nonresidents	✔ Yes
Lateral Transfers	➤Yes
Where to Apply	Above address
Web	*www.columbiasc.com*

SOUTH DAKOTA

Sioux Falls Police Department
500 North Dakota Avenue
Sioux Falls, SD 57104
(605) 367-7212

Anticipated Positions	Under 50
Profile of Department	
Sworn Officers:	150
Population:	113,200
Officer Benefits	
Starting Salary:	$26,000
Retirement:	25 years/age 50
Medical/Dental:	Yes
Educational:	Yes
Department Requirements	
Age:	21 minimum
Education:	High school
Vision:	20/40 corrected
Nonresidents	✔ Yes
Lateral Transfers	No
Where to Apply	City of Sioux Falls
	224 9th Street
	Sioux Falls, SD 57102
	(605) 367-7062
Web	*www.sioux-falls.org*

TENNESSEE

Nashville Metropolitan Police Department
200 James Robertson
Nashville, TN 37201
(615) 862-7785

Anticipated Positions	✪ Over 100
Profile of Department	
Sworn Officers:	1,200
Population:	511,000
Officer Benefits	
Starting Salary:	$21,000
Retirement:	25 years
Medical/Dental:	Yes
Educational:	Yes
Department Requirements	
Age:	21 minimum
Education:	60 college credits
Vision:	20/20 corrected
Nonresidents	✔ Yes
Lateral Transfers	No
Where to Apply	Above address
Web	*www.police.nashville.org*

Memphis Police Department
125 North Lane
Memphis, TN 38103
(901) 576-6509

Anticipated Positions	✪ Over 100
Profile of Department	
Sworn Officers:	1,490
Population:	560,700
Officer Benefits	
Starting Salary:	$23,000
Retirement:	25 years
Medical/Dental:	Yes
Educational:	Yes
Department Requirements	
Age:	21 minimum
Education:	60 college credits
Vision:	20/20 corrected
	20/70 uncorrected
Nonresidents	✔ Yes
Lateral Transfers	No
Comments	Two years of military service can replace college requirement.
Where to Apply	Above address
	(901) 357-1700
Web	*www.memphispolice.org*

TEXAS

Austin Police Department
715 East 8th Avenue
Austin, TX 78701
(512) 480-2124

Anticipated Positions	Over 50
Profile of Department	
Sworn Officers:	970
Population:	541,200
Officer Benefits	
Starting Salary:	$23,385
Retirement:	20 years
Medical/Dental:	Yes
Educational:	Yes
Department Requirements	
Age:	21 minimum
Education:	60 college credits
Vision:	20/30 corrected
	20/100 uncorrected
Nonresidents	✔ Yes

Lateral Transfers	No
Comments	Candidates with military or prior police experience receive credit.
Where to Apply	Above address
Web	*www.austinpolice.com*

Dallas Police Department
2014 Main Street
Dallas, TX 75201
1-800-527-2984

Anticipated Positions	✪ Over 100
Profile of Department	
Sworn Officers:	2,850
Population:	1,016,000
Officer Benefits	
Starting Salary:	$24,615
Retirement:	20 years/age 50
Medical/Dental:	Yes
Educational:	No
Department Requirements	
Age:	21 minimum
Education:	45 college credits
Vision:	20/20 corrected
	20/100 uncorrected
Nonresidents	✔ Yes
Lateral Transfers	No
Comments	Will accept applicants at $19\frac{1}{2}$ with 60 college credits.
Where to Apply	Above address
Web	*www.ci.dallas.tx.us*

El Paso Police Department
911 North Raynor Street
El Paso, TX 79903
(915) 564-7300

Anticipated Positions	50 to 100
Profile of Department	
Sworn Officers:	1,000
Population:	599,500
Officer Benefits	
Starting Salary:	$25,682
Retirement:	20 years/age 45
Medical/Dental:	Yes
Educational:	Yes

Department Requirements

Age:	21 minimum
Education:	30 college credits
Vision:	20/20 corrected
	20/100 uncorrected

Nonresidents ✔ Yes

Lateral Transfers No

Comments Credits applicants with two years of public service.

Where to Apply City of El Paso
Personnel Department
#2 Civic Center Plaza
El Paso, TX 79999
(915) 541-4504

Web *www.ci.el-paso.tx.us*

Fort Worth Police Department
350 West Belknap Street
Fort Worth, TX 76102
(817) 877-8202

Anticipated Positions ✪ Over 100

Profile of Department

Sworn Officers:	1,200
Population:	479,716

Officer Benefits

Starting Salary:	$28,104
Retirement:	25 years
Medical/Dental:	Yes
Educational:	Yes

Department Requirements

Age:	21 minimum
Education:	High school
Vision:	No requirement stated

Nonresidents ✔ Yes

Lateral Transfers ➤Yes

Where to Apply City of Fort Worth
Personnel Department
1000 Throckmorton Street
Fort Worth, TX 76102
(817) 871-7756

Web *www.ci.fort-worth.tx.us*

Houston Police Department
3300 Main
Houston, TX 77002
(713) 535-7500

Anticipated Positions	✪ Over 300
Profile of Department	
Sworn Officers:	5,300
Population:	1,700,000
Officer Benefits	
Starting Salary:	$23,912
Retirement:	20 years
Medical/Dental:	Yes
Educational:	Yes
Department Requirements	
Age:	21 minimum
Education:	60 college credits
Vision:	20/20 corrected
Nonresidents	✔ Yes
Lateral Transfers	➤Yes
Where to Apply	Above address
Web	*www.ci.houston.tx.us*

San Antonio Police Department
214 West Nueva
San Antonio, TX 78207
(800) 327-3586

Anticipated Positions	✪ Over 100
Profile of Department	
Sworn Officers:	1,900
Population:	1,014,300
Officer Benefits	
Starting Salary:	$22,980
Retirement:	20 years/age 55
Medical/Dental:	Yes
Educational:	Yes
Department Requirements	
Age:	21 minimum
Education:	High school
Vision:	No requirement stated
Nonresidents	✔ Yes
Lateral Transfers	No
Where to Apply	Above address
Web	*www.ci.sat.tx.us*

UTAH

Salt Lake City Police Department
315 East 200 S
Salt Lake City, UT 84111
(801) 799-3819

Anticipated Positions	50 to 100
Profile of Department	
Sworn Officers:	394
Population:	172,500
Officer Benefits	
Starting Salary:	$22,000
Retirement:	20 years
Medical/Dental:	Yes
Educational:	Yes
Department Requirements	
Age:	21 minimum
Education:	High school
Vision:	20/20 corrected
	20/100 uncorrected
Nonresidents	✔ Yes
Lateral Transfers	No
Where to Apply	Above address
Web	*www.slpa.com*

VERMONT

Burlington Police Department
1 North Avenue
Burlington, VT 05401
(802) 658-2704

Anticipated Positions	Under 10
Profile of Department	
Sworn Officers:	92
Population:	40,000
Officer Benefits	
Starting Salary:	$21,000
Retirement:	25 years
Medical/Dental:	Yes
Educational:	Yes
Department Requirements	
Age:	18 minimum
Education:	High school
Vision:	20/20 corrected
	20/200 uncorrected
Nonresidents	✔ Yes
Lateral Transfers	➤Yes
Where to Apply	Above address
Web	*www.ci.burlington.vt.us*

VIRGINIA

Fairfax County Police Department
10600 Page Avenue
Fairfax, VA 22030
(703) 246-7912

Anticipated Positions	✪ Over 100
Profile of Department	
Sworn Officers:	1,055
Population:	875,000
Officer Benefits	
Starting Salary:	$29,194
Retirement:	25 years
Medical/Dental:	Yes
Educational:	Yes
Department Requirements	
Age:	21 minimum
Education:	High school
Vision:	20/20 corrected
	20/100 uncorrected
Nonresidents	✔ Yes
Lateral Transfers	➤Yes
Where to Apply	Above address
	(703) 324-3303
Web	*www.ci.fairfax.va.us*

WASHINGTON

King County Police Department
516 3rd Avenue
Seattle, WA 98104
(206) 296-7528

Anticipated Positions	50 to 100
Profile of Department	
Sworn Officers:	579
Population:	1,619,410
Officer Benefits	
Starting Salary:	$33,383
Retirement:	20 years/age 55
Medical/Dental:	Yes
Educational:	Yes
Department Requirements	
Age:	21 minimum
Education:	High school
Vision:	20/30 corrected
	20/100 uncorrected
Nonresidents	✔ Yes
Lateral Transfers	➤Yes
Comments	Veterans receive credit.
Where to Apply	Above address or
	(206) 296-4069
Web	*www.metrokc.gov*

Seattle Police Department
610 3rd Avenue
Seattle, WA 98104
(206) 684-5473

Anticipated Positions	Over 50
Profile of Department	
Sworn Officers:	1,260
Population:	522,000
Officer Benefits	
Starting Salary:	$37,480
Retirement:	20 years
Medical/Dental:	Yes
Educational:	No
Department Requirements	
Age:	21 minimum
Education:	60 college credits
Vision:	20/20 corrected
Nonresidents	✔ Yes
Lateral Transfers	No
Where to Apply	Above address
Web	*www.ci.seattle.wa.us*

Tacoma Police Department
747 Market Street
Tacoma, WA 98402
(206) 591-5400

Anticipated Positions	Under 50
Profile of Department	
Sworn Officers:	390
Population:	177,500
Officer Benefits	
Starting Salary:	$30,401
Retirement:	20 years
Medical/Dental:	Yes
Educational:	Yes
Department Requirements	
Age:	21 minimum
Education:	High school
Vision:	20/20 corrected
	20/200 uncorrected
Nonresidents	✔ Yes
Lateral Transfers	No
Comments	Veterans receive credit.
Where to Apply	Above address or (206) 591-5400
Web	*www.ci.tacoma.wa.us*

WEST VIRGINIA

Charleston Police Department
P.O. Box 2749
Charleston, WV 25330
(304) 348-6460

Anticipated Positions	Under 50
Profile of Department	
Sworn Officers:	175
Population:	60,000
Officer Benefits	
Starting Salary:	$21,080
Retirement:	20 years/age 50
Medical/Dental:	Yes
Educational:	No
Department Requirements	
Age:	18 minimum
Education:	High school
Vision:	20/20 corrected
	20/100 uncorrected
Nonresidents	✔ Yes
Lateral Transfers	No
Where to Apply	Above address
Web	*www.charlestonwvpolice.org*

WISCONSIN

Milwaukee Police Department
809 North Broadway
Milwaukee, WI 53233
(414) 286-5000

Anticipated Positions	✪ Over 600
Profile of Department	
Sworn Officers:	2,151
Population:	590,500
Officer Benefits	
Starting Salary:	$26,000
Retirement:	25 years
Medical/Dental:	Yes
Educational:	Yes
Department Requirements	
Age:	21 minimum
Education:	60 college credits
Vision:	20/20 corrected
Nonresidents	✔ Yes
Lateral Transfers	No
Where to Apply	Above address
Web	*www.milw-police.org*

LARGE SHERIFF DEPARTMENTS

○ Deputy Sheriff

MISSION   County sheriff departments function exactly like municipal police departments, performing a variety of duties involving patrol and investigations. County jurisdictions are usually large in physical size, but population and crime rates vary greatly. In addition, each county sheriff is responsible for the operation of the county correctional facility.

PROFILE   There are more than 140,000 Deputy Sheriffs nationwide.

COMMENTS   *Employment Outlook:* The future outlook is excellent. Currently, the country is on a pro-law enforcement bandwagon and almost every municipality in the country is looking for ways to increase its police or sheriff department's ranks. In addition, the Crime Bill has added special funds for hiring police officers in many cities and towns.

Employment Conditions: Conditions vary from county to county nationwide, however, there is a trend for county law enforcement agencies to increase their educational requirement from high school to at least 60 college credits. Many sheriff departments require entry officers to serve in their corrections operation as jail officers before having other assignments such as road patrol.

WHERE TO APPLY   Apply directly to any of the Sheriff Departments listed or contact your local Sheriff Department.

SHERIFFS' DEPARTMENT STRUCTURE

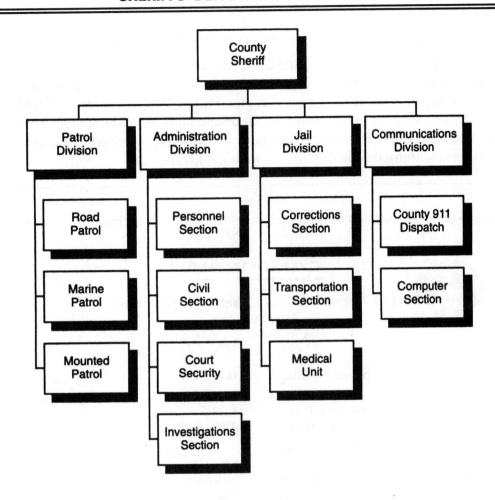

Opportunities

See page 5 for explanations of the entries in the following listings:

CALIFORNIA

Los Angeles County Sheriff Department
Temple Street
Los Angeles, CA 90012
(213) 526-5635

Anticipated Positions	✪ Over 400
Profile of Department	
Sworn Officers:	8,021
Population:	9,127,751
Officer Benefits	
Starting Salary:	$40,349
Retirement:	20 years
Medical/Dental:	Yes
Educational:	Yes
Department Requirements	
Age:	$19\frac{1}{2}$ minimum
Education:	High school
Vision:	20/30 corrected
Nonresidents	✔ Yes
Lateral Transfers	➤Yes
Where to Apply	Recruitment Unit
	11515 South Culima Street
	Whittier, CA 90604
	(310) 946-7012
Web	*www.la-sheriff.org*

Riverside County Sheriff Department
4095 Lemon Street
Riverside, CA 92501
(909) 275-6137

Anticipated Positions	✪ Over 100
Profile of Department	
Sworn Officers:	1,179
Population:	1,417,425
Officer Benefits	
Starting Salary:	$35,006
Retirement:	Age 50
Medical/Dental:	Yes
Educational:	No
Department Requirements	
Age:	21 minimum
Education:	High school
Vision:	20/20 corrected
	20/200 uncorrected
Nonresidents	✔ Yes
Lateral Transfers	➤Yes
Where to Apply	Riverside County Personnel Department
	4080 Lemon Street
	Riverside, CA 92502
	(909) 275-3500
Web	*www.co.riverside.ca.us*

San Diego County Sheriff Department
P.O. Box 429000
San Diego, CA 92142
(619) 565-5200

Anticipated Positions	✪ Over 100
Profile of Department	
Sworn Officers:	1,861
Population:	2,655,463
Officer Benefits	
Starting Salary:	$40,560
Retirement:	20 years/age 55
Medical/Dental:	Yes
Educational:	No
Department Requirements	
Age:	21 minimum
Education:	High school
Vision:	20/20 corrected
	20/100 uncorrected
Nonresidents	✔ Yes
Lateral Transfers	➤Yes
Where to Apply	Above address
Web	*www.co.san-diego.ca.us*

FLORIDA

Broward County Sheriff Department
2601 West Brue Blvd.
Fort Lauderdale, FL 33311
(954) 321-4400

Anticipated Positions	✪ Over 100
Profile of Department	
Sworn Officers:	1,906
Population:	1,438,228
Officer Benefits	
Starting Salary:	$29,169
Retirement:	20 years
Medical/Dental:	Yes
Educational:	Yes
Department Requirements	
Age:	19 minimum
Education:	High school
Vision:	20/20 corrected
Nonresidents	✔ Yes
Lateral Transfers	➤Yes
Where to Apply	Above address
Web	*www.sheriff.org*

Jacksonville Sheriff Department
501 East Bay Street
Jacksonville, FL 32202
(904) 630-2134

Anticipated Positions	Under 50
Profile of Department	
Sworn Officers:	1,438
Population:	679,792
Officer Benefits	
Starting Salary:	$28,692
Retirement:	25 years
Medical/Dental:	Yes
Educational:	Yes
Department Requirements	
Age:	21 minimum
Education:	60 college credits
Vision:	20/20 corrected
Nonresidents	✔ Yes
Lateral Transfers	In-state only
Where to Apply	Above address

Palm Beach County Sheriff Department
3228 Gun Club Road
West Palm Beach, FL 33406
(407) 688-3540

Anticipated Positions	✪ Over 100
Profile of Department	
Sworn Officers:	1,615
Population:	992,840
Officer Benefits	
Starting Salary:	$27,072
Retirement:	10 years/age 55
Medical/Dental:	Yes
Educational:	Yes
Department Requirements	
Age:	21 minimum
Education:	High school
Vision:	20/20 corrected
	20/100 uncorrected
Nonresidents	No
Lateral Transfers	No
Where to Apply	Above address
	(501) 371-4862 only
Web	*www.pbsd.org*

IDAHO

Ada County Sheriff Office
7200 Barrister Drive
Boise, ID 83704
(208) 377-6561

Anticipated Positions	Patrol services under 50
	Jail services over 100
Profile of Department	
Sworn Officers:	222
Population:	260,057
Officer Benefits	
Starting Salary:	$20,904
Retirement:	20 years/age 55
Medical/Dental:	Yes
Educational:	No
Department Requirements	
Age:	21 minimum
Education:	64 college credits
Vision:	20/20 corrected
	20/60 uncorrected
Nonresidents	✔ Yes
Lateral Transfers	No
Where to Apply	Above address
Web	*www.adasheriff.org*

ILLINOIS

Cook County Sheriff Department
704 Daley Center
Chicago, IL 60602
(312) 443-7938

Anticipated Positions	✪ Over 400
Profile of Department	
Sworn Officers:	5,600
Population:	5,096,540
Officer Benefits	
Starting Salary:	$32,000
Retirement:	20 years
Medical/Dental:	Yes
Educational:	Yes
Department Requirements	
Age:	21 minimum
Education:	High school
Vision:	20/20 corrected
Nonresidents	✔ Yes
Lateral Transfers	No
Where to Apply	Cook County Sheriff Merit Board
	118 North Clark Street
	Room 1079
	Chicago, IL 60602
Web	*www.cookcountysheriff.org*

NEW YORK

Erie County Sheriff Department
10 Delaware Avenue
Buffalo, NY 14202
(716) 858-7630

Anticipated Positions	Under 20
Profile of Department	
Sworn Officers:	530
Population:	954,621
Officer Benefits	
Starting Salary:	$29,197
Retirement:	20 years/age 55
Medical/Dental:	Yes
Educational:	No
Department Requirements	
Age:	21 minimum
Education:	60 college credits
Vision:	20/20 corrected
	20/40 uncorrected

Nonresidents	No
Lateral Transfers	No
Where to Apply	Erie County Civil Service
	95 Franklin, Room 604
	Buffalo, NY 14202
	(716) 858-8729
Web	*www.erie.gov*

Monroe County Sheriff Department
130 Plymouth Avenue
Rochester, NY 14614
(716) 428-3138

Anticipated Positions	50 to 100
Profile of Department	
Sworn Officers:	757
Population:	721,996
Officer Benefits	
Starting Salary:	$25,281
Retirement:	20 years/age 55
Medical/Dental:	Yes
Educational:	Yes
Department Requirements	
Age:	18 minimum
Education:	High school
Vision:	20/20 corrected
	20/40 uncorrected
Nonresidents	✔ Yes
Lateral Transfers	➤Yes
Where to Apply	Above address
Web	*www.co.monroe.ny.us*

TEXAS

Bexar County Sheriff Department
200 North Comal
San Antonio, TX 78207
(210) 270-6242

Anticipated Positions	✪ Over 100
Profile of Department	
Sworn Officers:	1,315
Population:	1,318,322
Officer Benefits	
Starting Salary:	$26,112
Retirement:	25 years
Medical/Dental:	Yes
Educational:	No

Department Requirements	
Age:	19 minimum
Education:	High school
Vision:	20/30 corrected
	20/100 uncorrected
Nonresidents	✔ Yes
Lateral Transfers	No
Comments	Combined organization of patrol, investigations, and jail services.
Where to Apply	Bexar County Civil Service Commission 100 Dolorosa San Antonio, TX 78205
Web	*www.co.bexar.tx.us*

Harris County Sheriff Department
1301 Franklin Street
Houston, TX 77002
(713) 921-8892

Anticipated Positions	✪ Over 100
Profile of Department	
Sworn Officers:	2,474
Population:	3,126,966
Officer Benefits	
Starting Salary:	$29,000
Retirement:	25 years
Medical/Dental:	Yes
Educational:	Yes
Department Requirements	
Age:	20 minimum
Education:	High school
Vision:	20/20 corrected
Nonresidents	✔ Yes
Lateral Transfers	➤Yes (Texas Only)
Where to Apply	Above address
Web	*www.co.harris.tx.us*

Chapter 6

STATE LAW ENFORCEMENT AGENCIES

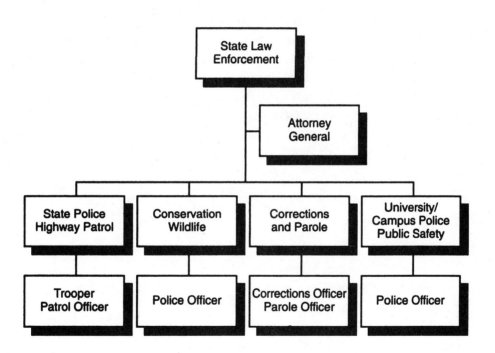

STATE LAW ENFORCEMENT

OVERVIEW   Each state in the nation has its own law enforcement system. Some state law enforcement agencies are considered direct hires, meaning that they can hire without approval from the state civil service or personnel department. Experienced law enforcement officers should explore career opportunities with a multitude of state investigative forces such as the state attorney general offices. Parole and probation departments usually hire candidates with at least a four-year degree or law enforcement experience. The problem with obtaining positions in these offices is that they are small in force number, meaning the competition will remain tight with other experienced law enforcement officers. Specialized offices such as these tend to have a large pool of candidates from which to choose. For that reason, we have profiled the four largest state agencies that hire at a significant level, and only listed the others as follows:

- State Police and Highway Patrol Agencies
- State Corrections Departments
- State Conservation, Wildlife, and Park Police Departments
- State College Law Enforcement Agencies
- State Parole and Probation Agencies
- State Attorney General Offices

STATE POLICE OFFICER/TROOPER
HIGHWAY PATROL OFFICER

⬭ **State Police Officer/Trooper**
⬭ **State Highway Patrol Officer**

MISSION   State Police or Highway Patrols serve as the main law enforcement agencies to ensure public safety on the highways, freeways, and turnpikes throughout the country. They direct traffic, assist motorists, deal with emergencies, and arrest violators for a variety of criminal offenses. In many states, officers work alone covering large areas of jurisdiction or posts. State Police Officers, or Troopers, differ from Highway Patrol Officers. State Troopers in many states are the major police agency responsible for a wide range of law enforcement to include criminal investigations and regulatory work, and are not restricted to highway patrol. Within the Texas State Police system exists the famous Texas Rangers, an elite investigative unit that has a primary function to investigate felony crimes. Hawaii is the only state that does not have a State Police Agency. There are over 54,000 State Police Officers nationwide.

COMMENTS   *Employment Outlook:* The overall outlook for State Police and Highway employment is good. Certain states will be hiring at an increased level. Check the profile section to note these agencies.

Employment Conditions: After graduation from State Police Academy, probationary officers may be assigned to any section of the state. State Police Officers can be reassigned to another part of the state without warning. The officer could also be required to move to the new post area, which could mean uprooting a family. Many officers spend their careers "working their way back home" before they retire. Officers work outdoors and in hazardous situations for extended periods of time. State Police are often sent to posts or barracks in remote areas and may work alone in very large sectors or regions.

WHERE TO APPLY   Directly to the agencies listed on page 117.

STATE POLICE DEPARTMENT STRUCTURE

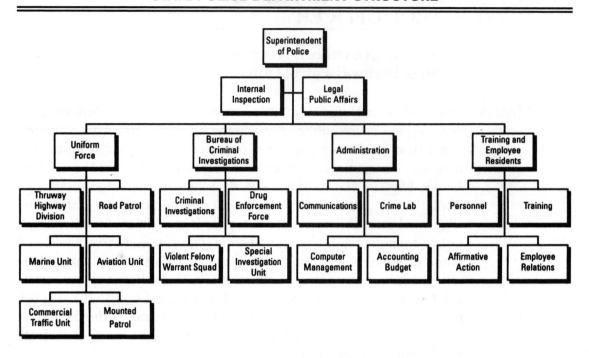

TYPICAL PROMOTION / CAREER LADDER

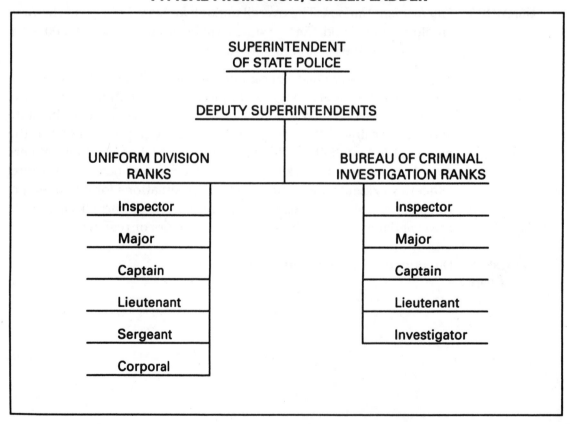

Opportunities

See page 5 for explanations of the entries in the following listings:

ALABAMA

Alabama Department of Public Safety
Public Safety Building
500 Dexter Avenue
Montgomery, AL 36130
(205) 242-4445

Anticipated Positions	✪ Over 100
Profile of Department	
Sworn Officers:	716
Population:	4,287,178
Officer Benefits	
Starting Salary:	$22,820
Retirement:	20 years/age 55
Medical/Dental:	Yes
Educational:	No
Department Requirements	
Age:	18 minimum
Education:	High school
Vision:	20/30 corrected
Nonresidents	✔ Yes
Lateral Transfers	No
Where to Apply	Above address
Web	*www.agencies.state.al.us*

ALASKA

State Troopers Division
5700 East Tudor Road
Anchorage, AK 99507
(907) 269-5511

Anticipated Positions	50 to 100
Profile of Department Jurisdiction	
Sworn Officers:	321
Population:	604,966
Officer Benefits	
Starting Salary:	$42,275
Retirement:	20 years/age 55
Medical/Dental:	Yes
Educational:	No
Department Requirements	
Age:	21 minimum
Education:	High school
Vision:	20/30 corrected
Nonresidents	✔ Yes
Lateral Transfers	Note comments
Comments	Certified officers can be hired in a more expeditious manner. Selection process includes Wildlife Law Enforcement Troopers.
Where to Apply	Above address
Web	*www.dps.state.ak.us*

ARIZONA

Arizona Highway Patrol
Department of Public Safety
Phoenix, AZ 85005
(602) 223-2000

Anticipated Positions	Undetermined
Profile of Department	
Sworn Officers:	966
Population:	4,434,340
Officer Benefits	
Starting Salary:	$28,723
Retirement:	20 years/age 55
Medical/Dental:	Yes
Educational:	Yes

Department Requirements

Age:	21 minimum
Education:	High school
Vision:	20/20 corrected
Nonresidents	✔ Yes
Lateral Transfers	No
Where to Apply	Above address
Web	*www.dps.state.az.us*

ARKANSAS

Arkansas State Police
Department of Public Safety
P.O. Box 5901
Little Rock, AR 72215
(501) 221-8240

Anticipated Positions	50 to 100
Profile of Department	
Sworn Officers:	505
Population:	2,506,293
Officer Benefits	
Starting Salary:	$20,140
Retirement:	10 years/age 52
Medical/Dental:	Yes
Educational:	Yes
Department Requirements	
Age:	22 minimum
Education:	High school
Vision:	20/20 corrected
	20/100 uncorrected
Nonresidents	No
Lateral Transfers	No
Comments	Higher education applicants are considered priority status. Those with military and prior law enforcement experience also receive special consideration.
Where to Apply	Above address
Web	*www.state.ar.us*

CALIFORNIA

California Highway Patrol
2555 First Avenue
Sacramento, CA 95818
(916) 657-7261

Anticipated Positions	✪ Over 100
Profile of Department	
Sworn Officers:	6,532
Population:	31,857,646
Officer Benefits	
Starting Salary:	$37,872
Retirement:	Age 50
Medical/Dental:	Yes
Educational:	Yes
Department Requirements	
Age:	21 minimum
Education:	High school
Vision:	20/20 corrected
	20/40 uncorrected
Nonresidents	No
Lateral Transfers	No
Where to Apply	California Highway Patrol
	444 North 3rd Street
	Sacramento, CA 95814
Web	*www.chp.ca.gov*

COLORADO

Colorado State Patrol
700 Kipling Street
Denver, CO 80215
(303) 239-4539

Anticipated Positions	✪ Over 100
Profile of Department	
Sworn Officers:	568
Population:	3,816,646
Officer Benefits	
Starting Salary:	$24,300
Retirement:	20 years/age 55
Medical/Dental:	Yes
Educational:	No
Department Requirements	
Age:	21 minimum
Education:	High school
Vision:	20/20 corrected

Nonresidents	✔ Yes
Lateral Transfers	No
Comments	Candidates with a college education are desired.
Where to Apply	Above address
Web	*www.state.co.us*

CONNECTICUT

Connecticut State Police
1111 Country Club Road
Middletown, CT 06457
(860) 685-8230

Anticipated Positions	✪ Over 100
Profile of Department	
Sworn Officers:	945
Population:	3,267,293
Officer Benefits	
Starting Salary:	$37,108
Retirement:	20 years
Medical/Dental:	Yes
Educational:	No
Department Requirements	
Age:	18 minimum
Education:	High school
Vision:	20/20 corrected
	20/70 uncorrected
Nonresidents	✔ Yes
Lateral Transfers	No
Where to Apply	Above address
Web	*www.state.ct.us*

FLORIDA

Florida Highway Patrol
2900 Apalachee Parkway
Tallahassee, FL 32399
(904) 487-3139

Anticipated Positions	Undetermined
Profile of Department	
Sworn Officers:	1,637
Population:	14,418,917
Officer Benefits	
Starting Salary:	$22,287
Retirement:	21 years
Medical/Dental:	Yes
Educational:	No

Department Requirements

Age:	19 minimum
Education:	60 college credits
Vision:	20/30 corrected
	20/100 uncorrected

Nonresidents	✔ Yes
Lateral Transfers	No
Where to Apply	Above address
	(904) 921-8961
Web	*www.fdle.state.fl.us*

IDAHO

Idaho State Police
Department of Law Enforcement
P.O. Box 700
Boise, ID 83680

Anticipated Positions	Under 50

Profile of Department

Sworn Officers:	195
Population:	1,187,597

Officer Benefits

Starting Salary:	$25,147
Retirement:	Age 50
Medical/Dental:	Yes
Educational:	No

Department Requirements

Age:	None
Education:	High school/Veteran
Vision:	20/20 corrected
	20/200 uncorrected

Nonresidents	✔ Yes
Lateral Transfers	No
Comments	Two years of work experience, military service, or college are required in addition.
Where to Apply	Idaho Personnel Commission
	700 West State Street
	Boise, ID 83720
	(208) 334-2263
Web	*www.state.id.us*

ILLINOIS

Illinois State Highway Police
201 East Adams
Springfield, IL 62701
(217) 782-6637

Anticipated Positions	✪ Over 100
Profile of Department	
Sworn Officers:	1,980
Population:	11,845,316
Officer Benefits	
Starting Salary:	$32,500
Retirement:	25 years/age 50
Medical/Dental:	Yes
Educational:	Yes
Department Requirements	
Age:	21 minimum
Education:	60 college credits
Vision:	20/20 corrected
Nonresidents	✔ Yes
Lateral Transfers	No
Where to Apply	Above address
Web	*www.state.il.us*

INDIANA

Indiana State Police
100 North Senate Avenue
Indianapolis, IN 46204
(312) 232-8277

Anticipated Positions	✪ Over 100
Profile of Department	
Sworn Officers:	1,222
Population:	5,828,090
Officer Benefits	
Starting Salary:	$22,438
Retirement:	25 years
Medical/Dental:	Yes
Educational:	No
Department Requirements	
Age:	22 minimum
Education:	Two-year college degree
Vision:	20/50 corrected
Nonresidents	✔ Yes
Lateral Transfers	No
Where to Apply	Above address
	(312) 232-8277
Web	*www.state.in.us*

IOWA

Iowa State Police
Wallace State Office Building
East 9th and Grand Avenue
Des Moines, IA 50319
(515) 281-7963

Anticipated Positions	50 to 100
Profile of Department	
Sworn Officers:	432
Population:	2,848,033
Officer Benefits	
Starting Salary:	$32,593
Retirement:	22 years/age 55
Medical/Dental:	Yes
Educational:	No requirement stated
Department Requirements	
Age:	22 minimum
Education:	High school
Vision:	20/20 corrected
	20/100 uncorrected
Nonresidents	✔ Yes
Lateral Transfers	No
Comments	Several position options with Iowa Department of Public Safety
Where to Apply	Above address
	(515) 281-5639
Web	*www.state.ia.us*

KANSAS

Kansas State Highway Patrol
122 SW 7th Street
Topeka, KS 66603
(913) 296-6800

Anticipated Positions	50 to 100
Profile of Department	
Sworn Officers:	526
Population:	2,579,149
Officer Benefits	
Starting Salary:	$25,376
Retirement:	25 years/age 50
Medical/Dental:	Yes
Educational:	No

Department Requirements

Age:	21 minimum
Education:	High school
Vision:	20/25 corrected

Nonresidents ✔ Yes

Lateral Transfers No

Where to Apply Above address

Web *www.state.ks.us*

KENTUCKY

Kentucky State Police
Department of Public Safety
919 Versailles Road
Frankfort, KY 40601
(502) 695-6341

Anticipated Positions ✪ Over 200

Profile of Department

Sworn Officers:	918
Population:	3,882,071

Officer Benefits

Starting Salary:	$24,588
Retirement:	20 years/age 50
Medical/Dental:	Yes
Educational:	Yes

Department Requirements

Age:	21 minimum
Education:	60 college credits
Vision:	No requirement stated

Nonresidents ✔ Yes

Lateral Transfers No

Where to Apply Above address

Web *www.state.ky.us*

LOUISIANA

Louisiana State Police
265 South Foster Drive
Baton Rouge, LA 70896
(504) 925-6202

Anticipated Positions	✪ Over 100
Profile of Department	
Sworn Officers:	909
Population:	4,340,818
Officer Benefits	
Starting Salary:	$20,124
Retirement:	20 years/age 50
Medical/Dental:	Yes
Educational:	No
Department Requirements	
Age:	18 minimum
Education:	60 college credits
Vision:	20/30 corrected
	20/200 uncorrected
Nonresidents	✔ Yes
Lateral Transfers	No
Where to Apply	Above address
Web	*www.spc.state.la.us*

MAINE

Maine State Police
36 Hospital Street
Augusta, ME 04330
(207) 624-7000

Anticipated Positions	50 to 100
Profile of Department	
Sworn Officers:	337
Population:	1,238,566
Officer Benefits	
Starting Salary:	$23,899
Retirement:	25 years/age 55
Medical/Dental:	Yes
Educational:	No
Department Requirements	
Age:	21 minimum
Education:	High school
Vision:	20/20 corrected
Nonresidents	✔ Yes
Lateral Transfers	No
Where to Apply	Above address
Web	*www.state.me.us*

MARYLAND

Maryland State Police
1201 Reistertown Road
Pikesville, MD 21208
(410) 653-4281

Anticipated Positions	✪ Over 100
Profile of Department	
Sworn Officers:	1,516
Population:	5,060,296
Officer Benefits	
Starting Salary:	$28,735
Retirement:	20 years/age 60
Medical/Dental:	Yes
Educational:	No
Department Requirements	
Age:	21 minimum
Education:	Four-year college degree
Vision:	20/30 corrected
	20/70 uncorrected
Nonresidents	No
Lateral Transfers	No
Where to Apply	Above address
Web	*www.state.md.us*

MASSACHUSETTS

Massachusetts State Police
470 Worcester Road
Framingham, MA 01701
(508) 820-2290

Anticipated Positions	Undetermined
Profile of Department	
Sworn Officers:	2,270
Population:	6,085,395
Officer Benefits	
Starting Salary:	$31,140
Retirement:	20 years/age 55
Medical/Dental:	Yes
Educational:	Yes
Department Requirements	
Age:	19 minimum
Education:	High school
Vision:	20/20 corrected
Nonresidents	✔ Yes
Lateral Transfers	No
Where to Apply	Above address
Web	*www.state.ma.us*

MICHIGAN

Michigan State Police
714 South Harrison Road
East Lansing, MI 48823
(517) 336-6686

Anticipated Positions	✪ Over 100
Profile of Department	
Sworn Officers:	2,054
Population:	9,730,925
Officer Benefits	
Starting Salary:	$28,814
Retirement:	25 years/age 55
Medical/Dental:	Yes
Educational:	Yes
Department Requirements	
Age:	21 minimum
Education:	High school
Vision:	20/20 corrected
Nonresidents	No
Lateral Transfers	No
Where to Apply	Above address
Web	*www.state.mi.us*

MINNESOTA

Minnesota Highway Patrol
444 Cedar Street
St. Paul, MN 55101
(612) 282-6870

Anticipated Positions	50 to 100
Profile of Department	
Sworn Officers:	499
Population:	4,648,596
Officer Benefits	
Starting Salary:	$32,823
Retirement:	Age 50
Medical/Dental:	Yes
Educational:	Yes
Department Requirements	
Age:	None
Education:	60 credits/Vetran
Vision:	20/30 corrected
	20/50 uncorrected

Nonresidents	✔ Yes
Lateral Transfers	No
Comments	Veterans receive credit, special recruitment for women and minorities.
Where to Apply	Minnesota Department of Employee Relations 658 Cedar Street St. Paul, MN 55155 (612) 296-2616
Web	*www.dps.state.mn.us*

MISSOURI

Missouri State Highway Patrol
P.O. Box 568
Jefferson City, MO 65102
(573) 751-3313

Anticipated Positions	50 to 100
Profile of Department	
Sworn Officers:	1,056
Population:	5,363,669
Officer Benefits	
Starting Salary:	$27,120
Retirement:	25 years
Medical/Dental:	No
Educational:	No
Department Requirements	
Age:	21 minimum
Education:	High school
Vision:	20/20 corrected 20/40 uncorrected
Nonresidents	✔ Yes
Lateral Transfers	No
Where to Apply	Human Resources Division
Web	*www.dps.state.mo.us*

MONTANA

Montana Highway Patrol
2550 Prospect Avenue
Helena, MT 59620
(406) 444-3780

Anticipated Positions	50 to 100
Profile of Department	
Sworn Officers:	212
Population:	876,684
Officer Benefits	
Starting Salary:	$22,882
Retirement:	20 years/age 50
Medical/Dental:	Yes
Educational:	No
Department Requirements	
Age:	18 minimum
Education:	60 college credits
Vision:	20/20 corrected
	20/50 uncorrected
Nonresidents	✔ Yes
Lateral Transfers	No
Where to Apply	Above address or
	(406) 444-3259
Web	*www.state.mt.us*

NEBRASKA

Nebraska State Patrol
1600 Nebraska Highway #2
Lincoln, NE 68502
(402) 471-4545

Anticipated Positions	50 to 100
Profile of Department	
Sworn Officers:	466
Population:	1,648,696
Officer Benefits	
Starting Salary:	$24,125
Retirement:	25 years/age 50
Medical/Dental:	Half
Educational:	No
Department Requirements	
Age:	21 minimum
Education:	High school
Vision:	20/20 corrected
	20/100 uncorrected

Nonresidents	✔ Yes
Lateral Transfers	No
Where to Apply	Nebraska State Patrol Training Academy
	3510 NW 36th Street
	Lincoln, NE 68524
	(402) 470-2404
Web	*www.nebraska-state-patrol.org*

NEVADA

Nevada State Highway Patrol
Division of Law Enforcement
357 Hammill Lane
Reno, NV 89511
(702) 688-2741

Anticipated Positions	✪ Over 100
Profile of Department	
Sworn Officers:	375
Population:	1,600,810
Officer Benefits	
Starting Salary:	$24,125
Retirement:	20 years/age 50
Medical/Dental:	Yes
Educational:	Yes
Department Requirements	
Age:	21 minimum
Education:	High school
Vision:	20/20 corrected
	20/40 uncorrected
Nonresidents	✔ Yes
Lateral Transfers	No
Comments	Residents receive extra points.
Where to Apply	Above address
Web	*www.state.nv.us*

NEW JERSEY

New Jersey State Police
P.O. Box 7068, River Road
West Trenton, NJ 08628
(609) 882-2000

Anticipated Positions	✪ Over 100
Profile of Department	
Sworn Officers:	2,555
Population:	8,001,850
Officer Benefits	
Starting Salary:	$34,714
Retirement:	20 years/age 55
Medical/Dental:	Yes
Educational:	No
Department Requirements	
Age:	18 minimum
Education:	Four-year college degree
Vision:	20/30 corrected
Nonresidents	✔ Yes
Lateral Transfers	No
Comments	New Jersey State Police have a "walk-in" exam system, gives credit for candidates with military service or law enforcement experience.
Where to Apply	Above address
Web	*www.state.nj.us*

NEW YORK

New York State Police
Campus, Public Security Building 22
Albany, NY 12226
(518) 457-2180

Anticipated Positions	✪ Over 100
Profile of Department	
Sworn Officers:	3,957
Population:	18,134,226
Officer Benefits	
Starting Salary:	$33,313
Retirement:	20 years/age 55
Medical/Dental:	Yes
Educational:	Yes

Department Requirements

Age:	21 minimum
Education:	60 college credits
Vision:	20/20 corrected
	20/40 uncorrected
Nonresidents	✔ Yes
Lateral Transfers	No
Where to Apply	Above address
Web	*www.troopers.state.ny.us*

NORTH CAROLINA

North Carolina Highway Patrol
512 North Salisbury Street
Raleigh, NC 27611
(919) 733-7952

Anticipated Positions	Undetermined
Profile of Department	
Sworn Officers:	1,298
Population:	7,309,055
Officer Benefits	
Starting Salary:	$24,838
Retirement:	30 years/age 55
Medical/Dental:	Yes
Educational:	Yes
Department Requirements	
Age:	21 minimum
Education:	High school
Vision:	20/20 corrected
	20/50 uncorrected
Nonresidents	No
Lateral Transfers	No
Where to Apply	Above address
Web	*www.ncshp.org*

NORTH DAKOTA

North Dakota Highway Patrol
600 East Boulevard Avenue
Bismarck, ND 58505
(701) 328-2456

Anticipated Positions	Under 50
Profile of Department	
Sworn Officers:	131
Population:	642,630
Officer Benefits	
Starting Salary:	$25,872
Retirement:	10 (years) vested
Medical/Dental:	Yes
Educational:	Yes
Department Requirements	
Age:	No requirement stated
Education:	Four years of college
Vision:	20/30 corrected
Nonresidents	✔ Yes
Lateral Transfers	No
Comments	Accepts combination of college and/or work experience.
Where to Apply	Above address
Web	*www.state.nd.us*

OHIO

Ohio State Highway Patrol
660 East Main Street
Columbus, OH 43205
(614) 752-2792

Anticipated Positions	✪ Over 100
Profile of Department	
Sworn Officers:	1,390
Population:	11,162,797
Officer Benefits	
Starting Salary:	$25,147
Retirement:	20 years/age 55
Medical/Dental:	Yes
Educational:	Yes

Department Requirements

Age:	21 minimum
Education:	High school
Vision:	20/20 corrected
	20/60 uncorrected
Nonresidents	✔ Yes
Lateral Transfers	No
Where to Apply	OSHP—Recruitment Section
	740 East 17th Avenue
	Columbus, OH 43211
	(614) 466-6019
Web	*www.state.oh.us*

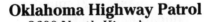

OKLAHOMA

Oklahoma Highway Patrol
3600 North King Avenue
Oklahoma City, OK 73136
(405) 425-2424

Anticipated Positions	✪ Over 100

Profile of Department

Sworn Officers:	747
Population:	3,295,315

Officer Benefits

Starting Salary:	$24,454
Retirement:	20 years
Medical/Dental:	Yes
Educational:	Yes

Department Requirements

Age:	23 minimum
Education:	30 college credits
Vision:	20/20 corrected
	20/70 uncorrected
Nonresidents	No
Lateral Transfers	No
Where to Apply	Above address
Web	*www.state.ok.us*

PENNSYLVANIA

Pennsylvania State Police
1800 Elmerton Avenue
Harrisburg, PA 17110
(717) 787-6941

Anticipated Positions	✪ Over 800
Profile of Department	
Sworn Officers:	4,098
Population:	12,040,084
Officer Benefits	
Starting Salary:	$33,612
Retirement:	10 years
Medical/Dental:	Yes
Educational:	No
Department Requirements	
Age:	21 minimum
Education:	60 college credits
Vision:	20/30 corrected
	20/70 uncorrected
Nonresidents	✔ Yes
Lateral Transfers	No
Comments	Credit is given for military and police experience.
Where to Apply	Above address
Web	*www.state.pa.us*

RHODE ISLAND

Rhode Island State Police
311 Danielson Pike
North Scituate, RI 02857
(401) 444-1000

Anticipated Positions	Under 50
Profile of Department	
Sworn Officers:	184
Population:	988,283
Officer Benefits	
Starting Salary:	$33,000
Retirement:	25 years/age 65
Medical/Dental:	Yes
Educational:	No

Department Requirements

Age:	18 minimum
Education:	High school
Vision:	20/20 corrected
	20/50 uncorrected

Nonresidents	✔ Yes
Lateral Transfers	No
Where to Apply	Above address or
	(401) 444-1192
Web	*www.state.ri.us*

SOUTH DAKOTA

South Dakota Highway Patrol
500 East Capitol Avenue
Pierre, SD 57501-5070
(605) 773-3105

Anticipated Positions	Under 50

Profile of Department

Sworn Officers:	154
Population:	737,561

Officer Benefits

Starting Salary:	$23,192
Retirement:	20 years/age 50
Medical/Dental:	Yes
Educational:	Yes

Department Requirements

Age:	21 minimum
Education:	High school
Vision:	20/20 corrected
	20/100 uncorrected

Nonresidents	✔ Yes
Lateral Transfers	No
Where to Apply	Above address or
	(605) 773-3148
Web	*www.state.sd.us*

TENNESSEE

Tennessee Highway Patrol Division
Department of Safety
1150 Foster Avenue
Nashville, TN 37210
(615) 251-5200

Anticipated Positions	✪ Over 100	
Profile of Department		
Sworn Officers:	913	
Population:	5,307,381	
Officer Benefits		
Starting Salary:	$22,944	
Retirement:	30 years	
Medical/Dental:	Yes	
Educational:	Yes	
Department Requirements		
Age:	21 minimum	
Education:	High school	
Vision:	20/30 corrected	
Nonresidents	✔ Yes	
Lateral Transfers	➤ Yes	
Where to Apply	Above address	
Web	*www.state.tn.us*	

TEXAS

Texas State Police
Department of Public Safety
5805 North Lamar Boulevard
Austin, TX 78752
(512) 465-2000

Anticipated Positions	✪ Over 100	
Profile of Department		
Sworn Officers:	2,757	
Population:	19,091,207	
Officer Benefits		
Starting Salary:	$23,796	
Retirement:	20 years	
Medical/Dental:	Yes	
Educational:	Yes	
Department Requirements		
Age:	21 minimum	
Education:	60 college credits	
Vision:	20/30 corrected	

Nonresidents	✔ Yes
Lateral Transfers	No
Comments	The elite Texas Rangers are selected from the ranks of the Texas State Police.
Where to Apply	Above address
Web	*www.thpa.org*

UTAH

Utah Highway Patrol
Department of Public Safety
4501 South 2700 West
Salt Lake City, UT 84119
(801) 965-4518

Anticipated Positions	Under 50
Profile of Department	
Sworn Officers:	389
Population:	2,017,572
Officer Benefits	
Starting Salary:	$24,847
Retirement:	20 years
Medical/Dental:	Yes
Educational:	Yes
Department Requirements	
Age:	21 minimum
Education:	High school
Vision:	20/20 corrected
	20/40 uncorrected
Nonresidents	✔ Yes
Lateral Transfers	No
Comments	Experienced personnel can be hired at a higher salary.
Where to Apply	Above address
Web	*www.state.ut.us*

VERMONT

Vermont State Police
Public Safety Department
Waterbury State Complex
103 South Main Street
Waterbury, VT 05676
(802) 244-8718

Anticipated Positions	Under 50
Profile of Department	
Sworn Officers:	263
Population:	586,461
Officer Benefits	
Starting Salary:	$20,488
Retirement:	20 years
Medical/Dental:	Yes
Educational:	Yes
Department Requirements	
Age:	21 minimum
Education:	High school
Vision:	20/40 corrected
Nonresidents	✔ Yes
Lateral Transfers	No
Where to Apply	Above address
Web	*www.dps.state.vt.us*

VIRGINIA

Department of State Police
P.O. Box 27472
Richmond, VA 23261-7472
(804) 674-2000

Anticipated Positions	Undetermined
Profile of Department	
Sworn Officers:	1,658
Population:	6,666,167
Officer Benefits	
Starting Salary:	$23,401
Retirement:	25 years/age 50
Medical/Dental:	Yes
Educational:	No
Department Requirements	
Age:	21 minimum
Education:	High school
Vision:	20/20 corrected
	20/100 uncorrected

Nonresidents	✔ Yes
Lateral Transfers	No
Where to Apply	Above address
Web	*www.state.va.us*

WASHINGTON

Washington State Patrol
Headquarters Administration Building
Olympia, WA 98504
(360) 753-6540

Anticipated Positions	✪ Over 100
Profile of Department	
Sworn Officers:	935
Population:	5,519,525
Officer Benefits	
Starting Salary:	$31,776
Retirement:	25 years/age 60
Medical/Dental:	Yes
Educational:	Yes
Department Requirements	
Age:	21 minimum
Education:	High school
Vision:	20/20 corrected
	20/50 uncorrected
Nonresidents	✔ Yes
Lateral Transfers	No
Where to Apply	WSP—Human Resources Division
	P.O. Box 42620
	Lacey, WA 98504
	(360) 438-5800
Web	*www.wa.gov*

WEST VIRGINIA

West Virginia State Police
725 Jefferson Road
South Charleston, WV 25309
(304) 746-2100

Anticipated Positions	50 to 100
Profile of Department	
Sworn Officers:	608
Population:	1,820,407
Officer Benefits	
Starting Salary:	$20,976
Retirement:	25 years
Medical/Dental:	Yes
Educational:	No
Department Requirements	
Age:	21 minimum
Education:	High school
Vision:	20/30 corrected
	20/100 uncorrected
Nonresidents	✔ Yes
Lateral Transfers	No
Where to Apply	Above address
Web	*www.state.wv.us*

WYOMING

Wyoming Highway Patrol
P.O. Box 1708
Cheyenne, WY 82003
(307) 777-4301

Anticipated Positions	Under 50
Profile of Department	
Sworn Officers:	155
Population:	480,611
Officer Benefits	
Starting Salary:	$20,460
Retirement:	Age 65
Medical/Dental:	Yes
Educational:	Yes
Department Requirements	
Age:	23 minimum
Education:	High school
Vision:	20/20 corrected
	20/100 uncorrected
Nonresidents	✔ Yes
Lateral Transfers	No
Where to Apply	Above address
Web	*www.state.wy.us*

STATE CORRECTIONS OFFICER

◯ State Corrections Officer

MISSION   Thousands of state corrections officers are hired every year to control and handle prisoners. State Corrections Officers are responsible for the custody, security, and well-being of inmates in State Correctional facilities. They also administer the rules and regulations to maintain law and order within the correctional facility. In addition, State Corrections Officers may be required to carry firearms. The conduct searches for contraband, supervise the movement and activities of inmates, and prepare written reports. They must be dependable, able to work without supervision, make decisions under pressure, take part in strenuous physical activities, and take action in physically dangerous situations.

PROFILE   State Corrections Officers: 192,674 nationwide

Adult Inmates: 860,632 nationwide

COMMENTS   *Employment Outlook:* The overall outlook for employment is excellent. Many states are now in the hiring mode and are expected to continue this into the 21st century. The trend is for a sharp increase in correction facilities to house the ever-increasing prison population. It is expected that thousands of officers will be hired. The requirements for being a State Corrections Officer, while they vary from state to state, are usually lower from that for most other law enforcement positions. For instance, vision requirements are minimal, if any, and many states require only a high school education, a clean record, and a minimum age of 18.

Employment Conditions: It should be noted that State Corrections Officers are usually required to attend an academy, after which they may be assigned to any facility within the state. They can be reassigned to another part of the state without notice. Corrections Officers work with large groups of dangerous inmates. They respond to inmates' situations that may include riots. They work overtime, including weekends and holidays. Officers may also be required to stand with a weapon in an elevated tower overseeing large groups of inmates. This is a difficult job with a significant turnover rate.

WHERE TO APPLY   Directly to the agencies beginning on page 147.

STATE CORRECTIONS DEPARTMENT STRUCTURE

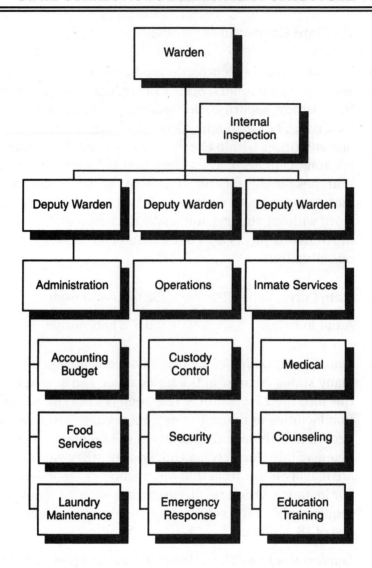

American Correctional Association (ACA)

The ACA is a professional organization that meets and holds conventions dealing with corrections matters. In addition, it puts out a yearly Directory of Correctional Departments. While no job opportunities are listed, the directory does provide up-to-date listings of departments and their facilities, however, it should be noted that at $75, it is somewhat costly.

Write to the Directory of Juvenile and Adult Correctional Departments (published each year) at 4380 Forbes Boulevard, Lanham, MD 20706, telephone (301) 918-1800.

Opportunities ——————————————

See page 5 for explanations of the entries in the following listings:

ALABAMA

Department of Corrections
1400 Lloyd Street
Montgomery, AL 36130
(334) 240-9500

Anticipated Positions	✪ Over 100
Profile of Department	
Corrections Officers:	2,257
Inmate Population:	23,326
Officer Benefits	
Starting Salary:	$21,000
Retirement:	25 years
Medical/Dental:	Yes
Educational:	No
Department Requirements	
Age:	21 minimum
Education:	High school
Vision:	20/30 corrected
Nonresidents	✔ Yes
Lateral Transfers	➤ Yes
Where to Apply	Above address
Web	*www.agencies.state.al.us*

ALASKA

Department of Corrections
P.O. Box 112000
Juneau, AK 99811

Anticipated Positions	✪ Over 100

Profile of Department

Corrections Officers:	779
Inmate Population:	4,097

Officer Benefits

Starting Salary:	$21,000
Retirement:	20 years
Medical/Dental:	Yes
Educational:	Yes

Department Requirements

Age:	21 minimum
Education:	High school
Vision:	No requirement stated
Nonresidents	No
Lateral Transfers	No
Where to Apply	Above address
Web	*www.state.ak.us*

ARIZONA

Department of Corrections
1601 West Jefferson
Phoenix, AZ 85007

Anticipated Positions	✪ Over 100

Profile of Department

Corrections Officers:	4,218
Inmate Population:	25,311

Officer Benefits

Starting Salary:	$21,000
Retirement:	20 years
Medical/Dental:	Yes
Educational:	Yes

Department Requirements

Age:	21 minimum
Education:	High school
Vision:	No requirement stated
Nonresidents	✔ Yes
Lateral Transfers	No
Where to Apply	Above address
Web	*www.state.az.us*

ARKANSAS

Department of Corrections
P.O. Box 8707
Pine Bluff, AR 71611
(501) 247-1800

Anticipated Positions	Undetermined
Profile of Department	
Corrections Officers:	1,919
Inmate Population:	10,638
Officer Benefits	
Starting Salary:	$17,292
Retirement:	30 years/age 65
Medical/Dental:	Yes
Educational:	No
Department Requirements	
Age:	18 minimum
Education:	High school
Vision:	No requirement stated
Nonresidents	No
Lateral Transfers	No
Where to Apply	Above address
Web	*www.state.ar.us*

CALIFORNIA

Department of Corrections
2201 Broadway
Sacramento, CA 95818
(916) 227-2110

Anticipated Positions	✪ Over 3,000
Profile of Department	
Corrections Officers:	16,856
Inmate Population:	161,904
Officer Benefits	
Starting Salary:	$23,316
Retirement:	20 years/age 50
Medical/Dental:	Yes
Educational:	No
Department Requirements	
Age:	21 minimum
Education:	High school
Vision:	20/20 corrected 20/60 uncorrected
Nonresidents	✔ Yes
Lateral Transfers	No
Where to Apply	Above address
Web	*www.cdc.state.ca.gov*

COLORADO

Department of Corrections
2862 South Circle Drive
Colorado Springs, CO 80906

Anticipated Positions	Undetermined
Profile of Department	
Corrections Officers:	2,001
Inmate Population:	14,312
Officer Benefits	
Starting Salary:	$22,044
Medical/Dental:	Yes
Educational:	No
Department Requirements	
Age:	21 minimum
Education:	High school
Vision:	No requirement stated
Nonresidents	No
Lateral Transfers	No
Where to Apply	Above address
Web	*www.state.co.us*

CONNECTICUT

Department of Corrections
340 Capitol Avenue
Hartford, CT 06106
(860) 566-7622

Anticipated Positions	✪ Over 100
Profile of Department	
Corrections Officers:	4,007
Inmate Population:	17,605
Officer Benefits	
Starting Salary:	$27,991
Retirement:	20 years
Medical/Dental:	Yes
Educational:	No
Department Requirements	
Age:	18 minimum
Education:	High school
Vision:	20/40 corrected
	20/80 uncorrected
Nonresidents	✔ Yes
Lateral Transfers	No
Where to Apply	Above address
Web	*www.state.ct.us*

DELAWARE

Department of Corrections
80 Monrovia Avenue
Smyrna, DE 19977

Anticipated Positions	Undetermined
Profile of Department	
Corrections Officers:	911
Inmate Population:	5,558
Officer Benefits	
Starting Salary:	$18,598
Medical/Dental:	Yes
Educational:	No
Department Requirements	
Age:	21 minimum
Education:	High school
Vision:	No requirement stated
Nonresidents	No
Lateral Transfers	No
Where to Apply	Above address
Web	*www.state.de.us*

FLORIDA

Department of Corrections
2601 Blairstone Road
Tallahassee, FL 32399
(904) 488-3130

Anticipated Positions	✪ Over 100
Profile of Department	
Corrections Officers:	10,301
Inmate Population:	67,224
Officer Benefits	
Starting Salary:	$18,301
Retirement:	25 years
Medical/Dental:	Yes
Educational:	Yes
Department Requirements	
Age:	19 minimum
Education:	High school
Vision:	No requirement stated
Nonresidents	✔ Yes
Lateral Transfers	No
Where to Apply	Above address
Web	*www.dc.state.fl.us*

GEORGIA

Department of Corrections
2 Martin Luther King Drive
Atlanta, GA 30334

Anticipated Positions	Undetermined
Profile of Department	
Corrections Officers:	7,932
Inmate Population:	39,262
Officer Benefits	
Starting Salary:	$17,646
Medical/Dental:	Yes
Educational:	No
Department Requirements	
Age:	21 minimum
Education:	High school
Vision:	No requirement stated
Nonresidents	No
Lateral Transfers	No
Where to Apply	Above address
Web	*www.state.ga.us*

IDAHO

Department of Corrections
500 South 10th Street
Boise, ID 83720

Anticipated Positions	Undetermined
Profile of Department	
Corrections Officers:	669
Inmate Population:	4,924
Officer Benefits	
Starting Salary:	$20,883
Retirement:	Age 50
Medical/Dental:	Yes
Educational:	No
Department Requirements	
Age:	21 minimum
Education:	High school
Vision:	No requirement stated
Nonresidents	✔ Yes
Lateral Transfers	No
Where to Apply	Idaho Personnel Commission
	700 West State Street
	Boise, ID 83720
Web	*www.idoc.state.id.us*

ILLINOIS

Department of Corrections
1301 Concordia Court
Springfield, IL 62794

Anticipated Positions	Undetermined
Profile of Department	
Corrections Officers:	7,321
Inmate Population:	43,051
Officer Benefits	
Starting Salary:	$24,236
Retirement:	25 years
Medical/Dental:	Yes
Educational:	Yes
Department Requirements	
Age:	18 minimum
Education:	High school
Vision:	No requirement stated
Nonresidents	No
Lateral Transfers	No
Where to Apply	Above address
Web	*www.idoc.state.il.us*

INDIANA

Department of Corrections
302 West Washington Street
Indianapolis, IN 46204
1-800-638-3940

Anticipated Positions	✪ Over 1,000
Profile of Department	
Corrections Officers:	4,000
Inmate Population:	19,100
Officer Benefits	
Starting Salary:	$19,300
Retirement:	30 years
Medical/Dental:	Yes
Educational:	No
Department Requirements	
Age:	18 minimum
Education:	High school
Vision:	No requirement stated
Nonresidents	✔ Yes
Lateral Transfers	No
Where to Apply	Above address
Web	*www.state.in.us*

KANSAS

Department of Corrections
900 SW Jackson
Topeka, KS 66612
(913) 296-4495

Anticipated Positions	Undetermined
Profile of Department	
Corrections Officers:	1,816
Inmate Population:	8,100
Officer Benefits	
Starting Salary:	$17,868
Retirement:	20 years
Medical/Dental:	Yes
Educational:	No
Department Requirements	
Age:	21 minimum
Education:	High school
Vision:	No requirement stated
Nonresidents	✔ Yes
Lateral Transfers	No
Comments	Veterans receive extra points.
Where to Apply	Above address
Web	*www.state.ks.us*

KENTUCKY

Department of Corrections
State Office Building
Frankfort, KY 40601

Anticipated Positions	Undetermined
Profile of Department	
Corrections Officers:	1,681
Inmate Population:	14,987
Officer Benefits	
Starting Salary:	$13,668
Retirement:	Age 50
Medical/Dental:	Yes
Educational:	No
Department Requirements	
Age:	21 minimum
Education:	High school
Vision:	No requirement stated
Nonresidents	No
Lateral Transfers	No
Where to Apply	Above address
Web	*www.state.ky.us*

LOUISIANA

Department of Public Safety and Corrections
Box 94304
Baton Rouge, LA 70804
(504) 342-6620

Anticipated Positions	✪ Over 100
Profile of Department	
Corrections Officers:	4,405
Inmate Population:	32,227
Officer Benefits	
Starting Salary:	$14,736
Retirement:	20 years/age 50
Medical/Dental:	Yes
Educational:	No
Department Requirements	
Age:	18 minimum
Education:	High school
Vision:	No requirement stated
Nonresidents	✔ Yes
Lateral Transfers	➤ Yes
Where to Apply	Above address
Web	*www.dps.state.la.us*

MAINE

Department of Corrections
State House Station 111
Augusta, ME 04333
(207) 287-4368

Anticipated Positions	50 to 100
Profile of Department	
Corrections Officers:	407
Inmate Population:	1,610
Officer Benefits	
Starting Salary:	$17,721
Retirement:	25 years
Medical/Dental:	Yes
Educational:	Yes
Department Requirements	
Age:	No requirement stated
Education:	High school
Vision:	No requirement stated
Nonresidents	No
Lateral Transfers	➤ Yes
Where to Apply	Above address
Web	*www.state.me.us*

MARYLAND

Department of Corrections
6776 Reistertown Road
Baltimore, MD 21215
(410) 764-4189

Anticipated Positions	Undetermined
Profile of Department	
Corrections Officers:	4,219
Inmate Population:	22,572
Officer Benefits	
Starting Salary:	$20,772
Retirement:	Age 50
Medical/Dental:	Yes
Educational:	No
Department Requirements	
Age:	21 minimum
Education:	High school
Vision:	No requirement stated
Nonresidents	No
Lateral Transfers	No
Where to Apply	Above address
Web	*www.state.md.us*

MASSACHUSETTS

Department of Corrections
100 Cambridge Street
Boston, MA 02202
(617) 727-3300

Anticipated Positions	Undetermined
Profile of Department	
Corrections Officers:	3,271
Inmate Population:	11,832
Officer Benefits	
Starting Salary:	$28,114
Retirement:	Age 50
Medical/Dental:	Yes
Educational:	No
Department Requirements	
Age:	21 minimum
Education:	High school
Vision:	No requirement stated
Nonresidents	No
Lateral Transfers	No
Where to Apply	Above address
Web	*www.state.ma.us*

MICHIGAN

Department of Corrections
206 East Michigan
P.O. Box 30003
Lansing, MI 48909
(517) 373-6391

Anticipated Positions	✪ Over 500
Profile of Department	
Corrections Officers:	8,147
Inmate Population:	45,879
Officer Benefits	
Starting Salary:	$21,924
Retirement:	25 years/age 51
Medical/Dental:	Yes
Educational:	Yes
Department Requirements	
Age:	18 minimum
Education:	15 college credits
Vision:	No requirement stated
Nonresidents	✔ Yes
Lateral Transfers	No
Comments	Department appears to be in a hiring mode for the next several years.
Where to Apply	At above address or at any Michigan Employment Security Commission office
Web	*www.state.mi.us*

MINNESOTA

Department of Corrections
1450 Energy Park Drive
St. Paul, MN 55108
(612) 642-0201

Anticipated Positions	✪ Over 100
Profile of Department	
Corrections Officers:	1,418
Inmate Population:	5,572
Officer Benefits	
Starting Salary:	$23,115
Retirement:	30 years
Medical/Dental:	Yes
Educational:	Yes
Department Requirements	
Age:	No minimum stated
Education:	High school
Vision:	20/40 corrected
Nonresidents	✔ Yes
Lateral Transfers	No
Where to Apply	Above address or (612) 603-0013
Web	*www.state.mn.us*

MISSISSIPPI

Department of Corrections
723 North President Street
Jackson, MS 39202
(601) 359-5600

Anticipated Positions	✪ Over 100
Profile of Department	
Corrections Officers:	1,810
Inmate Population:	16,678
Officer Benefits	
Starting Salary:	$16,237
Retirement:	25 years
Medical/Dental:	Yes
Educational:	No
Department Requirements	
Age:	21 minimum
Education:	High school
Vision:	No requirement stated
Nonresidents	✔ Yes
Lateral Transfers	No
Where to Apply	State Personnel Board
	301 North Lamar Street
	Jackson, MS 39201
	(601) 359-1406
Web	*www.dps.state.ms.us*

MISSOURI

Division of Corrections
2729 Plaza Drive
P.O. Box 236
Jefferson City, MO 65102
(573) 751-2389

Anticipated Positions	✪ 200 to 300
Profile of Department	
Corrections Officers:	3,350
Inmate Population:	24,974
Officer Benefits	
Starting Salary:	$17,600
Retirement:	Age 65
Medical/Dental:	Yes
Educational:	Yes
Department Requirements	
Age:	21 minimum
Education:	High school
Vision:	20/20 corrected
Nonresidents	✔ Yes
Lateral Transfers	No
Where to Apply	Above address
Web	*www.state.mo.us*

MONTANA

Department of Corrections
1538 11th Avenue
Helena, MT 59620
(406) 444-0445

Anticipated Positions	Undetermined
Profile of Department	
Corrections Officers:	222
Inmate Population:	2,734
Officer Benefits	
Starting Salary:	$16,064
Retirement:	Age 50
Medical/Dental:	Yes
Educational:	No
Department Requirements	
Age:	21 minimum
Education:	High school
Vision:	No requirement stated
Nonresidents	No
Lateral Transfers	No
Where to Apply	Above address
Web	*www.doc.state.mt.gov*

NEBRASKA

Department of Correctional Services
P.O. Box 94661
Lincoln, NE 68509
(402) 471-2654

Anticipated Positions	✪ Over 100
Profile of Department	
Corrections Officers:	600
Inmate Population:	3,674
Officer Benefits	
Starting Salary:	$18,589
Retirement:	30 years
Medical/Dental:	Yes
Educational:	No
Department Requirements	
Age:	18 minimum
Education:	High school
Vision:	No requirement stated
Nonresidents	✔ Yes
Lateral Transfers	No
Where to Apply	Above address
Web	*www.state.ne.us*

NEVADA

Department of Prisons
P.O. Box 7011
Carson City, NV 89702

Anticipated Positions	Undetermined
Profile of Department	
Corrections Officers:	1,088
Inmate Population:	9,651
Officer Benefits	
Starting Salary:	$22,484
Retirement:	Age 50
Medical/Dental:	Yes
Educational:	No
Department Requirements	
Age:	21 minimum
Education:	High school
Vision:	No requirement stated
Nonresidents	No
Lateral Transfers	No
Where to Apply	Above address
Web	*www.state.nv.us*

NEW HAMPSHIRE

Department of Corrections
P.O. Box 1806
Concord, NH 03302

Anticipated Positions	Undetermined
Profile of Department	
Corrections Officers:	478
Inmate Population:	2,160
Officer Benefits	
Starting Salary:	$20,249
Retirement:	Age 50
Medical/Dental:	Yes
Educational:	No
Department Requirements	
Age:	21 minimum
Education:	High school
Vision:	No requirement stated
Nonresidents	No
Lateral Transfers	No
Where to Apply	Above address
Web	*www.state.nh.us*

NEW JERSEY

Department of Corrections
CN863
Whittlesey Road
Trenton, NJ 08625

Anticipated Positions	Undetermined
Profile of Department	
Corrections Officers:	5,367
Inmate Population:	31,121
Officer Benefits	
Starting Salary:	$29,125
Retirement:	Age 55
Medical/Dental:	Yes
Educational:	Yes
Department Requirements	
Age:	21 minimum
Education:	High school
Vision:	No requirement stated
Nonresidents	No
Lateral Transfers	No
Where to Apply	Above address
Web	*www.state.nj.us*

NEW YORK

Department of Correctional Services
State Campus
Albany, NY 12226
(518) 457-5393

Anticipated Positions	Undetermined
Profile of Department	
Corrections Officers:	20,099
Inmate Population:	72,638
Officer Benefits	
Starting Salary:	$23,000
Retirement:	20 years/age 55
Medical/Dental:	Yes
Educational:	Yes
Department Requirements	
Age:	21 minimum
Education:	High school
Vision:	No requirement stated
Nonresidents	✔ Yes
Lateral Transfers	No
Where to Apply	Above address
Web	*www.state.ny.us*

NORTH CAROLINA

Department of Corrections
214 West Jones Street
Raleigh, NC 27626
(919) 733-4926

Anticipated Positions	Undetermined
Profile of Department	
Corrections Officers:	11,200
Inmate Population:	31,810
Officer Benefits	
Starting Salary:	$19,645
Retirement:	Age 55
Medical/Dental:	Yes
Educational:	No
Department Requirements	
Age:	20 minimum
Education:	High school
Vision:	No requirement stated
Nonresidents	No
Lateral Transfers	➤ Yes
Where to Apply	Above address
Web	*www.doc.state.nc.us*

NORTH DAKOTA

Department of Corrections
P.O. Box 1898
Bismarck, ND 58505

Anticipated Positions	Undetermined
Profile of Department	
Corrections Officers:	118
Inmate Population:	915
Officer Benefits	
Starting Salary:	$15,948
Retirement:	Age 50
Medical/Dental:	Yes
Educational:	No
Department Requirements	
Age:	No requirement stated
Education:	High school
Vision:	No requirement stated
Nonresidents	✔ Yes
Lateral Transfers	No
Where to Apply	Above address
Web	*www.state.nd.us*

OHIO

Department of Corrections
1050 Freeway Drive
Columbus, OH 43229

Anticipated Positions	Undetermined
Profile of Department	
Corrections Officers:	6,072
Inmate Population:	48,450
Officer Benefits	
Starting Salary:	$21,258
Retirement:	Age 55
Medical/Dental:	Yes
Educational:	Yes
Department Requirements	
Age:	21 minimum
Education:	High school
Vision:	No requirement stated
Nonresidents	✔ Yes
Lateral Transfers	No
Where to Apply	Above address
Web	*www.state.oh.us*

OKLAHOMA

Department of Corrections
3400 Martin Luther King Avenue
Oklahoma City, OK 73136

Anticipated Positions	Undetermined
Profile of Department	
Corrections Officers:	1,711
Inmate Population:	20,892
Officer Benefits	
Starting Salary:	$15,965
Retirement:	Age 50
Medical/Dental:	Yes
Educational:	No
Department Requirements	
Age:	21 minimum
Education:	High school
Vision:	No requirement stated
Nonresidents	No
Lateral Transfers	No
Where to Apply	Above address
Web	*www.doc.state.ok.us*

OREGON

Department of Corrections
2575 Center Street
Salem, OR 97310
(503) 945-9018

Anticipated Positions	✪ Over 100
Profile of Department	
Corrections Officers:	1,181
Inmate Population:	8,927
Officer Benefits	
Starting Salary:	$21,864
Retirement:	25 years/age 50
Medical/Dental:	Yes
Educational:	No
Department Requirements	
Age:	21 minimum
Education:	High school
Vision:	No requirement stated
Nonresidents	No
Lateral Transfers	No
Comments	Residents receive extra credit.
Where to Apply	Above address
Web	*www.doc.state.or.us*

PENNSYLVANIA

Department of Corrections
P.O. Box 598
Camp Hill, PA 17001

Anticipated Positions	Undetermined
Profile of Department	
Corrections Officers:	5,447
Inmate Population:	36,377
Officer Benefits	
Starting Salary:	$19,362
Retirement:	Age 50
Medical/Dental:	Yes
Educational:	No
Department Requirements	
Age:	21 minimum
Education:	High school
Vision:	No requirement stated
Nonresidents	No
Lateral Transfers	No
Where to Apply	Above address
Web	*www.state.pa.gov*

RHODE ISLAND

Department of Corrections
39 Howard Avenue
Cranston, RI 02920
(401) 464-3250

Anticipated Positions	✪ Over 100
Profile of Department	
Corrections Officers:	895
Inmate Population:	3,450
Officer Benefits	
Starting Salary:	$23,521
Retirement:	20 years/age 50
Medical/Dental:	Yes
Educational:	No
Department Requirements	
Age:	18 minimum
Education:	High school
Vision:	No requirement stated
Nonresidents	✔ Yes
Lateral Transfers	No
Where to Apply	Above address
Web	*www.doa.state.ri.us*

SOUTH CAROLINA

Department of Corrections
4444 Broad River Road
Columbia, SC 29210
(803) 896-1646

Anticipated Positions	✪ Over 100
Profile of Department	
Corrections Officers:	3,947
Inmate Population:	22,115
Officer Benefits	
Starting Salary:	$15,310
Retirement:	25 years/age 55
Medical/Dental:	Yes
Educational:	No
Department Requirements	
Age:	21 minimum
Education:	High school
Vision:	20/40 corrected
Nonresidents	✔ Yes
Lateral Transfers	➤ Yes
Where to Apply	Recruitment and Employment Branch 4330 Broad Road Columbia, SC 29210 (803) 896-1649
Web	*www.state.sc.us*

SOUTH DAKOTA

Department of Corrections
115 East Dakota Street
Pierre, SD 57501

Anticipated Positions	Undetermined
Profile of Department	
Corrections Officers:	318
Inmate Population:	2,430
Officer Benefits	
Starting Salary:	$15,000
Retirement:	Age 50
Medical/Dental:	Yes
Educational:	No
Department Requirements	
Age:	21 minimum
Education:	High school
Vision:	No requirement stated
Nonresidents	✔ Yes
Lateral Transfers	No
Where to Apply	Above address
Web	*www.state.sd.us*

TENNESSEE

Department of Corrections
320 6th Avenue
Nashville, TN 37243

Anticipated Positions	Undetermined
Profile of Department	
Corrections Officers:	3,122
Inmate Population:	17,738
Officer Benefits	
Starting Salary:	$14,100
Retirement:	30 years
Medical/Dental:	Yes
Educational:	No
Department Requirements	
Age:	21 minimum
Education:	High school
Vision:	No requirement stated
Nonresidents	No
Lateral Transfers	No
Where to Apply	Above address
Web	*www.state.tn.us*

TEXAS

Department of Criminal Justice
Institutional Division
P.O. Box 99
Huntsville, TX 77342

Anticipated Positions	Undetermined

Profile of Department

Corrections Officers:	20,019
Inmate Population:	144,510

Officer Benefits

Starting Salary:	$15,576
Retirement:	Age 55
Medical/Dental:	Yes
Educational:	No

Department Requirements

Age:	20 minimum
Education:	High school
Vision:	No requirement stated
Nonresidents	No
Lateral Transfers	No
Where to Apply	Above address
Web	*www.txpds.state.tx.us*

UTAH

Department of Corrections
6100 South Fashion Street
Murray, UT 84107

Anticipated Positions	Undetermined

Profile of Department

Corrections Officers:	938
Inmate Population:	4,391

Officer Benefits

Starting Salary:	$17,748
Retirement:	Age 55
Medical/Dental:	Yes
Educational:	No

Department Requirements

Age:	21 minimum
Education:	High school
Vision:	No requirement stated
Nonresidents	No
Lateral Transfers	No
Where to Apply	Above address
Web	*www.cr.ex.state.ut.us*

VERMONT

Department of Corrections
103 South Main Street
Waterbury, VT 05602
(802) 241-2291

Anticipated Positions	✪ Over 100
Profile of Department	
Corrections Officers:	407
Inmate Population:	1,426
Officer Benefits	
Starting Salary:	$20,000
Retirement:	20 years
Medical/Dental:	Yes
Educational:	Yes
Department Requirements	
Age:	18 minimum
Education:	High school
Vision:	No requirement stated
Nonresidents	No
Lateral Transfers	No
Where to Apply	Above address
Web	*www.state.vt.us*

VIRGINIA

Department of Corrections
P.O. Box 26963
West Broad Street
Richmond, VA 23261
(804) 674-3507

Anticipated Positions	✪ Over 100
Profile of Department	
Corrections Officers:	5,625
Inmate Population:	28,560
Officer Benefits	
Starting Salary:	$19,188
Retirement:	30 years
Medical/Dental:	Yes
Educational:	No
Department Requirements	
Age:	21 minimum
Education:	High school
Vision:	No requirement stated
Nonresidents	No
Lateral Transfers	No
Where to Apply	Above address
Web	*www.state.va.us*

WASHINGTON

Department of Corrections
410 West 5th
Olympia, WA 98504
(360) 753-9654

Anticipated Positions	50 to 100
Profile of Department	
Corrections Officers:	2,550
Inmate Population:	14,161
Officer Benefits	
Starting Salary:	$24,000
Retirement:	Age 55
Medical/Dental:	Yes
Educational:	Yes
Department Requirements	
Age:	No requirement stated
Education:	High school
Vision:	No requirement stated
Nonresidents	✔ Yes
Lateral Transfers	No
Where to Apply	Above address
Web	*www.wa.gov*

WEST VIRGINIA

Department of Corrections
112 California Avenue
Charleston, WV 25305

Anticipated Positions	Undetermined
Profile of Department	
Corrections Officers:	545
Inmate Population:	3,470
Officer Benefits	
Starting Salary:	$16,000
Retirement:	25 years
Medical/Dental:	Yes
Educational:	No
Department Requirements	
Age:	21 minimum
Education:	High school
Vision:	No requirement stated
Nonresidents	No
Lateral Transfers	No
Where to Apply	Above address
Web	*www.state.wv.us*

WYOMING

Department of Corrections
Hershler Building
Cheyenne, WY 82002

Anticipated Positions	Undetermined
Profile of Department	
Corrections Officers:	241
Inmate Population:	1,570
Officer Benefits	
Starting Salary:	$15,700
Retirement:	Age 65
Medical/Dental:	Yes
Educational:	No
Department Requirements	
Age:	21 minimum
Education:	High school
Vision:	No requirement stated
Nonresidents	No
Lateral Transfers	No
Where to Apply	Above address
Web	*www.state.wy.us*

LARGE CITY CORRECTIONS DEPARTMENTS

Opportunities

See page 5 for explanations of the entries in the following listings:

New York City Department of Corrections
60 Hudson Street
New York, NY 10013
(212) 728-7000

Anticipated Positions	✪ Over 100
Profile of Department	
Corrections Officers:	10,248
Inmate Population:	18,460
Officer Benefits	
Starting Salary:	$27,838
Retirement:	20 years/age 55
Medical/Dental:	Yes
Educational:	Yes
Department Requirements	
Age:	22 minimum
Education:	High school
Vision:	No requirement stated
Nonresidents	✔ Yes
Lateral Transfers	No
Comments	Residents receive extra credit.
Where to Apply	NYC Department of Personnel 18 Washington Street New York, NY 10004
Web	*www.ci.nyc.ny.us*

Philadelphia Prison System
7901 State Road
Philadelphia, PA 19136

Anticipated Positions	Undetermined
Profile of Department	
Corrections Officers:	1,510
Inmate Population:	4,640
Officer Benefits	
Starting Salary:	$24,000
Retirement:	Age 55
Medical/Dental:	Yes
Educational:	No
Department Requirements	
Age:	21 minimum
Education:	High school
Vision:	No requirement stated
Nonresidents	No
Lateral Transfers	No
Where to Apply	Above address
Web	*www.phila.gov*

District of Columbia
Department of Corrections
1923 Vermont Avenue
Washington, DC 20001

Anticipated Positions	Undetermined
Profile of Department	
Corrections Officers:	2,530
Inmate Population:	9,940
Officer Benefits	
Starting Salary:	$26,000
Retirement:	Age 55
Medical/Dental:	Yes
Educational:	No
Department Requirements	
Age:	21 minimum
Education:	High school
Vision:	No requirement stated
Nonresidents	No
Lateral Transfers	No
Where to Apply	Above address

STATE CONSERVATION/WILDLIFE OFFICER
PARK POLICE OFFICER

⬭ **State Conservation/Wildlife Officer**
⬭ **State Park Police Officer**

MISSION   Conservation and Wildlife law enforcement officers maintain law and order outdoors. They maintain vehicle and foot patrol in various weather and traffic conditions for extended periods of time, patrol for investigation of fish and wildlife violations and hunting and trapping violations, investigate the trafficking of endangered species, and respond to nuisance and distress wildlife complaints. In states that border the oceans they enforce marine resources laws and patrol and investigate shellfish harvesting violations and marine finfish, lobster, and crab harvesting violations. They enforce laws relating to marine fish and marine mammals and provide public education. They participate in search and rescue efforts, investigate hunting accidents, investigate petroleum/hazardous material spills, and investigate criminal dumping of wastes. Park Police Officers maintain law enforcement throughout state-owned parks and reservations. Like their counterparts, the Conservation and Wildlife Officers, Park Police Officers are also specially trained to protect the environment they patrol.

COMMENTS   *Employment Outlook:* The general outlook for employment is fair. Most openings occur due to retirements.

Employment Conditions: These officers work with minimal direction or supervision. They usually work alone and frequently in areas where backup assistance is not immediately available. These are physically demanding jobs, requiring heavy lifting, running over uneven terrain, and spending long periods of time outdoors in adverse weather conditions.

WHERE TO APPLY   Directly to the agencies beginning on page 176.

SAMPLE CONSERVATION POLICE DEPARTMENT STRUCTURE

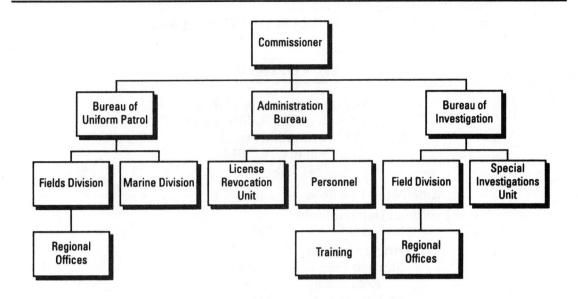

Opportunities ———————————————

See page 5 for explanations of the entries in the following listings:

ALABAMA

Alabama Game & Fish
Department of Law Enforcement
64 North Union Street
Montgomery, AL 36130
(334) 242-3467

Anticipated Positions	Under 50
Profile of Department	
Sworn Officers:	158
Officer Benefits	
Starting Salary:	$24,500
Retirement:	20 years/age 50
Medical/Dental:	Yes
Educational:	No
Department Requirements	
Age:	26 minimum
Education:	High school
Vision:	20/25 corrected
	20/200 uncorrected
Nonresidents	✔ Yes
Lateral Transfers	No
Comments	Title: Conservation Enforcement Officer
Where to Apply	Alabama Department of Personnel
	Above address
Web	*www.dcnr.state.al.us*

ARIZONA

Arizona Game and Fish Department
Law Enforcement Division
2221 West Greenway Road
Phoenix, AZ 85023
(602) 942-3000

Anticipated Positions	Under 50
Profile of Department	
Sworn Officers:	137
Officer Benefits	
Starting Salary:	$24,414
Retirement:	20 years
Medical/Dental:	Yes
Educational:	Yes
Department Requirements	
Age:	21 minimum
Education:	Four-year college degree
Vision:	20/20 corrected
Nonresidents	✔ Yes
Lateral Transfers	No
Where to Apply	Above address
Web	*www.gf.state.az.us*

CALIFORNIA

California Park and Recreation Police
P.O. Box 942896
Sacramento, CA 95814
(916) 653-4272

Anticipated Positions	50 to 100
Profile of Department	
Sworn Officers:	702
Officer Benefits	
Starting Salary:	$34,000
Retirement:	Age 50
Medical/Dental:	Yes
Educational:	Yes
Department Requirements	
Age:	18 minimum
Education:	Two-year college degree
Vision:	20/20 corrected
	20/40 uncorrected
Nonresidents	✔ Yes
Lateral Transfers	No
Where to Apply	Above address
Web	*www.cal-parks.ca.gov*

COLORADO

Colorado Division of Wildlife
6060 Broadway
Denver, CO 80216
(303) 291-7371

Anticipated Positions	Under 50
Profile of Department	
Sworn Officers:	200
Officer Benefits	
Starting Salary:	$26,000
Retirement:	Varies
Medical/Dental:	Yes
Educational:	Yes
Department Requirements	
Age:	21 minimum
Education:	Four-year college degree
Vision:	No requirement stated
Nonresidents	No
Lateral Transfers	No
Comments	Candidates must have a degree in Wildlife Biology or similar field.
Where to Apply	State Personnel Department 1313 Sherman Denver, CO 80203
Web	*www.state.co.us*

CONNECTICUT

Connecticut Environmental Protection
Law Enforcement Division
79 Elm Street
Hartford, CT 06106
(806) 424-3012

Anticipated Positions	Under 10
Profile of Department	
Sworn Officers:	55
Officer Benefits	
Starting Salary:	$42,000
Retirement:	20 years
Medical/Dental:	Yes
Educational:	Yes
Department Requirements	
Age:	21 minimum
Education:	High school
Vision:	No requirement stated
Nonresidents	✔ Yes
Lateral Transfers	No
Where to Apply	Above address
Web	*www.dep.state.ct.us*

FLORIDA

Florida Game and Fresh Water Fish Commission
Law Enforcement Division
620 South Meridian Street
Tallahassee, FL 32399
(904) 488-6251

Anticipated Positions	50 to 100
Profile of Department	
Sworn Officers:	356
Officer Benefits	
Starting Salary:	$22,287
Retirement:	25 years
Medical/Dental:	Yes
Educational:	Yes
Department Requirements	
Age:	19 minimum
Education:	High school
Vision:	20/20 corrected
Nonresidents	No
Lateral Transfers	➤ Yes
Where to Apply	Above address
Web	*www.state.fl.us*

GEORGIA

Department of Natural Resources
Law Enforcement Division
781 Red Top Mountain Road SE
Cartersville, GA 30120
(770) 975-4230

Anticipated Positions	Under 50
Profile of Department	
Sworn Officers:	233
Officer Benefits	
Starting Salary:	$22,260
Retirement:	30 years
Medical/Dental:	Yes
Educational:	No
Department Requirements	
Age:	21 minimum
Education:	High school
Vision:	20/40 corrected
	20/60 uncorrected
Nonresidents	✔ Yes
Lateral Transfers	No
Where to Apply	Wildlife Resources Division
	2070 U.S. Highway 278, SE
	Social Circle, GA 30279
	(770) 918-6403
Web	*www.dnr.state.ga.us*

IDAHO

Fish and Game Department
Law Enforcement Division
600 South Walnut
Boise, ID 83707
(208) 334-3736

Anticipated Positions	Under 10
Profile of Department	
Sworn Officers:	115
Officer Benefits	
Starting Salary:	$13.25/hour
Retirement:	Age 55
Medical/Dental:	Yes
Educational:	No
Department Requirements	
Age:	20 minimum
Education:	Four-year college degree
Vision:	20/20 corrected
Nonresidents	✔ Yes
Lateral Transfers	No
Where to Apply	Above address
Web	*www.state.id.us*

KANSAS

Department of Wildlife and Parks
Law Enforcement Division
512 SE 25th Avenue
Pratt, KS 67124
(316) 672-5911

Anticipated Positions	Under 50
Profile of Department	
Sworn Officers:	173
Officer Benefits	
Starting Salary:	$25,128
Retirement:	20 years
Medical/Dental:	Yes
Educational:	Yes
Department Requirements	
Age:	21 minimum
Education:	Four-year college degree
Vision:	No requirement stated
Nonresidents	✔ Yes
Lateral Transfers	➤ Yes
Where to Apply	Above address
Web	*www.state.ks.us*

KENTUCKY

Department of Fish and Wildlife Resources
Law Enforcement Division
1 Game Farm Road
Frankfort, KY 40601
(502) 564-3176

Anticipated Positions	Under 50
Profile of Department	
Sworn Officers:	144
Officer Benefits	
Starting Salary:	$19,812
Retirement:	20 years
Medical/Dental:	Yes
Educational:	Yes
Department Requirements	
Age:	21 minimum
Education:	Four-year college degree
Vision:	No requirement stated
Nonresidents	✔ Yes
Lateral Transfers	No
Where to Apply	Kentucky Department of Personnel
	200 Fair Oaks Lane
	Frankfort, KY 40601
	(502) 564-8030
Web	*www.state.ky.us*

LOUISIANA

Department of Wildlife and Fisheries
Law Enforcement Division
P.O. Box 98000
Baton Rouge, LA 70898
(504) 765-2985

Anticipated Positions	Under 50
Profile of Department	
Sworn Officers:	215
Officer Benefits	
Starting Salary:	$18,000
Retirement:	20 years
Medical/Dental:	Yes
Educational:	No
Department Requirements	
Age:	18 minimum
Education:	60 college credits
Vision:	No requirement stated
Nonresidents	✔ Yes
Lateral Transfers	No
Where to Apply	Above address
Web	*www.dnr.state.la.us*

MAINE

Maine Conservation Department
Inland Fisheries and Wildlife
Law Enforcement Division
Augusta, ME 04333
(207) 287-5211

Anticipated Positions	Under 50
Profile of Department	
Sworn Officers:	122
Officer Benefits	
Starting Salary:	$24,411
Retirement:	25 years
Medical/Dental:	Yes
Educational:	Yes
Department Requirements	
Age:	21 minimum
Education:	60 college credits
Vision:	20/20 corrected
Nonresidents	✔ Yes
Lateral Transfers	No
Where to Apply	Above address
Web	*www.state.me.us*

MARYLAND

Maryland Forest and Park Service
Tawes State Office Building E-3
Annapolis, MD 21401
(410) 974-3771

Anticipated Positions	Under 50
Profile of Department	
Sworn Officers:	187
Officer Benefits	
Starting Salary:	$23,624
Retirement:	25 years
Medical/Dental:	Yes
Educational:	No
Department Requirements	
Age:	21 minimum
Education:	High school
Vision:	20/20 corrected
Nonresidents	No
Lateral Transfers	No
Where to Apply	Above address
Web	*www.mde.state.md.us*

MINNESOTA

Department of Natural Resources
Law Enforcement Division
500 Lafayette Road
St. Paul, MN 55155
(612) 296-0657

Anticipated Positions	Under 50
Profile of Department Jurisdiction	
Sworn Officers:	191
Officer Benefits	
Starting Salary:	$32,970
Retirement:	30 years
Medical/Dental:	Yes
Educational:	No
Department Requirements	
Age:	21 minimum
Education:	Four-year college degree
Vision:	No requirement stated
Nonresidents	✔ Yes
Lateral Transfers	No
Where to Apply	Above address
Web	*www.dnr.state.mn.us*

NEBRASKA

Game and Parks Commission
Law Enforcement Division
2200 North 33rd Street
Lincoln, NE 68503
(402) 464-0641

Anticipated Positions	Under 50
Profile of Department	
Sworn Officers:	55
Officer Benefits	
Starting Salary:	$23,000
Retirement:	30 years
Medical/Dental:	Yes
Educational:	Yes
Department Requirements	
Age:	21 minimum
Education:	High school
Vision:	No requirement stated
Nonresidents	✔ Yes
Lateral Transfers	No
Where to Apply	Above address
Web	*www.nrc.state.ne.us*

NEW MEXICO

Game and Fish Department
Law Enforcement Division
P.O. Box 25112
Santa Fe, NM 87504
(505) 827-7934

Anticipated Positions	Under 50
Profile of Department	
Sworn Officers:	118
Officer Benefits	
Starting Salary:	$24,414
Retirement:	25 years
Medical/Dental:	Yes
Educational:	No
Department Requirements	
Age:	21 minimum
Education:	Four-year college degree
Vision:	20/20 corrected

Nonresidents	✔ Yes
Lateral Transfers	➤ Yes
Where to Apply	New Mexico State Personnel P.O. Box 26127 Santa Fe, NM 87505 (505) 827-8110
Web	*www.gmfsh.state.nm.us*

NEW YORK

New York State Park Police
Empire State Plaza
Albany, NY 12238

Anticipated Positions	Under 50
Profile of Department	
Sworn Officers:	319
Officer Benefits	
Starting Salary:	$24,900
Retirement:	20 years
Medical/Dental:	Yes
Educational:	Yes
Department Requirements	
Age:	21 minimum
Education:	High school
Vision:	20/20 corrected
Nonresidents	✔ Yes
Lateral Transfers	No
Where to Apply	New York State Civil Service State Campus Albany, NY 12239
Web	*www.nysparks.state.ny.us*

NORTH CAROLINA

Wildlife Resources Commission
Law Enforcement Division
512 North Salisbury Street
Raleigh, NC 27604
(919) 733-7191

Anticipated Positions	Under 50
Profile of Department	
Sworn Officers:	208
Officer Benefits	
Starting Salary:	$23,719
Retirement:	30 years/age 55
Medical/Dental:	Yes
Educational:	Yes
Department Requirements	
Age:	21 minimum
Education:	High school
Vision:	20/30 corrected
	20/100 uncorrected
Nonresidents	✔ Yes
Lateral Transfers	No
Where to Apply	Above address
Web	*www.state.nc.us*

NORTH DAKOTA

State Game and Fish Department
Law Enforcement Division
100 North Bismarck Expressway
Bismarck, ND 58501
(701) 328-6324

Anticipated Positions	Under 50
Profile of Department	
Sworn Officers:	29
Officer Benefits	
Starting Salary:	$24,400
Retirement:	5 years (vested)
Medical/Dental:	Yes
Educational:	No
Department Requirements	
Age:	21 minimum
Education:	Four-year college degree
Vision:	20/20 corrected
Nonresidents	✔ Yes
Lateral Transfers	➤ Yes
Where to Apply	Above address
Web	*www.state.nd.us*

OHIO

Department of Natural Resources
Law Enforcement Division
1952 Belcher Drive
Columbus, OH 43224
(614) 265-6561

Anticipated Positions	Under 50
Profile of Department	
Sworn Officers:	300
Officer Benefits	
Starting Salary:	$26,333
Retirement:	25 years/age 48
Medical/Dental:	Yes
Educational:	Yes
Department Requirements	
Age:	21 minimum
Education:	High school
Vision:	No requirement stated
Nonresidents	No
Lateral Transfers	No
Comments	Currently revising educational requirements.
Where to Apply	Above address
Web	*www.state.oh.us*

OKLAHOMA

Department of Wildlife Conservation
Law Enforcement Division
1801 North Lincoln Blvd.
Oklahoma City, OK 73105
(405) 521-4640

Anticipated Positions	Under 50
Profile of Department	
Sworn Officers:	125
Officer Benefits	
Starting Salary:	$24,861
Retirement:	20 years
Medical/Dental:	Yes
Educational:	No
Department Requirements	
Age:	21 minimum
Education:	Four-year college degree
Vision:	No requirement stated
Nonresidents	✔ Yes
Lateral Transfers	No
Where to Apply	Above address
Web	*www.state.ok.us*

PENNSYLVANIA

Pennsylvania Game Commission
Law Enforcement Division
2001 Elmerton Avenue
Harrisburg, PA 17110
(717) 783-6528

Anticipated Positions	Under 50
Profile of Department	
Sworn Officers:	221
Officer Benefits	
Starting Salary:	$24,414
Retirement:	35 years
Medical/Dental:	Yes
Educational:	Yes
Department Requirements	
Age:	21 minimum
Education:	High school
Vision:	20/20 corrected
	20/70 uncorrected
Nonresidents	No
Lateral Transfers	➤ Yes
Where to Apply	Above address
Web	*www.state.pa.us*

TEXAS

Parks and Wildlife Department
Law Enforcement Division
4200 Smith School Road
Austin, TX 78744
(800) 792-1112

Anticipated Positions	50 to 100
Profile of Department	
Sworn Officers:	540
Officer Benefits	
Starting Salary:	$25,461
Retirement:	10 years
Medical/Dental:	Yes
Educational:	Yes
Department Requirements	
Age:	21 minimum
Education:	Four-year college degree
Vision:	20/20 corrected
Nonresidents	✔ Yes
Lateral Transfers	No
Where to Apply	Above address
Web	*www.state.tx.us*

WASHINGTON

Department of Fish and Wildlife
Enforcement Division
600 Capital Way
Olympia, WA 98501
(206) 902-2936

Anticipated Positions	Under 50
Profile of Department	
Sworn Officers:	180
Officer Benefits	
Starting Salary:	$28,020
Retirement:	25 years
Medical/Dental:	Yes
Educational:	No
Department Requirements	
Age:	21 minimum
Education:	Four-year college degree
Vision:	No requirement stated
Nonresidents	✔ Yes
Lateral Transfers	No
Where to Apply	Above address
Web	*www.state.wa.us*

WYOMING

Game and Fish Department
Law Enforcement Division
5400 Bishop Blvd.
Cheyenne, WY 82006
(307) 777-4507

Anticipated Positions	Under 50
Profile of Department	
Sworn Officers:	71
Officer Benefits	
Starting Salary:	$18,500
Retirement:	Age 55
Medical/Dental:	Yes
Educational:	Yes
Department Requirements	
Age:	21 minimum
Education:	Four-year college degree
Vision:	No requirement stated
Nonresidents	✔ Yes
Lateral Transfers	No
Comments	Candidates must have a degree in natural resources.
Where to Apply	Above address
Web	*www.state.wy.us*

STATE PAROLE/PROBATION OFFICER

⬭ **State Parole Officers**
⬭ **State Probation Officers**

MISSION   Parole Officers provide supervision and guidance to an assigned case load of releasees from state and local correctional facilities and help releasees comply with the terms of their release from incarceration. Probation Officers supervise probationers and advise them on their rehabilitation. They make probation investigations of persons coming before the courts to ascertain previous criminal and delinquent records, social history, and physical, mental, and psychiatric data. Both are required to conduct surveillance, enforce the conditions of the probation or parole, and submit written reports on investigations to supervisors. They make reports and recommendations regarding the status of the subject involved and cooperate with social and law enforcement agencies.

COMMENTS   *Employment Outlook:* The general outlook for employment as a parole or probation officer is fair. For the most part, openings are due to retirements.

Employment Conditions: Officers work with criminals who have histories of committing violent crimes, and who may have an openly hostile attitude. They work overtime, including weekends and holidays, and may be required to work in high crime areas and/or conduct surveillance on parolees.

WHERE TO APPLY   Directly to the agencies that follow.

Listings

ALABAMA

Pardon and Parole Board
P.O. Box 302405
Montgomery, AL 36130

ALASKA

State Corrections Department
Division of Community Corrections
4500 Diplomacy Drive
Anchorage, AK 99508

ARIZONA

Department of Corrections
Community Corrections Division
363 North 1st Avenue
Phoenix, AZ 85002

ARKANSAS

Department of Corrections
Community Punishment
323 Center Street
Little Rock, AR 72201

CALIFORNIA

Parole and Community
Services Division
1515 South Street
Sacramento, CA 95815

COLORADO

Division of Adult Parole
710 Kipling Street
Lakewood, CO 80215

CONNECTICUT

Division of Corrections
Adult Parole Services
340 Capitol Avenue
Hartford, CT 06106

DELAWARE

Division of Community Corrections
Adult Parole and Probation Services
State Office Building
Wilmington, DE 19801

FLORIDA

Department of Corrections
Parole and Probation Services
2501 Blair Stone Road
Tallahassee, FL 32399

GEORGIA

Pardons and Paroles Board
2 Martin Luther King Drive
Atlanta, GA 30334

HAWAII

State Parole Department
250 South King Street
Honolulu, HI 96813

IDAHO

Division of Field and
Community Services
Adult Parole and Probation
State House Mail
Boise, ID 83720

ILLINOIS

Administrative Office of
the Illinois Courts
Probation Division
300 East Monroe Street
Springfield, IL 62701

INDIANA

Department of Corrections
Division of Community Services
302 West Washington Street
Indianapolis, IN 46204

IOWA

Department of Corrections
Division of Community Corrections
Adult Parole and Probation Services
Capitol Annex
Des Moines, IA 50319

KANSAS

Department of Corrections
Division of Community and Field
Services
900 SW Jackson
Topeka, KS 66612

KENTUCKY

Division of Parole and Probation
Services
State Office Building
Frankfort, KY 40601

LOUISIANA

Division of Adult Parole and
Probation
Box 94304
Baton Rouge, LA 70804

MAINE

Department of Corrections
Division of Parole and Probation
State House Station 111
Augusta, ME 04333

MARYLAND

Department of Corrections
Division of Parole and Probation
6776 Reisterstown Road
Baltimore, MD 21215

MASSACHUSETTS

State Parole Board
27-43 Wormwood Street
Boston, MA 02210

Probation Department
1 Ashburn Place
Boston, MA 02108

MICHIGAN

Department of Corrections
Field Operations Unit
Parole and Probation Services
P.O. Box 30003
Lansing, MI 48909

MINNESOTA

Department of Corrections
Parole and Probation Services
1450 Engery Street
St. Paul, MN 55108

MISSISSIPPI

Community Service Division
Adult Parole and Probation Services
723 North President Street
Jackson, MS 39202

MISSOURI

Board of Parole and Probation
117 Commerce Street
Jefferson City, MO 65102

MONTANA

Parole and Probation Services
1539 11th Avenue
Helena, MT 59620

NEBRASKA

Board of Parole
P.O. Box 94754
Lincoln, NE 68509

NEVADA

Department of Parole and Probation
5500 East Snyder
Carson City, NV 89710

NEW HAMPSHIRE

Department of Corrections
Adult Probation Services
105 Pleasant Street
Concord, NH 03302

NEW JERSEY

Bureau of Parole
CN863, Whittlesey Road
Trenton, NJ 08625

NEW MEXICO

Probation and Parole Division
P.O. Box 27116
Santa Fe, NM 87502

NEW YORK

Division of Parole
97 Central Avenue
Albany, NY 12206

NORTH CAROLINA

Department of Corrections
4000 Wake Forest Road
Raleigh, NC 27609

NORTH DAKOTA

Parole and Probation
P.O. Box 5521
Bismarck, ND 58506

OHIO

Department of Corrections
Division of Parole and Community
Services
1050 Freeway Drive
Columbus, OH 43229

OKLAHOMA

Department of Corrections
Parole and Probation Division
3400 Martin Luther King Avenue
Oklahoma City, OK 73136

OREGON

Division of Community Corrections
2575 Center Street
Salem, OR 97310

PENNSYLVANIA

Board of Parole and Probation
3101 North Front Street
Harrisburg, PA 17105

RHODE ISLAND

Division of Rehabilitative Service
Parole and Probation
40 Howard Street
Cranston, RI 02920

SOUTH CAROLINA

Department of Parole, Probation
and Pardons Services
P.O. Box 50666
2221 Devinest
Columbia, SC 29250

SOUTH DAKOTA

Parole Services
408 South 2nd Avenue
Sioux Falls, SD 57102

TENNESSEE

Division of Field Service
Adult Parole Services
320 Sixth Avenue
Nashville, TN 37243

TEXAS

Parole Division
Capital Station
P.O. Box 13401
Austin, TX 78711

UTAH

Department of Corrections
Division of Field Operations
6100 South 300 East
Murray, UT 84107

VERMONT

Department of Corrections
Parole and Probation Services
103 South Main Street
Waterbury, VT 05676

WASHINGTON

Department of Corrections
Division of Community Corrections
410 West 5th Avenue
Olympia, WA 98504

WEST VIRGINIA

Department of Corrections
Division of Parole and Probation
112 California Street
South Charleston, WV 25305

WISCONSIN

Department of Corrections
Division of Parole and Probation
P.O. Box 7925
Madison, WI 53707

WYOMING

Department of Corrections
Division of Field Services
Herschler Building
Cheyenne, WY 82002

STATE COLLEGE LAW ENFORCEMENT

◯ **University Police Officer**
◯ **Campus Public Safety Officer**

MISSION Most states have large university systems with campuses the size of small cities. Campus Police Officers or Public Safety Officers are certified law enforcement officers who work on an assigned campus or university and are responsible for the protection and well-being of the residents, and the protection of the university facilities. They wear uniforms and maintain vehicle and foot patrols in various weather and traffic conditions for extended periods of time. They may be required to be proficient in firearms; however, in many states campus/university law enforcement officers do not carry firearms.

COMMENTS *Employment Outlook:* The outlook for general employment is fair. University police departments or campus public safety departments are currently staffing to a full complement after years of being treated as a necessary evil. Colleges are now being rated on their safety and crime records, which has translated into an increase in the hiring of campus and university law enforcement officers; however, these departments do not have massive hiring as do large cities. Most campus law enforcement positions require a high standard of education largely due to their surroundings—the academic environment.

Employment Conditions: Campus/universities law enforcement officers must be responsive to a college community made up of young people who may not always respect their authority. Candidates must be able to handle young subjects in a capable manner. Many colleges/universities allow and encourage their officers to continue a college education, which may allow the officer to not only gather experience, but also to obtain a higher degree of education.

Internships: Campus and university law enforcement offices offer outstanding intern opportunities largely due to the interconnectedness with the facility's criminal justice program. Many interns have gone straight from the criminal justice college program into a campus police officer position by being in the right place at the right time.

WHERE TO APPLY Apply directly with cover letter and résumé to the offices that follow.

Listings

ALABAMA

University of Alabama
Public Safety Department
Birmingham, AL 35205

ALASKA

University of Alaska
Public Safety Department
Anchorage, AK 99508

ARIZONA

Arizona State University
Public Safety Department
Tempe, AZ 85287

ARKANSAS

University of Arkansas
Public Safety Department
Little Rock, AR 72204

CALIFORNIA

California State University
Public Safety Department
Los Angeles, CA 90032

California State University
Public Safety Department
Long Beach, CA 90840

California State University
Public Safety Department
Sacramento, CA 95819

COLORADO

Colorado State University
Campus Police Department
Fort Collins, CO 80523

CONNECTICUT

University of Connecticut
Campus Police Department
Storrs, CT 06268

Yale University
Police Department
100 Sachem Street
New Haven, CT 06520

DELAWARE

University of Delaware
Public Safety Department
Newark, DE 19716

DISTRICT OF COLUMBIA

American University
Public Safety Department
4400 Washington
Washington, DC 20016

George Washington University
Public Safety Department
2033 G Street, NW
Washington, DC 20052

FLORIDA

Florida State University
Police Department
Tallahassee, FL 32306

University of Florida
Police Department
Gainesville, FL 32611

GEORGIA

Georgia State University
Police Department
Atlanta, GA 30303

IDAHO

Idaho State University
Public Safety Department
Pocatello, ID 83209

ILLINOIS

Southern Illinois University
at Carbondale
Public Safety Department
Carbondale, IL 62901

Illinois State University
Police Department
Normal, IL 61780

INDIANA

Indiana University
Police Department
Bloomington, IN 47405

Indiana University
Police Department
Indianapolis, IN 46202

IOWA

Iowa State University
Public Safety Department
Ames, IA 50011

KANSAS

University of Kansas
Police Department
Lawrence, KS 66044

KENTUCKY

University of Kentucky
Campus Police Department
Lexington, KY 40506

LOUISIANA

Louisiana State University
Police Department
Baton Rouge, LA 70803

MARYLAND

University of Maryland
Police Department
College Park, MD 20742

MASSACHUSETTS

Harvard University
Police Department
Cambridge, MA 02138

University of Massachusetts
Public Safety Department
Amherst, MA 01003

MICHIGAN

Michigan State University
Police Department
East Lansing, MI 48824

MINNESOTA

University of Minnesota
Police Department
Minneapolis, MN 55414

MISSISSIPPI

Mississippi Valley State University
Public Safety Department
Itta Bena, MS 38941

MISSOURI

University of Missouri
Police Department
St. Louis, MO 63121

MONTANA

University of Montana
Police Department
Missoula, MT 59812

NEBRASKA

University of Nebraska
Police Department
Lincoln, NE 68588

NEVADA

University of Nevada
Police Department
Reno, NV 89507

NEW HAMPSHIRE

University of New Hampshire
Police Department
Durham, NH 03824

NEW JERSEY

Rutgers University
Police Department
New Brunswick, NJ 08903

NEW MEXICO

University of New Mexico
Police Department
Las Cruces, NM 88003

NEW YORK

John Jay College of Criminal Justice
City University of New York (CUNY)
Public Safety Department
New York, NY 10019

State University of New York (SUNY)
at Albany
Police Department
Albany, NY 12222

State University of New York (SUNY)
at Buffalo
Public Safety Department
Buffalo, NY 14260

NORTH CAROLINA

North Carolina University
Public Safety Department
Raleigh, NC 27695

NORTH DAKOTA

North Dakota University
Police Department
Fargo, ND 58105

OHIO

Ohio State University
Police Department
Columbus, OH 43210

OKLAHOMA

Oklahoma State University
Police Department
Stillwater, OK 74078

OREGON

Oregon State University
Police Department
Corvallis, OR 97330

PENNSYLVANIA

Pennsylvania State University
Campus Police Department
Reading, PA 19610

RHODE ISLAND

University of Rhode Island
Public Safety Department
Kingston, RI 02881

SOUTH CAROLINA

University of South Carolina
Public Safety Department
Columbia, SC 29208

SOUTH DAKOTA

South Dakota State University
Police Department
Brookings, SD 57007

TENNESSEE

Tennessee State University
Campus Police Department
Knoxville, TN 37996

TEXAS

University of Texas
Campus Police Department
Austin, TX 78705

University of Texas
Campus Police Department
El Paso, TX 79968

Sam Houston University
Public Safety Department
Huntsville, TX 77341

UTAH

University of Utah
Public Safety Department
Salt Lake City, UT 84112

VERMONT

University of Vermont
Police Department
Burlington, VT 05405

VIRGINIA

University of Virginia
Police Department
Charlottesville, VA 22901

WASHINGTON

University of Washington
Police Department
Seattle, WA 98105

WEST VIRGINIA

West Virginia University
Public Safety Department
Morgantown, WV 26506

WISCONSIN

University of Wisconsin
Police Department
Madison, WI 53711

WYOMING

University of Wyoming
Campus Police Department
Laramie, WY 82071

STATE ATTORNEY GENERAL OFFICES INVESTIGATOR

○ **State Attorney General Investigator**

MISSION Attorney general investigators conduct a wide variety of complex investigations that may involve organized crime, public corruption, narcotics, white collar crime, and consumer protection. Investigators in the State Attorney General's office may work undercover and in high crime areas. They testify in court in a wide variety of civil and criminal actions. Due to the complexity of the cases, investigators may be required to gather, collect, analyze, and prepare graphs and link charts on career criminal and conspiracy cases. Investigators coordinate efforts with other agencies, serve warrants, and take individuals into custody.

COMMENTS *Employment Outlook:* Experienced law enforcement officers and/or candidates with college degrees in criminal justice, law, and accounting have an advantage.

WHERE TO APPLY Apply directly with cover letter and résumé to the offices that follow.

Listings

ALABAMA

Attorney General
11 Union Street
Montgomery, AL 36130
(334) 242-7300

ALASKA

Attorney General
P.O. Box 110300
Juneau, AK 99811
(907) 465-3600

ARIZONA

Attorney General
1275 West Washington
Phoenix, AZ 85007
(602) 542-4266

ARKANSAS

Attorney General
Tower Building
Little Rock, AR 72201
(501) 682-2007

CALIFORNIA

Attorney General
P.O. Box 944255
Sacramento, CA 94244
(916) 324-5437

COLORADO

Attorney General
1525 Sherman Street
Denver, CO 80203
(303) 866-3052

CONNECTICUT

Attorney General
55 Elm Street
Hartford, CT 06106
(860) 808-5318

DELAWARE

Attorney General
820 North French Street
Wilmington, DE 19601
(302) 577-8400

FLORIDA

Attorney General
State Capitol
Tallahassee, FL 32399
(850) 487-1963

GEORGIA

Attorney General
40 Capitol Square
Atlanta, GA 30334
(404) 656-4585

HAWAII

Attorney General
425 Queen Street
Honolulu, HI 96813
(808) 586-1292

IDAHO

Attorney General
State House
Boise, ID 83720
(208) 334-2400

ILLINOIS

Attorney General
500 South Second
Springfield, IL 62706
(312) 814-2503

INDIANA

Attorney General
State House
Indianapolis, IN 46204
(317) 233-4386

IOWA

Attorney General
State Office Building
Des Moines, IA 50319
(515) 281-3053

KANSAS

Attorney General
Kansas Judicial Center
Topeka, KS 66612
(785) 296-2215

KENTUCKY

Attorney General
Capitol Building
Frankfort, KY 40602
(502) 696-5300

LOUISIANA

Attorney General
P.O. Box 94005
Baton Rouge, LA 70804
(225) 342-7013

MAINE

Attorney General
State House Station 6
Augusta, ME 04333
(207) 626-8800

MARYLAND

Attorney General
200 St. Paul
Baltimore, MD 21202
(410) 576-6300

MASSACHUSETTS

Attorney General
1 Ashburton
Boston, MA 02108
(617) 727-2200

MINNESOTA

Attorney General
State Capitol
St. Paul, MN 55155
(651) 296-6196

MISSISSIPPI

Attorney General
P.O. Box 220
Jackson, MS 39205
(601) 359-3692

MISSOURI

Attorney General
P.O. Box 899
Jefferson City, MO 65102
(573) 751-3321

MONTANA

Attorney General
Justice Building
Helena, MT 59620
(406) 444-2026

NEBRASKA

Attorney General
State Capitol Building
Lincoln, NE 68509
(402) 471-2682

NEVADA

Attorney General
Capitol Complex
Carson City, NV 89710
(775) 684-1108

NEW HAMPSHIRE

Attorney General
33 Capitol Street
Concord, NH 03301
(603) 271-3658

NEW JERSEY

Attorney General
Justice Complex
Trenton, NJ 08625
(609) 292-4925

NEW MEXICO

Attorney General
P.O. Drawer 1508
Santa Fe, NM 87504
(505) 827-6000

NEW YORK

Attorney General
State Capitol
Albany, NY 12224
(518) 474-7330

NORTH CAROLINA

Attorney General
P.O. Box 629
Raleigh, NC 27602
(919) 716-6400

NORTH DAKOTA

Attorney General
600 Boulevard Avenue
Bismarck, ND 58505
(701) 328-2210

OHIO

Attorney General
30 Broad Street
Columbus, OH 43215
(614) 466-3376

OKLAHOMA

Attorney General
State Capitol Building
Oklahoma City, OK 73105
(405) 521-3921

OREGON

Attorney General
Justice Building
Salem, OR 97310
(503) 378-6002

PENNSYLVANIA

Attorney General
Strawberry Square
Harrisburg, PA 17120
(717) 787-3391

RHODE ISLAND

Attorney General
72 Pine Street
Providence, RI 02903
(401) 274-4400

SOUTH CAROLINA

Attorney General
P.O. Box 11549
Columbia, SC 29211
(803) 734-3970

SOUTH DAKOTA

Attorney General
500 East Capitol
Pierre, SD 57501
(605) 773-3215

TEXAS

Attorney General
P.O. Box 12548
Austin, TX 78711
(512) 463-2191

UTAH

Attorney General
State Capitol
Salt Lake City, UT 84114
(801) 538-1326

VERMONT

Attorney General
109 State Street
Montpelier, VT 05609
(802) 828-3171

WASHINGTON

Attorney General
P.O. Box 40100
Olympia, WA 98504
(360) 753-6200

WEST VIRGINIA

Attorney General
State Capitol
Charleston, WV 25305
(304) 558-2021

WISCONSIN

Attorney General
P.O. Box 7857
Madison, WI 53707
(608) 266-1221

WYOMING

Attorney General
123 Capitol Building
Cheyenne, WY 82002
(307) 777-7841

Chapter 7

GENERAL LAW ENFORCEMENT APPLICATION PROCESS

Follow this procedure in applying to Municipal and State Law Enforcement Agencies:

1. Call or write to ask for position announcements and required applications.

2. Read the announcements carefully, then fill out the applications.

3. Submit the applications (and résumé if applicable).

4. Take the required tests. Wait for results and next steps.

5. If at first you don't succeed, reexamine what went wrong and TRY . . . TRY . . . AGAIN!

Municipal Police and County Sheriff Departments

Local law enforcement agencies at the municipal and county level usually act as recruiters for candidates and may issue the applications directly; however, the application issued by the law enforcement agency may need to be submitted to the civil service or personnel department for processing. In these areas the civil service or personnel departments may act as a central handler for all local agencies.

State Law Enforcement Agencies

The procedures to apply vary slightly from state to state; however, for the most part, the applicant is advised to contact the hiring agency directly for information and to request an application. In some states the applicant may be redirected to the state civil service or personnel department for the application and examination requirements. As with municipal and county law enforcement agencies, the state-level civil service and personnel departments act as the central handler for the collective agencies within the state; however, our best advice is to send a letter to the state agencies and the corresponding civil service and personnel departments—you will not only receive the information you are looking for, but may also receive information you need but did not know to ask for.

SAMPLE LAW ENFORCEMENT ANNOUNCEMENT

**POLICE DEPARTMENT
CIVIL SERVICE ANNOUNCEMENT**

POLICE OFFICER EXAMINATION

An application fee of $10.00 must accompany your application.

Benefits:
Salary: $31,489 year
Full Pay during Academy Training
Family and Domestic Partner Health and Dental Coverage
Paid Vacations, Sick Leave, and Holidays

TEST DATES: To be announced
LOCATION: To be announced

An Equal Opportunity Employer

SELECTION PROCESS

- Written examination
- Physical agility test
- Psychological evaluation
- Extensive background investigation
- Polygraph test
- Medical screening and examination
- Urinalysis (to test for drugs)

GENERAL REQUIREMENTS

In addition to successfully completing the competitive examinations given by the state's Civil Service Division, candidates must meet several standards established by the state's Law Enforcement Division:

Area of Recruitment: Candidates must be citizens of the United States. Residents of the city will be given preference in appointments to the position of Police Officer.

Minimum Age: Candidates must be at least 20 years old on the date of the competitive examination and at least 21 years old on the date of appointment.

Maximum Age: Candidates must not have reached their 35th birthday on the date of appointment. Candidates with military service in their background, as defined in Section 243 of the military law, may use good service time to extend the age limit up to a five-year limit. Applicable provisions of federal law may also have an impact on the maximum age requirement.

Education: Candidates must have graduated from a registered high school or possess a state High School Equivalency Diploma prior to appointment. Military GED and High School Equivalency Diplomas from other states must be converted to each state's standards. *(Possible)* In addition, all candidates must have completed a minimum of 45 credit hours at an accredited college at the time of appointment. The State Law Enforcement Administration may waive 30 credit hours for candidates who have an honorable discharge from the United States military, or for candidates who have prior law enforcement experience and have successfully graduated from a certified police academy.

Residence: Candidates must be U.S. citizens, and must be residents of the state in question on the date of employment, and maintain that residency as long as employed by the state Law Enforcement Agency.

Criminal Record: Candidates with felony convictions are automatic disqualifications. Conviction for other crimes and offenses are subject to evaluation by the administrative staff.

Driver's License: Candidates must possess a valid state driver's license at the time of appointment.

Veterans' Preference: Candidates who have active duty service in their background and possess an honorable discharge may apply for a veteran's credit on the examination.

Medical Fitness: Since the physical activities of the position as a State Law Enforcement Officer often demand extreme physical exertion in emergency situations, sound health and good physical condition are required of all candidates. A complete medical examination will be given prior to appointment, during which hearing, vision, weight, dental, and general fitness will be determined.

Vision must be no worse than 20/40 in each eye uncorrected, corrected to 20/20. Color blindness is disqualifying. Weight must be in proportion to height and build (minimum/maximum height standards have been removed from many states).

Candidates will be required to provide blood and urine samples for analysis of drug abuse.

GENERAL INFORMATION

Eligible List: The term of the eligible list resulting from this examination will be one year and may be extended for four years. Candidates will be ranked on the resulting eligible list in the order of their final ratings, with the name of the candidates with the highest final rating first.

Salary: The salary for this position is subject to change from time to time.

Veterans: If you are entitled to veterans' credits, you should claim these credits when you file your application.

Residence: Residence is required for all positions at appointment date.

THE GENERAL APPLICATION FORM

Most local and state law enforcement agencies use the personnel or civil service application forms for the initial application process. These forms request certain information for the position the candidate is seeking. Blocks are designated for background, experience, education, and veterans' preference. In addition, questions regarding employment background, criminal records, and financial history also may be asked.

SAMPLE CIVIL SERVICE APPLICATION FORM

FORM OC-APP (3/95)

APPLICATION FOR NYS EXAMINATIONS
OPEN TO THE PUBLIC

New York State Department of Civil Service
Building 1, State Campus
Albany, NY 12239

- Read instructions on Page 4 First
- Please Print Clearly

Announced Test Date: ___ mo ___ day ___ yr

Exam No(s). ___   Title(s) ___

Last Name ___   First Name ___   MI ___

Mailing Address: No., Street, Apt., or P.O. Box

City or Post Office ___   State ___   ZIP Code ___

Social Security Number ___

Home Phone ( ) ___   Day Phone ( ) ___

SPECIAL ACCOMMODATIONS IN TESTING
☐ I require special accommodations to take this test. (See Page 4)

SATURDAY RELIGIOUS OBSERVER
☐ I am a religious observer and cannot be tested on the scheduled test date. (See Page 4)

W ○   G ○   U ○

ADDITIONAL QUESTIONS

YES☐ NO☐ Are you currently in default on any outstanding student loan(s) made or guaranteed by the New York State Higher Education Services Corporation?

If you answer YES to any of the following questions, give specifics under REMARKS on Page 3. If you do not provide specifics a confidential investigation supplement will be sent to you.

YES☐ NO☐ Were you ever discharged from any employment except for lack of work or funds, disability or medical condition?

YES☐ NO☐ Did you ever resign from any employment rather than face discharge?

YES☐ NO☐ Did you ever receive a discharge from the Armed Forces of the United States which was other than "Honorable" or which was issued under other than honorable conditions?

YES☐ NO☐ Have you ever been convicted of any crime (felony or misdemeanor)?

YES☐ NO☐ Are you now under charges for any crime?

PROCESSING FEE   *Please read exam announcement and information on Page 4.*

Check One

☐ I have enclosed the fee. (The fee will NOT BE REFUNDED if your application is DISAPPROVED)

NO FEE IS DUE BECAUSE:

☐ I am a NY State employee and my fee is paid by my union (CSEA or PEF).

☐ I am unemployed and primarily responsible for the support of a household.

☐ I am receiving public assistance as described on Page 4.

I affirm under penalties of perjury that statements made on this application (including any attached papers) are true. I understand that all statements made by me in connection with this application are subject to investigation and verification and that a material misstatement or fraud may disqualify me from consideration and/or lead to revocation of my appointment.

X _____
Signature of Applicant   Date

_____
Please print any other last name by which you are or have been known.

DO NOT COMPLETE THIS SECTION UNLESS YOU:
1. Wish to claim Part Time Veterans Credits, AND
2. Have NOT used veterans credits for appointment to a position in NY State or Local Government employment since January 1, 1951.

EXTRA CREDITS FOR WAR TIME VETERANS
YOUR ANSWERS MUST BE "YES" TO BE ELIGIBLE FOR ADDITIONAL CREDITS.

YES☐ NO☐ I served on an active duty basis other than active duty for training purposes during one or more of the following Time of War periods.

YES☐ NO☐ I received a discharge which was honorable or I was released under honorable circumstances from the Armed Forces of the United States. (The "Armed Forces of the United States" means the Army, Navy, Marine Corps, Air Force and Coast Guard, including all components thereof, and the National Guard when in the service of the United States pursuant to call as provided by law on a full-time active duty basis other than active duty for training purposes.)

In the Armed Forces:
- Aug. 2, 1990 to the date when the Persian Gulf hostilities ends;
- Dec. 22, 1961 to May 7, 1975;
- June 27, 1950 to Jan. 31, 1955;
- Dec. 7, 1941 to Dec. 31, 1946;

or earned the armed forces, navy, or marine corps expeditionary medal for service in:
- (Panama) Dec. 20, 1989 to Jan. 31, 1990;
- (Lebanon) June 1, 1983 to Dec. 1, 1987;
- (Grenada) Oct. 23, 1983 to Nov. 21, 1983;

or in the U.S. Public Health Service;
- June 28, 1950 to July 3, 1952;
- July 29, 1945 to Sept. 2, 1945.

YES☐ NO☐ I am a United States citizen or an alien lawfully admitted for permanent residence.

YES☐ NO☐ I am a New York State resident.

To claim additional credits as a Disabled Veteran, you must also answer YES to this question:

YES☐ NO☐ I am receiving payments from the U.S. Dept. of Veterans Affairs for a service connected disability rated at 10% or more incurred during a "Time of War" period listed above.

• NEW YORK STATE • AN EQUAL OPPORTUNITY/AFFIRMATIVE ACTION EMPLOYER

It is the policy of the New York State Department of Civil Service to provide accommodations in testing to individuals with disabilities and religious observers and to provide for and promote equal opportunity in employment, compensation and other terms and conditions of employment without discrimination because of age, race, creed, color, national origin, gender, sexual orientation, disability or marital status.

OC–APP (1/96)   Page 2

READ THE REQUIRED QUALIFICATIONS ON THE EXAMINATION ANNOUNCEMENT(S) AND ANSWER THESE QUESTIONS

EDUCATION: Read exam announcement for educational requirements, if any. If specialized coursework is required, attach a list transcript or list of the required courses and semester credit hours you completed.

Do you have a High School or Equivalency Diploma? ☐ Yes ☐ No   If YES, Name and location of High School or Issuing Governmental Authority: Date Graduated or Date Issued: Mo / Yr

College, University, Professional or Technical School(s)	Dates of Attendance (Month/Year) From	To	No. of Years Credited	Full or Part Time	Did You Graduate?	No. of Credits Received	Type of Degree Received	Major Subject or Type of Course	Date Degree Received or Expected
Name									
Address (Street, City, State)									
Name									
Address (Street, City, State)									

LICENSE OR CERTIFICATION: Complete the following if a license, certificate or other authorization to practice a trade or profession is required. If not currently licensed, check this box: ☐

Name of Trade or Profession	License Number	Granted by (licensing agency)	City or State
Specialty	Date License First Issued	Current Regisration: From: (Mo./Yr.)	To: (Mo./Yr.)

DESCRIBE YOUR EXPERIENCE: Beginning with your most recent, list all employment, military service, or volunteer experience that shows you meet the minimum qualifications for the examination(s). We cannot interpret omissions or vagueness in your favor. You are responsible for an accurate and clear description of your experience. Do not send your resume. Under DUTIES describe the nature of the work which you personally performed including the estimated percentage of time spent on each type of activity. If you supervised, state how many people and the nature of such supervision.

LENGTH OF EMPLOYMENT MO YR MO YR
FROM / TO /
EARNINGS (Circle One) / WK / MO / YR
$
TYPE OF BUSINESS
YOUR EXACT TITLE
NAME OF YOUR SUPERVISOR
SUPERVISOR'S TITLE
No. of hours worked per week (exclusive of overtime):
FIRM NAME ADDRESS CITY AND STATE
DUTIES:

LENGTH OF EMPLOYMENT MO YR MO YR
FROM / TO /
EARNINGS (Circle One) / WK / MO / YR
$
TYPE OF BUSINESS
YOUR EXACT TITLE
NAME OF YOUR SUPERVISOR
SUPERVISOR'S TITLE
No. of hours worked per week (exclusive of overtime):
FIRM NAME ADDRESS CITY AND STATE
DUTIES:

LENGTH OF EMPLOYMENT MO YR MO YR
FROM / TO /
EARNINGS (Circle One) / WK / MO / YR
$
TYPE OF BUSINESS
YOUR EXACT TITLE
NAME OF YOUR SUPERVISOR
SUPERVISOR'S TITLE
No. of hours worked per week (exclusive of overtime):
FIRM NAME ADDRESS CITY AND STATE
DUTIES:

ALL STATEMENTS ARE SUBJECT TO VERIFICATION

OC–APP (1/96)   **Page 3**

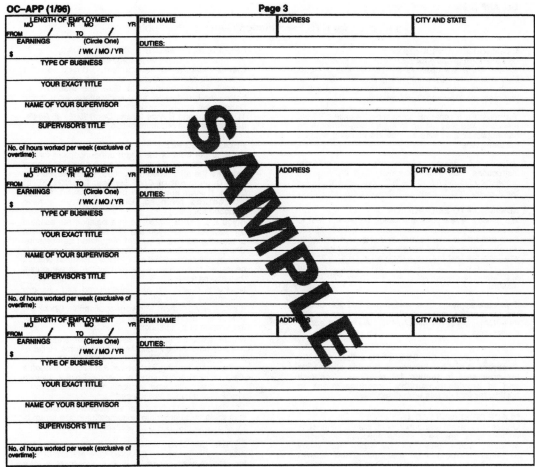

REMARKS: (Use this space to provide any additional information as necessary. Attach additional 8 1/2" x 11" sheets if necessary.)

OC–APP (3/95)   Page 4

Application for NYS Examinations Open to the Public

EXAMINATION APPLICATION
Use this form to apply for New York State Civil Service exams which are open to the public (The five-digit Examination Numbers beginning with 2 or 8). Read each exam announcement carefully to be sure that you meet the Minimum Qualifications.

You must file a separate application for each different test date. You may list up to eight exam numbers on one application, as long as they are all being held on the same date.

Unless the exam announcement has different instructions, mail your application (and the required processing fee, if any) to the NYS Department of Civil Service, Building 1, State Campus, Albany, NY 12239.

ADMISSION TO EXAMINATION
We usually review your application before the test to be sure that you qualify. Generally we will advise you if we need more information. You may be admitted to the test pending a full review of your application. If you take the test but your application is disapproved later, you will not receive a test score. If your application is disapproved, we will notify you of the reason.

If you are applying for a written test and you do not receive a notice from us by three days before the test date, CALL US at (518) 457-5405. We cannot accept collect calls.

It is the policy of the State of New York and the Department of Civil Service to provide alternative arrangements in testing for religious observers and to provide reasonable accommodations in testing for individuals with disabilities.

PLACE OF EXAMINATION
Unless the exam announcement states otherwise, written tests are held in the following locations, although some may not be open for every examination. You will be assigned to the nearest location based on the postal ZIP code for your mailing address.

Albany	Nyack
Amsterdam	Plattsburgh
Batavia	Poughkeepsie
Binghamton	Rochester
Buffalo	Saranac Lake
Fredonia	Saratoga
Hicksville	Selden
Hornell	Syracuse
Kingston	Troy
Middletown	Utica
New York City (Bronx)	Watertown
New York City (Manhattan)	

Oral tests are usually held in Albany only.

SATURDAY RELIGIOUS OBSERVER
Most written tests are held on Saturdays. If you are a religious observer and you cannot take the test on the announced test date, check the box, "I am a religious observer and cannot be tested on the scheduled test date." We will make arrangements for you to take the test on a different date (usually the following day).

SPECIAL ACCOMMODATIONS IN TESTING
We provide reasonable accommodations for persons with a disability to take a test. If you need a reasonable accommodation, check the box, "I require special accommodations to take this test." On or before the last date for filing applications, write to the Department of Civil Service or call (518) 457-3416 or TDD (Telephone Device for the Deaf) (518) 457-8480 and describe the accommodation you need.

PROCESSING FEE
Refer to the front of the exam announcement for the required processing fee. Enclose a check or money order for the total amount required, **made payable to NYS Department of Civil Service.** DO NOT SEND CASH. **If your application is disapproved, the fee will not be refunded.** Check the box, "I have enclosed the fee."

If you are a NYS employee in a position represented by CSEA or PEF, you are not required to submit a processing fee under current negotiated agreements. Check the box "I am a NYS employee and my fee is paid by my union (**CSEA** or **PEF**)." Refunds will not be issued to employees covered by the agreements if they submit a fee.

No fee is due if you are unemployed and primarily responsible for the support of a household. Do not enclose any payment with your application. Check the box, "I am unemployed and primarily responsible for the support of a household."

No fee is due if you are receiving Supplemental Social Security payments, Public Assistance (Home Relief or Aid to Dependent Children), Foster Care, or are certified Job Training Partnership Act eligible through a state or local social service agency. Do not enclose any payment with your application. Check the box, "I am receiving public assistance."

All claims are subject to verification. Those not supported by appropriate documentation are grounds for barring or rescinding an appointment.

EXTRA CREDITS FOR WAR TIME VETERANS
War Time Veterans and Disabled Veterans are eligible for extra credits added to their exam score if they pass. These extra credits can be used only once for any permanent government employment in New York State. If you want to have the extra credits added to your exam score, you must answer the questions now. You can waive the extra credits later if you wish. At the time of interview and appointment you will be required to produce the documentation, such as discharge papers, to prove that you are eligible for the extra credits.

Answering these questions means that you are requesting the extra credits. Do not answer the questions if you are not a war time veteran or if you do not want to request the extra credits.

PERSONAL PRIVACY PROTECTION LAW NOTIFICATION
The information which you are providing on this application is being requested pursuant to Section 50.3 of the New York State Civil Service Law for the principal purpose of determining the eligibility of applicants to participate in the examination(s) for which they have applied. This information will be used in accordance with Section 96(1) of the Personal Privacy Protection Law, particularly subdivisions (b), (e), and (f). Failure to provide this information may result in disapproval of the application. This information will be maintained by the Director, Division of Staffing Services, Department of Civil Service, The W. Averell Harriman State Office Building Campus, Albany, New York 12239. For further information, relating *only* to the Personal Privacy Protection Law, call (518) 457-9375. (For examination information, call (518) 457-6216.)

SAMPLE LETTER TO LAW ENFORCEMENT AGENCY

Name
Address
City, State, Zip Code
Phone Number

Police Department
Address
City, State, Zip Code

Date

Personnel Administrator:

I am interested in applying for a position as a police officer with the _____
Police Department. Please send me the position's announcement, required application
forms, information on the selection process, and qualifications.

Thank you for your time and consideration.

Sincerely,

Your Name

RÉSUMÉ HINTS   For the most part, applicants to law enforcement positions are required to fill out an official form that is essentially a narrative résumé, however, law enforcement candidates and veteran law enforcement officers should have a narrative history style of résumé on hand that lists their education or experience in reverse chronological order, meaning their most recent employment first.

- Type your résumé on standard $8\frac{1}{2} \times 11$-inch paper. If possible, have your résumé printed on a laser printer in order to provide the best quality lettering.

- Make clear and presentable copies. Nothing is worse than a hazy photocopy of a résumé. It sends a message that the person who submitted it has sent out a mass of copies and may not really care about this particular position. Remember, your résumé is the first impression a prospective employer will have of you.

- Avoid long-winded descriptions of your experience; write short and concise sentences, using the key words of targeted experience.

- Proofread your résumé or have someone else do it for you—misspelled words or grammar errors can be a fatal mistake.

SAMPLE RÉSUMÉ

Chris Candidate
123 Address Street
Buffalo, New York 12345
(716) 123-4567

EDUCATION

1995–1997   SUNY Empire State College at Buffalo, New York
Bachelor Degree: Criminal Justice

1993–1995   Sam Houston State University, Huntsville, Texas
Associate Degree: Criminal Justice

INTERNSHIP

1995   Sam Houston State University,
Public Safety Department, Huntsville, Texas
Public Safety Intern
Conducted safety patrol as assigned by Campus Police Supervisor; instructed and completed Uniform Crime report for department; assigned a special statistical project and received a letter of recommendation from the chief of the department for my assistance.

EXPERIENCE

1997–2000   United States Customs Service, Niagara Falls, New York
U.S. Customs Inspector (Summer)
Protected the United States border; controlled carriers, persons, and cargo entering and departing the United States; prevented fraud and smuggling; assessed and collected customs duties and excise tax on imported goods; worked during summer break from college.

1996–1997   State Protection Services, Huntsville, Texas
Security Officer
Worked as a uniform security guard assigned to high crime areas; conducted both foot and vehicle patrols; entrusted with several special protection projects.

SAMPLE LETTER TO CIVIL SERVICE OR PERSONNEL DEPARTMENTS

Name
Address
City, State, Zip Code
Phone Number

Civil Service Department
Address
City, State, Zip Code

Date

Personnel Administrator:

I am interested in applying for the position of _____ officer. Please send me any announcement of current law enforcement positions, the required application forms, information on the selection process, and qualifications.

Thank you for your time and consideration.

Sincerely,

Your Name

STATE PERSONNEL AND CIVIL SERVICE DEPARTMENTS

Listings

ALABAMA

Department of Personnel
64 North Union Street
Montgomery, AL 36130

ALASKA

State Division of Personnel
P.O. Box 110208
Juneau, AK 99811

ARIZONA

State Personnel Division
1831 West Jefferson
Phoenix, AZ 85007

ARKANSAS

State Office of Personnel Management
P.O. Box 3278
Little Rock, AR 72203

CALIFORNIA

State Personnel Department
801 Capitol Mall
Sacramento, CA 95814

COLORADO

State Personnel Department
1313 Sherman Street
Denver, CO 80203

CONNECTICUT

State Human Resources Bureau
165 Capitol Avenue
Hartford, CT 06106

DELAWARE

State Personnel Department
Townsend Building
Dover, DE 19903

DISTRICT OF COLUMBIA

DC Personnel Department
441 Fourth Street NW
Washington, DC 20001

FLORIDA

State Personnel Management
Division
Knight Building
Tallahassee, FL 32399

GEORGIA

Personnel Administration
200 Piedmount Avenue
Atlanta, GA 30334

HAWAII

State Human
Resources Department
830 Punchbowl Street
Honolulu, HI 96813

IDAHO

State Personnel Department
700 West State Street
Boise, ID 83720

ILLINOIS

Civil Service Department
William Stratton Building
401 South Spring Street
Springfield, IL 62706

INDIANA

State Personnel Department
402 West Washington Street
Indianapolis, IN 46204

IOWA

State Personnel Department
Grimes State Office Building
Des Moines, IA 50319

KANSAS

State Personnel Department
Landon State Office Building
Topeka, KS 66612

KENTUCKY

State Personnel Department
200 Fair Oaks
Frankfort, KY 40601

LOUISIANA

State Civil Service Department
Capitol Station
Baton Rouge, LA 70804

MAINE

State Personnel Department
State Office Building
Augusta, ME 04333

MARYLAND

State Personnel Department
301 West Present Street
Baltimore, MD 21201

MASSACHUSETTS

State Civil Service Department
One Ashburton Place
Boston, MA 02108

MICHIGAN

State Civil Service Department
P.O. Box 30002
Lansing, MI 48909

MINNESOTA

State Personnel Department
658 Cedar Street
St. Paul, MN 55155

MISSISSIPPI

State Personnel Department
301 North Lamar Street
Jackson, MS 39201

MISSOURI

State Division of Personnel
Harry S Truman Building
Jefferson City, MO 65102

MONTANA

Division of State Personnel
Mitchell Building
Helena, MT 59620

NEBRASKA

State Personnel Department
301 Centennial Mall Street
Lincoln, NE 94905

NEVADA

State Personnel Department
209 East Musser Street
Carson City, NV 89710

NEW HAMPSHIRE

State Personnel Department
25 Capitol Street
Concord, NH 03301

NEW JERSEY

State Personnel Department
44 South Clinton Avenue
Trenton, NJ 08625

NEW MEXICO

State Personnel Department
P.O. Box 26127
Santa Fe, NM 87505

NEW YORK

State Civil Service Department
W. Averell Harriman State Office
Albany, NY 12239

NORTH CAROLINA

State Personnel Department
116 West Jones Street
Raleigh, NC 27603

NORTH DAKOTA

State Personnel Department
600 East Blvd.
Bismarck, ND 58505

OHIO

State Human Resources Division
30 East Broad Street
Columbus, OH 43266

OKLAHOMA

State Personnel Office
2101 North Lincoln Blvd.
Oklahoma City, OK 73105

OREGON

State Human Resources Division
155 Cottage Street
Salem, OR 97310

PENNSYLVANIA

State Civil Service Department
207 Finance Building
Harrisburg, PA 17120

RHODE ISLAND

State Personnel
Administration Department
One Capitol Hill
Providence, RI 02908

SOUTH CAROLINA

State Human
Resources Department
1201 Main Street
Columbia, SC 29201

SOUTH DAKOTA

State Personnel Department
500 East Capitol Avenue
Pierre, SD 57501

TENNESSEE

State Personnel Department
James Polk Building
Nashville, TN 37243

TEXAS

State Employment Commission
101 15th Street
Austin, TX 78778

UTAH

State Department
Employment Security
140 East 300 South
Salt Lake City, UT 84145

VERMONT

State Personnel Department
110 State Street
Montpelier, VT 05620

VIRGINIA

State Personnel Division
Monroe Building
101 North 14th Street
Richmond, VA 23219

WASHINGTON

State Personnel Department
P.O. Box 47500
Olympia, WA 98504

WEST VIRGINIA

State Personnel Division
State Capitol
Charleston, WV 25305

WISCONSIN

State Personnel Commission
131 West Wilson Street
Madison, WI 53707

WYOMING

State Personnel Department
2001 Capitol Avenue
Cheyenne, WY 82002

STATE LAW ENFORCEMENT STANDARDS, TRAINING COUNCILS, AND COMMISSIONS

A list of state law enforcement standards, training councils, and commissions has been provided for law enforcement officers considering transfers or laterals to agencies in other states. Officers should contact these agencies and research the state's requirements for law enforcement certification and standards.

Listings

ALASKA

Alaska Police Standards Council
P.O. Box 111200
Juneau, AK 99981
(907) 465-4378

ALABAMA

Alabama Peace Officer
Standards and Training Commission
472 South Lawrence Street
Montgomery, AL 36104
(205) 242-4045

ARKANSAS

Law Enforcement Standards and
Training Advisory Council
P.O. Box 3106
East Camden, AR 71701
(501) 574-1810

ARIZONA

Arizona Peace Officer Standards and
Training
2643 East University Drive
Phoenix, AZ 85005
(602) 244-0477

CALIFORNIA

Commission on Peace Officer
Standards and Training
1601 Alhambra Blvd.
Sacramento, CA 95816
(916) 227-2802

COLORADO

Colorado Peace Officer Standards and
Training
1525 Sherman Avenue
Denver, CO 80203
(303) 866-5671

CONNECTICUT

Municipal Police Training Council
285 Preston Avenue
Meriden, CT 06450
(203) 238-6505

DELAWARE

Delaware State Police
P.O. Box 430
Dover, DE 19901
(302) 739-5945

FLORIDA

Division of Criminal Justice
Standards and Training
P.O. Box 1489
Tallahassee, FL 32302
(904) 487-0491

GEORGIA

Peace Officer Standards and Training
Council
351 Thornton Road
Lithia Springs, GA 30057
(404) 739-5217

HAWAII

Honolulu Police Department
93-093 Waipahu Depot Road
Waipahu, HI 96797
(808) 677-1474

IOWA

Iowa Law Enforcement Academy
P.O. Box 130
Johnston, IA 50131
(515) 242-5357

IDAHO

Peace Officer Standards and Training
Academy
P.O. Box 700
Meridian, ID 83680
(208) 884-7250

ILLINOIS

Law Enforcement Officers Training
Board
600 South Second Street
Springfield, IL 62704
(217) 782-4540

INDIANA

Law Enforcement Training Board
P.O. Box 313
Plainfield, IN 46168
(317) 839-5191

KANSAS

Kansas Law Enforcement Training
Center
P.O. Box 647
Hutchinson, KS 67504
(316) 662-3378

KENTUCKY

Kentucky Department of Criminal
Justice Training
Kit Carson Drive
Richmond, KY 40475
(606) 622-6164

LOUISIANA

Commission on Law Enforcement
1885 Wooddale Blvd.
Baton Rouge, LA 70806
(504) 925-1997

MASSACHUSETTS

Criminal Justice Training Council
41 Terrace Hall Avenue
Burlington, MA 01803
(617) 727-7827

MARYLAND

Maryland Police and Correctional
Training Commission
3085 Hernwood Road
Woodstock, MD 21163
(410) 442-2700

MAINE

Maine Criminal Justice Academy
93 Silver Street
Waterville, ME 04901
(207) 873-4691

MICHIGAN

Law Enforcement Officers Training
Council
7426 North Canal Road
Lansing, MI 48913
(517) 322-1947

MINNESOTA

Minnesota Board of Peace Officer
Standards and Training
1600 University Avenue
St. Paul, MN 55104
(612) 643-3060

MISSOURI

Department of Public Safety
P.O. Box 749
Jefferson City, MO 65102
(314) 751-4905

MISSISSIPPI

Board of Law Enforcement Officer
Standards and Training
P.O. Box 23039
Jackson, MS 39225
(601) 359-7880

MONTANA

Montana Peace Officer Standards
and Training Advisory Council
303 North Roberts
Helena, MT 59620
(406) 444-3605

NORTH CAROLINA

Training and Standards Division
P.O. Box 629
Raleigh, NC 27602
(919) 733-3377

NORTH DAKOTA

Training Division
Bureau of Criminal Investigation
P.O. Box 1054
Bismarck, ND 58502
(701) 221-6180

NEBRASKA

Law Enforcement Training Center
4600 North Academy Road
Grand Island, NE 68801
(308) 381-5700

NEW HAMPSHIRE

Police Standards and Training Council
17 Fan Road
Concord, NH 03301
(603) 271-2133

NEW JERSEY

Police Training Commission
Division of Criminal Justice
CN-085
Trenton, NJ 08625
(609) 984-2140

NEW MEXICO

Department Public Safety
Training Center
4491 Cerrillos Road
Santa Fe, NM 87505
(505) 827-9255

NEVADA

Peace Officer Standards and Training
555 Wright Way
Carson City, NV 89711
(702) 687-3283

NEW YORK

NYS Division of Criminal Justice
Services
Bureau for Municipal Police
Executive Park Tower
Stuyvesant Plaza
Albany, NY 12203
(518) 457-6101

OHIO

Ohio Peace Officer Training Council
P.O. Box 309
London, OH 43140
(614) 466-7771

OKLAHOMA

Council on Law Enforcement
Education and Training
P.O. Box 11476
Cimarron Station
Oklahoma City, OK 73136
(405) 425-2750

OREGON

Board on Public Safety Standards and
Training
550 North Monmouth Avenue
Monmouth, OR 97361
(503) 378-2100

PENNSYLVANIA

Municipal Police Officers'
Education and Training Commission
75 East Derry Road
Hershey, PA 17033
(717) 533-5987

RHODE ISLAND

Rhode Island Police Academy
Community College of Rhode Island
Flanagan Campus
Lincoln, RI 02865
(401) 277-3753

SOUTH CAROLINA

Criminal Justice Academy
5400 Broad River Road
Columbia, SC 29210
(803) 896-7779

SOUTH DAKOTA

Criminal Justice Training Center
East Highway 34
500 East Capitol
Pierre, SD 57501
(605) 773-3331

TENNESSEE

Law Enforcement Training Academy
3025 Lebanon Road
Nashville, TN 37214
(615) 741-4448

TEXAS

Texas Commission on Law
Enforcement Officer Standards
and Education
1033 La Posada
Austin, TX 78752
(512) 450-0188

UTAH

Peace Officer Standards and Training
4525 South 2700 West
Salt Lake City, UT 84119
(801) 965-4669

VIRGINIA

Department of Criminal Justice
Services
805 East Broad Street
Richmond, VA 23219
(804) 786-8475

VERMONT

Criminal Justice Training Council
RR2, Box 2160
Pittsford, VT 05763
(802) 483-6228

WASHINGTON

Criminal Justice Training Commission
P.O. Box 40905
Olympia, WA 98504
(206) 459-6342

WISCONSIN

Training and Standards Bureau
Wisconsin Department of Justice
P.O. Box 7857
Madison, WI 53707
(608) 266-7864

WEST VIRGINIA

CJ and Highway Safety
Law Enforcement Training
1204 Kanawha Blvd., East
Charleston, WV 25301
(304) 348-8814

WYOMING

Peace Officer Standards and Training
1710 Pacific Avenue
Cheyenne, WY 82002
(307) 777-6619

SECTION

Chapter 8

FEDERAL LAW ENFORCEMENT AGENCIES

TABLE OF ORGANIZATION/FEDERAL AGENCIES AND DEPARTMENTS

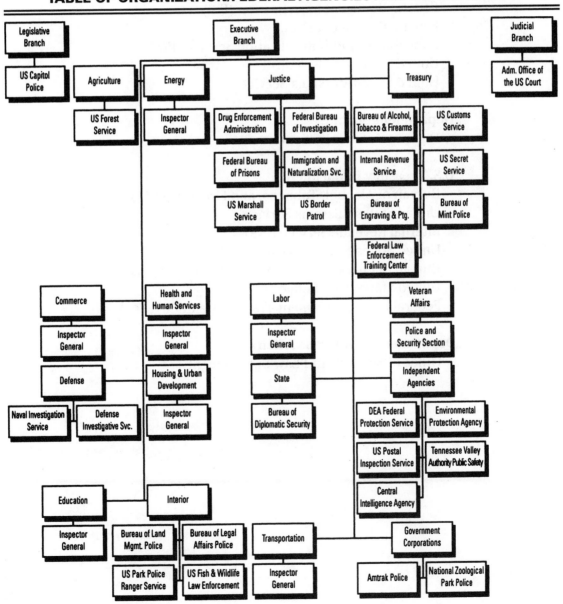

Department of Agriculture
United States Forest Service

Department of Defense
Naval Criminal Investigative Service
Defense Criminal Investigative Service

Department of Interior
United States Fish and Wildlife Service
National Park Service
Bureau of Indian Affairs (BIA)
Bureau of Land Management (BLM)

Department of Justice
Drug Enforcement Administration (DEA)
Federal Bureau of Investigation (FBI)
Federal Bureau of Prisons
Immigration and Naturalization Service (INS)
United States Border Patrol
United States Marshals Service

Department of State
Diplomatic Security Service

U.S. Treasury Department
Bureau of Alcohol, Tobacco, and Firearms (ATF)
United States Customs Service
Internal Revenue Service (IRS)
United States Secret Service
Bureau of Engraving and Printing Police
United States Mint Police
Federal Law Enforcement Training Center

Department of Veterans Affairs
Office of Security and Law Enforcement

Independent Federal Agencies
General Service Administration
Federal Protective Service
Environmental Protection Agency
United States Postal Inspection Service
Tennessee Valley Authority (TVA)
Central Intelligence Agency (CIA)

Judicial Branch
Administrative Offices of the United States Court
Parole Division

Legislative Branch
United States Capitol Police

Quasi-Official Agencies
Amtrak Police
National Zoological Park Police

United States Inspector General Offices
Federal Agencies and Departments

DEPARTMENT OF AGRICULTURE

United States Forest Service
Law Enforcement
14th and Independence Avenue SW
Washington, DC 20250
(703) 235-3440

◻ **Law Enforcement Officer (GS-5)**
◻ **Special Agent (GS-7)**

MISSION The United States Forest Service law enforcement personnel protect the national forest lands, animals, and resources from harm, damage, and illegal harvest. U.S. Forest Service Special Agents/Law Enforcement Officers patrol the vast territory for illegal activities and conduct investigations of criminal activities.

Anticipated Positions	Under 100 nationwide.
Profile of Agency	
Law Enforcement Personnel:	700+
Major States of Assignment:	Arizona, California, Colorado, Idaho, Montana, Oregon
Qualifications	
Age:	21 to 37 years
Education:	Bachelor's Degree and/or
Experience:	Three years general (GS-5)
	One year specialized (GS-7)

COMMENTS *Employment Outlook:* DOA maintains internship programs and various summer employment opportunities.
Preferred Degree Fields: Range Conservation, Forestry, Criminal Justice.
Training Location: Federal Law Enforcement Training Center, Glynco, GA
Retirement: 20 years/age 55

WHERE TO APPLY The Washington Personnel Office or the nearest Regional Office.

WEB *www.usda.gov*

REGIONAL OFFICES

Alaska Region
U.S. Forest Service
Juneau, AK 99802
(907) 586-8802

Pacific Southwest Region
U.S. Forest Service
630 Sansome Street
San Francisco, CA 94111
(415) 556-9907

Rocky Mountain Region
U.S. Forest Service
11177 West 8th Avenue
Lakewood, CO 89225
(303) 236-9630

Southern Region
U.S. Forest Service
1720 Peachtree Road, NW
Atlanta, GA 30367
(404) 347-2384

Northern Region
U.S. Forest Service
Federal Building
Missoula, MT 59807
(406) 329-3535

Southwestern Region
U.S. Forest Service
Federal Building
517 Gold Street
Albuquerque, NM 87102
(505) 842-3382

Pacific Northwest Region
U.S. Forest Service
319 SW Pine Street
Portland, OR 97208
(503) 423-3655

Intermountain Region
U.S. Forest Service
Federal Building
324 25th Street
Ogden, UT 84401
(801) 625-5310

Eastern Region
U.S. Forest Service
Federal Building
310 West Wisconsin Avenue
Milwaukee, WI 53203
(414) 291-3719

DEPARTMENT OF DEFENSE

U.S. Naval Criminal Investigative Service
Career Services Department
716 Sicaro Street SE, Suite 2000
Washington, DC 20388
(800) 616-8891

◌ NCIS Special Agent

MISSION The U.S. Naval Criminal Investigative Service is a centrally directed, largely civilian organization responsible for criminal investigations and counterintelligence operations for the U.S. Navy. NCIS Special Agents are frequently detailed for protective service to U.S. Military Officials and are trained in antiterrorism tactics. In addition, the NCIS Special Agent Afloat program stations an agent aboard military vessels to be responsible for all major criminal investigations and counterintelligence matters.

Anticipated Positions	✪ Over 100
Profile of Agency	
Law Enforcement Personnel:	1,200 NCIS Special Agents
Qualifications	
Age:	21 to 37 years
Education:	Bachelor's Degree and/or
Experience:	Three years general (GS-5)
	One year specialized (GS-7)
Vision:	20/20 corrected
	20/70 uncorrected

COMMENTS *Employment Conditions:* During a 20-year career, an NCIS Special Agent can expect to do at least two years of duty overseas. Some NCIS Special Agents may be assigned to a military vessel for up to a one-year tour of duty.
Training Location: Federal Law Enforcement Training Center, Glynco, GA
Retirement: 20 years/age 55

WHERE TO APPLY Above address or Regional Office

WEB *www.ncis.navy.mil*

REGIONAL OFFICES
New York, NY
Washington, DC
Norfolk, VA
Charleston, SC
San Francisco, CA
San Diego, CA
London, England
Pearl Harbor, HI
Yosuka, Japan
Subic Bay, Philippines

Defense Criminal Investigative Service
1340 Braddock Place
Alexandria, VA 22315
(703) 325-5324

⬭ Special Agent

MISSION   The Defense Criminal Investigative Service conducts all personnel security investigations for the Department of Defense components. These include the investigation of allegations of subversive affiliations, adverse suitability information, or any other situation that requires resolution to complete the personnel security investigation. Agents conduct field interviews and investigations that require extensive travel.

Anticipated Positions	Undetermined
Profile of Agency	
Law Enforcement Personnel:	Undetermined
Qualifications	
Age:	21 to 37 years
Education:	Bachelor's Degree and/or
Experience:	Three years general (GS-5)
	One year specialized (GS-7)
Vision:	20/20 corrected
	20/70 uncorrected

COMMENTS   *Employment Conditions:* Extensive travel involved
Training Location: Federal Law Enforcement Training Center, Glynco, GA
Retirement: 20 years/age 55

WHERE TO APPLY   Above address or Regional Office

WEB   *www.dia.mil*

REGIONAL OFFICES

Defense Investigative Office
Long Beach, CA 90807

Defense Investigative Office
Smyrna, GA 30080

Defense Investigative Office
Cherry Hill, NJ 08034

Defense Investigative Office
Irving, TX 75062

Defense Investigative Office
Alexandria, VA 22331

DEPARTMENT OF INTERIOR

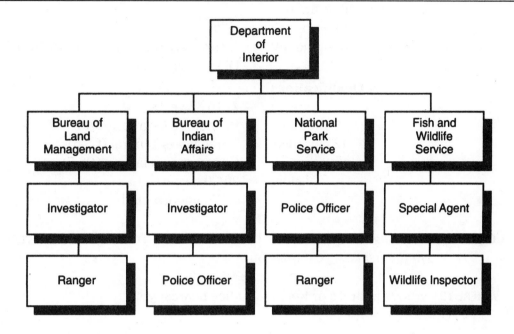

The Department of Interior maintains an Automated Vacancy Announcement Distribution System Bulletin Board, which contains lists of current position vacancies within the Department of Interior. It is accessible through a personal computer and is free of charge by using a modem to dial 1-800-368-3321. You can also call toll free 1-800-336-4562, for prerecorded vacancy information if you do not have access to the electronic bulletin board.

U.S. Fish and Wildlife Service
Law Enforcement Division
1849 C Street NW
Washington, DC 20240
(703) 358-2120

◌ **Special Agent GS-5/7**
◌ **Wildlife Inspector GS-5/7**

MISSION   Special Agents enforce wildlife laws through both standard investigations and covert operations. They also are involved in public education and assistance. Wildlife inspectors, at ports of entry into the United States, examine shipping containers, live animals, wildlife products such as animal skins, and documents. Inspectors, who work closely with Special Agents, may seize shipments as evidence, participate in investigations, and testify in court.

Anticipated Positions	Under 100
Profile of Agency	
Law Enforcement Personnel:	1,000 +
Major States of Assignment:	Alaska, Arizona, Missouri, North Dakota, Oklahoma, Texas
Qualifications	
Age:	21 to 37 years
Education:	Bachelor's Degree and/or
Experience:	Three years general (GS-5)
	One year specialized (GS-7)
Vision:	20/20 corrected
	20/70 uncorrected

COMMENTS *Training Location:* Federal Law Enforcement Training Center, Glynco, GA
Retirement: 20 years/age 55

WHERE TO APPLY Above address or Regional Office nearest you.

WEB *www.fws.gov*

REGIONAL OFFICES

Alaska Region
U.S. Fish and Wildlife Service
1011 East Tudor Road
Anchorage, AK 99503
(907) 786-3301

Mountain-Prairie Region
U.S. Fish and Wildlife Service
P.O. Box 25486
Denver Federal Center
Denver, CO 80225
(303) 236-4733
(Job Information Line)

Southeast Region
U.S. Fish and Wildlife Service
1875 Century Center Blvd. NE
Atlanta, GA 30345
(404) 679-4014

Northeast Region
U.S. Fish and Wildlife Service
300 Westgate Center Drive
Hadley, MA 01035-9589
(413) 253-8200
(Job Information Line)

Great Lakes-Big Rivers Region
U.S. Fish and Wildlife Service
Federal Building, Fort Snelling
Twin Cities, MN 55111-4056
(612) 725-3585

Southwest Region
U.S. Fish and Wildlife Service
500 Gold Avenue SW
P.O. Box 1306
Albuquerque, NM 87103
(505) 766-2033

Pacific Region
U.S. Fish and Wildlife Service
911 NE 11th Avenue
Eastside Federal Complex
Portland, OR 97232-4181
(503) 231-2018
(Job Information Line)
(503) 231-6136 (Personnel Office)

National Park Service
1849 C Street NW
Washington, DC 20240
(202) 208-5093

○ **U.S. Park Police Officer (GS-5/7)**
○ **U.S. Park Ranger (GS-4/7)**

MISSION The U.S. Park Police and Rangers contribute to resource protection through the use of law enforcement methods, and techniques designed to fit the nature of the offenses committed or suspected on national park system properties. Offenses may range from homicides, rapes, assaults, burglaries, car theft, excessive use of alcoholic beverages, and use of and trafficking in illegal drugs. Rangers perform duties educating the public about the park's resources and requirements pertaining to their use, and specialized duties directed toward protection of the park's natural and cultural resources, safety, and security of park visitors, park employees, contractor and concessionaire employees, and other members of the public, and protection of public and private property.

Anticipated Positions	✪ Over 200
Profile of Agency	
Law Enforcement Personnel:	660 Police Officers/1,500 Rangers
Qualifications	
Age:	21 to 31 years (Park Police)
	21 to 37 years (Ranger)
Education:	Bachelor's Degree and/or
Experience:	Three years general (GS-5)
	One year specialized (GS-7)
Vision:	20/20 corrected
	20/70 uncorrected

COMMENTS *Employment Conditions:* Both Park Police and Rangers may be required to work weekends, holidays, evenings, and during special events or snow emergencies. This is a required-occupancy position. Rangers will be required to live in government quarters, if available. Prolonged walking, standing, and occasional running may be required. They may be required to work frequent overtime with little or no notice.
Training Location: Federal Law Enforcement Training Center, Glynco, GA
Retirement: Park Police—age 50/20 years service.
Rangers—age 60/20 years of service.

WHERE TO APPLY   Above address or at the following personnel offices:

WEB   *www.nps.gov*

National Park Service
Seasonal Employment Unit
P.O. Box 37127
Washington, DC 20013

U.S. Ranger Division
1849 C Street NW
Washington, DC 20240
(202) 208-5093

U.S. Park Police
1100 Ohio Drive SW
Washington, DC 20242
(202) 619-7056

**Bureau of Indian Affairs
Law Enforcement Division**
615 First Street NW
Albuquerque, NM 87102
(505) 248-7937
(505) 346-7108

☐ **BIA Police Officer GS-5/7**
☐ **BIA Criminal Investigator GS-5/7**

MISSION   The Bureau of Indian Affairs (BIA) was created to encourage and to assist Native American and Alaskan people to manage their own affairs under the trust relationship of the federal government. BIA Police Officers and Criminal Investigators are responsible for law enforcement and investigations on the designated Indian territories and jurisdiction.

Anticipated Positions	Under 50
Profile	
Law Enforcement Personnel:	330
Qualifications	
Age:	21 to 37 years
Education:	High school and
Experience:	Three years general (GS-5)
	One year specialized (GS-7)

COMMENTS   *Employment Outlook:* Currently BIA is experiencing problems with funding. Native American candidates are given preference in hiring by federal law.
Training Location: Federal Law Enforcement Training Center, Glynco, GA
Retirement: 20 years/age 55

WHERE TO APPLY   Above address or Regional Offices

WEB   *www.doi.gov*

REGIONAL OFFICES

Bureau of Indian Affairs
9109 Mendenhall Road
Suite 5
Juneau, AK 99802
(907) 586-7177

Bureau of Indian Affairs
P.O. Box 10
1 North 1st Street
Phoenix, AZ 85001
(602) 379-6600

Bureau of Indian Affairs
P.O. Box M, WR-1 BIA Building
Window Rock Blvd.
Window Rock, AZ 86515
(602) 871-5151

Bureau of Indian Affairs
2800 Cottage Way
Sacramento, CA 95825
(916) 484-4682

Bureau of Indian Affairs
331 South 2nd Avenue
Minneapolis, MN 55401
(612) 349-3631

Bureau of Indian Affairs
316 North 26th Street
Billings, MT 59101
(406) 657-6315

Bureau of Indian Affairs
P.O. Box 26567
615 1st Street NW
Albuquerque, NM 87125
(505) 766-3170

Bureau of Indian Affairs
P.O. Box 1060
Gallup, NM 83705
(505) 863-8314

Bureau of Indian Affairs
P.O. Box 368
WCD Office Complex, Highway 8
Anadarko, OK 75003
(405) 247-6673

Bureau of Indian Affairs
Old Federal Building 5th
and West Okmulgee
Muskogee, OK 74401
(918) 687-2296

Bureau of Indian Affairs
911 NE 11th Avenue
Portland, OR 97232
(503) 231-6702

Bureau of Indian Affairs
115 4th Avenue
Aberdeen, SD 57401
(605) 226-7343

Bureau of Indian Affairs
3701 North Fairfax Drive
Suite 260
Arlington, VA 22203
(703) 235-2571

**Bureau of Land Management
Law Enforcement Division**
18th and C Street NW
Washington, DC 20240
(202) 653-8815

◯ **BLM Rangers (GS-5/7)**
◯ **Criminal Investigator (GS-9/12)**

MISSION   The Bureau of Land Management (BLM) is responsible for the total management of 270 million acres of public lands and for an additional 300 million acres where the mineral rights are owned by the federal government. Resources managed by the BLM include timber, solid minerals, oil and gas, wildlife habitat, endangered plant and animal species, rangeland vegetation, recreation and cultural values, wild and scenic rivers, designated conservation and wilderness areas, and open space. Rangers and Criminal Investigators protect the massive land and its resources and conduct investigations of violations of federal laws.

Anticipated Positions	Under 50
Qualifications	
Age:	21 to 37 years
Education:	Bachelor's Degree and/or
Experience:	Three years general (GS-5)
	One year specialized (GS-7)

COMMENTS   *Training Location:* Federal Law Enforcement Training Center, Glynco, GA
Retirement: 20 years/age 55

WHERE TO APPLY   Above address or regional offices (on next page)

WEB   *www.blm.gov*

REGIONAL OFFICES

Bureau of Land Management
222 West 7th Avenue, No. 13
Anchorage, AK 99513
(907) 271-5076

Bureau of Land Management
P.O. Box 16563
3707 North 7th Street
Phoenix, AZ 85011
(602) 650-0500

Bureau of Land Management
2800 Cottage Way
Rm E-2841
Sacramento, CA 95825
(916) 979-2845

Bureau of Land Management
2850 Youngfield Street
Lakewood, CO 80215
(303) 239-3700

Bureau of Land Management
3380 Americana Terrace
Boise, ID 83706
(208) 384-3001

Bureau of Land Management
P.O. Box 36800
222 North 32nd Street
Billings, MT 59107
(406) 255-2904

Bureau of Land Management
P.O. Box 12000
850 Harvard Way
Reno, NV 89520
(702) 785-6590

Bureau of Land Management
P.O. Box 27115
1474 Rodeo Road
Santa Fe, NM 87502
(505) 438-7501

Bureau of Land Management
P.O. Box 2965
1515 SW 5th Avenue
Portland, OR 97208
(503) 952-6024

Bureau of Land Management
P.O. Box 45155
324 South State Street
Salt Lake City, UT 84145
(801) 539-4010

Bureau of Land Management
7450 Boston Blvd.
Springfield, VA 22153
(703) 440-1700

Bureau of Land Management
P.O. Box 1828
2515 Warren Avenue
Cheyenne, WY 82003
(307) 775-6001

DEPARTMENT OF JUSTICE

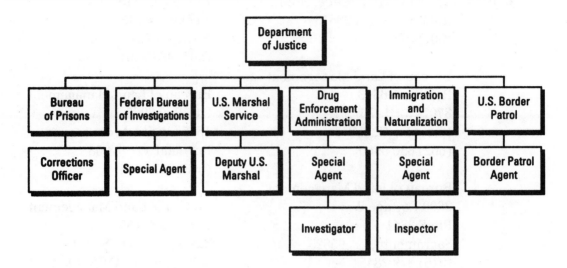

Drug Enforcement Administration
700 Army/Navy Drive
Arlington, VA 20537-0001
(202) 307-4088 or 1-800-DEA-4288

○ **Special Agent (GS-7/9)**
○ **Investigator (GS-5/7)**

MISSION The Drug Enforcement Agency (DEA) is the primary federal agency for the enforcement of narcotics and controlled substances laws and regulations. Formed in 1973, the Drug Enforcement Administration enforces the federal drug laws of our nation. The agency has grown to over 3,700 Special Agents, who work in American towns and cities and in over 50 countries around the world to target the most notorious drug traffickers and dismantle their global networks. Working with fellow law enforcement agencies, DEA has aggressively attacked drug trafficking organizations at home and abroad. DEA Agents are on the cutting edge of criminal investigations, and use sophisticated tools to identify and immobilize traffickers and their assets.

DEA has offices in 170 U.S. cities and 74 foreign posts of duty.

Anticipated Positions ✪ Over 100
Profile of Agency
Law Enforcement Personnel: 3,000 Special Agents
Major States of Assignment: Alabama, California, D.C., Florida, Illinois, New York, Texas

Qualifications

Age:	21 to 37 years
Education:	Bachelor's Degree (minimum)
Vision:	20/20 corrected
	20/200 uncorrected
	Radial keratotomy is disqualifying

COMMENTS *Preferred Degree Fields:* Accounting, Chemistry, Criminal Justice, Language, Law, and Pharmacology.

Employment Conditions: Must be willing to accept an assignment throughout career anywhere in the United States. There is a possibility of foreign assignment, with a typical tour of duty in a foreign office two to three years.

Training Location: FBI Academy, Quantico, Virginia.

Retirement: 20 years/age 55

WHERE TO APPLY Directly to the Regional Office or call 1-800-DEA-4288.

WEB *www.usdoj.gov*

REGIONAL OFFICES

Phoenix Division
3010 North 2nd Street
Suite 301
Phoenix, AZ 85012
(602) 664-5600

Los Angeles Division
255 East Temple Street
20th Floor
Los Angeles, CA 90012
(213) 894-4258

San Diego Division
402 West 35th Street
National City, CA 91950
(619) 585-4241

San Francisco Division
450 Golden Gate Avenue
Room 12215
San Francisco, CA 94102
(415) 436-7814

Rocky Mountain Division
115 Inverness Drive
East Englewood, CO 80112
(303) 705-7300

Washington, DC Division
400 Sixth Street SW
Room 2558
Washington, DC 20024
(202) 401-7512

Miami Division
8400 NW 53rd Street
Miami, FL 33166
(305) 590-4812

Atlanta Division
75 Spring Street SW
Room 740
Atlanta, GA 30303
(404) 331-4401

Chicago Division
230 South Dearborn Street
Suite 1200
Chicago, IL 60604
(312) 353-7875

New Orleans Division
3838 North Causeway Blvd.
3 Lakeway Center
Suite 1800
Metairie, LA 70002
(504) 840-1100

New England Division
50 Stanford Street
Suite 200
Boston, MA 02114
(617) 557-2100

Detroit Division
431 Howard Street
Detroit, MI 48226
(313) 234-4000

Midwest Division
7911 Forsythe Blvd.
Suite 500
St. Louis, MO 63105
(314) 425-3241

Newark Division
Federal Office Building
970 Broad Street
Room 806
Newark, NJ 07102
(201) 645-3344

New York Division
99 Tenth Avenue
New York, NY 10011
(212) 337-3900

Philadelphia Division
Wm. J. Green Federal Building
600 Arch Street
Room 10224
Philadelphia, PA 19106
(215) 597-7870

Caribbean Division
Casa Lee Building
2432 Loiza Street
Santurce, PR 00913
(809) 253-4200

Dallas Division
1880 Regal Row
Dallas, TX 75235
(214) 767-7151

Houston Division
333 West Loop North
Suite 300
Houston, TX 77024
(713) 681-1771

Seattle Division
220 West Mercer
Suite 104
Seattle, WA 98119
(206) 553-5443

Federal Bureau of Investigation (FBI)
Headquarters
Ninth Street and Pennsylvania Avenue NW
Washington, DC 20535
(202) 324-3000

○ Special Agent (GS-10)

MISSION The mission of the FBI is to uphold the law through the investigation of violations of federal criminal law, to protect the United States from foreign intelligence activities, to provide leadership and law enforcement assistance to federal, state, local, and international agencies, and to perform these responsibilities in a manner that is responsive to the needs of the public and is faithful to the Constitution of the United States. Investigative programs include: Civil rights and applicant matters with additional national priority given to organized crime/drugs, counterterrorism, foreign counterintelligence, violent crimes, and white collar crime. The FBI is a unique institution in the federal government in that it is responsible for sensitive foreign counterintelligence matters, important civil investigations, background inquiries on persons nominated for high public office, and criminal investigations that may involve prominent figures in both the public and private sectors. In recognition of these diverse responsibilities, the FBI has traditionally been provided broader discretion in personnel matters than is afforded most other federal agencies.

Anticipated Positions	❂ Over 1,000 nationwide
Profile of Agency	
Law Enforcement Personnel:	Special Agents: 10,000 + Support Personnel: 13,500
Major States of Assignment:	California, D.C., Florida, Illinois, New York, Pennsylvania, Virginia, Texas
Qualifications	
Age:	23 to 37 years
Education:	Bachelor's Degree (minimum)
Vision:	20/20 corrected 20/40 uncorrected Radial keratotomy is disqualifying.

COMMENTS *Preferred Degree Fields:* Accounting, Engineering, Science, Law, Language, Diversified.

Employment Conditions: Candidates must be willing to accept assignments throughout their career anywhere in the United States with the possibility of foreign assignments. The FBI has a rigorous application process. Candidates must complete a series of written tests and a formal interview, and are rated on education, language ability, and experience.

Training Location: The FBI Academy, Quantico, Virginia.

Retirement: 20 years/age 55

WHERE TO APPLY The FBI is authorized to hire its own personnel directly; unlike most federal agencies it does not hire through the Office of Personnel Management. The FBI recruits candidates through its 56 field offices. FBI Headquarters finalizes all appointments. Contact the FBI office nearest you for an application.

WEB *www.fbi.gov*

FIELD OFFICES

Federal Bureau of Investigation
Room 1400
2121 Building
Birmingham, AL 35203
(205) 252-7705

Federal Bureau of Investigation
St. Louis Centre
1 St. Louis Street
Mobile, AL 36602
(334) 438-3674

Federal Bureau of Investigation
101 East Sixth Avenue
Anchorage, AK 99501
(907) 276-4441

Federal Bureau of Investigation
Suite 400
201 East Indianola
Phoenix, AZ 85012
(602) 279-5511

Federal Bureau of Investigation
Suite 200
10825 Financial Center Parkway
Little Rock, AR 72211
(501) 221-9100

Federal Bureau of Investigation
Federal Office Building
11000 Wilshire Blvd.
Los Angeles, CA 90024
(310) 477-6565

Federal Bureau of Investigation
Suite E 1606
2800 Cottage Way
Sacramento, CA 95825
(916) 481-9110

Federal Bureau of Investigation
9797 Aero Drive
San Diego, CA 92123-1800
(619) 565-1255

Federal Bureau of Investigation
450 Golden Gate Avenue
San Francisco, CA 94102
(415) 553-7400

Federal Bureau of Investigation
Federal Office Building
Suite 1823
1961 Stout Street
Denver, CO 80294
(303) 629-7171

Federal Bureau of Investigation
Federal Office Building
150 Court Street
New Haven, CT 06510
(203) 777-6311

Federal Bureau of Investigation
Washington Metropolitan Field
Office
1900 Half Street SW
Washington, DC 20535-0001
(202) 252-7801

Federal Bureau of Investigation
Suite 200
7820 Arlington Expressway
Jacksonville, FL 32211
(904) 721-1211

Federal Bureau of Investigation
16320 Northwest Second Avenue
North Miami Beach, FL 33169
(305) 944-9101

Federal Bureau of Investigation
500 Zack Street
Tampa, FL 33602
(813) 273-4566

Federal Bureau of Investigation
Suite 400
2635 Century Parkway NE
Atlanta, GA 30345
(404) 679-9000

Federal Bureau of Investigation
Room 4307
300 Ala Moana Blvd.
Honolulu, HI 96850
(808) 521-1411

Federal Bureau of Investigation
Room 905 E.M.
Dirksen Federal Office Building
219 South Dearborn Street
Chicago, IL 60604
(312) 431-1333

Federal Bureau of Investigation
Suite 400
400 West Monroe Street
Springfield, IL 62704
(217) 522-9675

Federal Bureau of Investigation
Room 679
575 North Pennsylvania Street
Indianapolis, IN 46204
(317) 639-3301

Federal Bureau of Investigation
Room 500
600 Martin Luther King Place
Louisville, KY 40202
(502) 583-3941

Federal Bureau of Investigation
Suite 2200
1250 Poydras Street
New Orleans, LA 70113
(504) 522-4671

Federal Bureau of Investigation
7142 Ambassador Road
Baltimore, MD 21244
(410) 265-8080

Federal Bureau of Investigation
Suite 600
One Center Plaza
Boston, MA 02108
(617) 742-5533

Federal Bureau of Investigation
Suite 1100
111 Washington Avenue South
Minneapolis, MN 55401
(612) 376-3200

Federal Bureau of Investigation
Federal Office Building
477 Michigan Avenue
Detroit, MI 48226
(313) 965-2323

Federal Bureau of Investigation
Room 1553
100 West Capitol Street
Jackson, MS 39269
(601) 948-5000

Federal Bureau of Investigation
Room 300
U.S. Courthouse
Kansas City, MO 64106
(816) 221-6100

Federal Bureau of Investigation
2222 Market Street
St. Louis, MO 63103
(314) 589-2500

Federal Bureau of Investigation
700 East Charleston Blvd.
Las Vegas, NV 89104
(702) 385-1281

Federal Bureau of Investigation
1 Gateway Centre
Market Street
Newark, NJ 07102
(973) 792-3000

Federal Bureau of Investigation
Suite 300
415 Silver Street SW
Albuquerque, NM 87102
(505) 224-2000

Federal Bureau of Investigation
200 McCarty Avenue
Albany, NY 12209
(518) 465-7551

Federal Bureau of Investigation
1 FBI Plaza
Buffalo, NY 14202
(716) 856-7800

Federal Bureau of Investigation
26 Federal Plaza
New York, NY 10278
(212) 335-2700

Federal Bureau of Investigation
Suite 900
400 South Tyron Street
Charlotte, NC 28285
(704) 377-9200

Federal Bureau of Investigation
Room 9023
550 Main Street
Cincinnati, OH 45202
(513) 421-4310

Federal Bureau of Investigation
Room 3005
Federal Office Building
1240 East 9th Street
Cleveland, OH 44199
(216) 522-1400

Federal Bureau of Investigation
3301 West Memorial Drive
Oklahoma City, OK 73134
(405) 290-7770

Federal Bureau of Investigation
10755 Burt Street
Omaha, NE 68114
(402) 493-8688

Federal Bureau of Investigation
Crown Plaza
1500 Southwest First Avenue
Portland, OR 97201
(503) 224-4181

Federal Bureau of Investigation
8th Floor
600 Arch Street
Philadelphia, PA 19106
(215) 418-4000

Federal Bureau of Investigation
Suite 300
U.S. Post Office Building
700 Grant Street
Pittsburgh, PA 15219
(412) 471-2000

Federal Bureau of Investigation
U.S. Courthouse and Federal
Office Building
Hato Rey
San Juan, PR 00918
(809) 754-6000

Federal Bureau of Investigation
Room 1357
1835 Assembly Street
Columbia, SC 29201
(803) 254-3011

Federal Bureau of Investigation
6th Floor
710 Locust Street
Knoxville, TN 37901
(423) 544-0751

Federal Bureau of Investigation
225 North Humphreys Blvd.
Memphis, TN 38120-2107
(901) 747-4300

Federal Bureau of Investigation
Room 300
1801 North Lamar
Dallas, TX 75202
(214) 720-2200

Federal Bureau of Investigation
Suite C-600
700 East San Antonio Avenue
El Paso, TX 79901
(915) 533-7451

Federal Bureau of Investigation
Room 200
2500 East TC Jester
Houston, TX 77008
(713) 868-2266

Federal Bureau of Investigation
Room 200
615 East Houston Street
San Antonio, TX 78205
(210) 225-6741

Federal Bureau of Investigation
Suite 1200
257 East 200 Street South
Salt Lake City, UT 84111
(801) 579-1400

Federal Bureau of Investigation
150 Corporate Boulevard
Norfolk, VA 23502
(804) 455-0100

Federal Bureau of Investigation
111 Greencourt Road
Richmond, VA 23228
(804) 261-1044

Federal Bureau of Investigation
915 Second Avenue
Seattle, WA 98174
(206) 622-0460

Federal Bureau of Investigation
Suite 600
330 East Kilbourn Avenue
Milwaukee, WI 53202
(414) 276-4684

Federal Bureau of Prisons
Headquarters
320 First Street NW
Washington, DC 20534
(202) 514-2000

⬡ Federal Corrections Officer (GS-5/6)

MISSION   The Federal Bureau of Prisons Corrections Officers have the responsibility for the safekeeping, care, protection, instruction, and discipline of all persons charged or convicted of offenses against the United States. Corrections Officers may be required to use force to subdue unruly inmates who are armed or assaultive.

Anticipated Positions	✪ Over 1,000

Profile of Agency

Law Enforcement Personnel:	11,300 +
Number of Correction Institutions:	71
Inmate Population:	84,900
Major States of Assignment:	California, Colorado, Florida, Kentucky, Pennsylvania, New York, Texas

Qualifications

Age:	21 to 37 years
Education:	Four-year degree and/or
Experience:	Three years general (GS-5)
	One year specialized (GS-6)
Vision:	20/20 corrected
	20/70 uncorrected

COMMENTS   *Training Location:* Federal Law Enforcement Training Center, Glynco, GA
Retirement: 20 years/age 55

WHERE TO APPLY   Above address or Regional Offices nearest you.

WEB   *www.bop.gov*

REGIONAL OFFICES

Federal Bureau of Prisons	Federal Bureau of Prisons
Western Regional Office	Southeast Regional Office
7950 Dublin Blvd.	5213 McDonough Blvd.
Dublin, CA 94568	Atlanta, GA 30315

Federal Bureau of Prisons
North Central Regional Office
Airworld Center
10920 Ambassador Drive
Kansas City, MO 64153

Federal Bureau of Prisons
South Central Regional Office
4211 Cedar Springs Road
Dallas, TX 75219

Federal Bureau of Prisons
Northeast Regional Office
U.S. Customs House
2nd and Chestnut Street
Philadelphia, PA 19106

Immigration & Naturalization Service
425 I Street NW
Washington, DC 20536
(202) 514-2690

☐ **Special Agent (GS-5/7)**
☐ **Inspector (GS-5/7)**
☐ **Deportation Officer (GS-5/7)**

MISSION The Immigration and Naturalization Service (INS) mission involves inspections, investigations, detention, and deportation, as well as U.S. Border Patrol. INS is charged with preventing unlawful entry, employment, or receipt of benefits by those not entitled to receive them, and apprehending those aliens who enter and remain illegally in the United States.

Special Agents investigate illegal entry activities and other criminal matters relating to Immigration and Naturalization laws. Immigration Inspectors are stationed anywhere that people enter the United States, primarily at land ports, seaports, and airports. They prevent ineligible persons from entering the United States. Deportation Officers provide control and removal of persons who have been ordered deported or otherwise required to leave the United States.

Anticipated Positions ✪ Over 1,000 nationwide
Profile of Agency
Law Enforcement Personnel: 12,400 nationwide

Qualifications

Age:	21 to 37 years
Education:	Bachelor's Degree and/or
Experience:	Three years general (GS-5)
	One year specialized (GS-7)
Vision:	20/20 corrected
	20/200 uncorrected

COMMENTS ○ *Special Opportunity:* U.S. INS hires a large number of "Summer" INS Inspectors at key border crossings/certain areas. The hiring takes place mainly in the summer months due to the influx of tourism and the regular staff taking vacations. While the employment usually lasts only for the summer, it is an ideal opportunity for experience.
Training Location: Federal Law Enforcement Training Center, Glynco, GA
Retirement: 20 years/age 55

WHERE TO APPLY   Above address or Regional Offices

WEB   *www.usdoj.gov*

REGIONAL OFFICES   Western Region
Terminal Island
San Pedro, CA 90731

Northern Region
Federal Building
Fort Snelling
Twin Cities, MN 55111

Southern Region
Skyline Center, Building C
311 North Stemmons Freeway
Dallas, TX 75207

Immigration and Naturalization Service
Eastern Region
Federal Building
Elmwood Avenue
Burlington, VT 05401

U.S. Border Patrol
425 I Street NW
Washington, DC 20536
1-800-238-1945

○ Border Patrol Agent (GS-5)

MISSION   Border Patrol Agents must interdict aliens and narcotics or other contraband between ports of entry; detain and deport illegal aliens; and perform intelligence functions related to INS responsibilities. Historically, Border Patrol involve the linewatch, which is the detection and apprehension of illegal aliens and smugglers on U.S. borders.

Anticipated Positions	✪ Over 3,000 nationwide
Profile of Agency	
Law Enforcement Personnel:	3,900 Border Patrol Agents
Major States of Assignment:	Arizona, California, New Mexico, Texas
Qualifications	
Age:	21 to 37 years
Education:	Bachelor's Degree and/or
Experience:	Three years general (GS-5)
	One year specialized (GS-7)
Language:	Spanish
Vision:	20/20 corrected
	20/70 uncorrected

COMMENTS   *Employment Conditions:* Must learn Spanish. Border Patrol Agents' first duty station is on the United States-Mexican border. Agents may be stationed in small isolated communities that may not be near adequate schools or medical facilities. Border Patrol Agents routinely work overtime.
Training Location: Federal Law Enforcement Training Center, Glynco, GA
Retirement: 20 years/age 55

WHERE TO APPLY   Above address or Regional Offices

WEB   *www.usborderpatrol.gov*

REGIONAL Immigration and Naturalization Service
OFFICES Western Region
Terminal Island
San Pedro, CA 90731

Immigration and Naturalization Service
Northern Region
Federal Building
Fort Snelling
Twin Cities, MN 55111

Immigration and Naturalization Service
Southern Region
Skyline Center, Building C
311 North Stemmons Freeway
Dallas, TX 75207

Immigration and Naturalization Service
Eastern Region
Federal Building
Elmwood Avenue
Burlington, VT 05401

U.S. Marshals Service
600 Army/Navy Drive
Arlington, VA 22202-4210
(202) 307-9065

○ Deputy U.S. Marshal (GS-5)

MISSION The United States Marshal Service is the nation's oldest federal law enforcement agency, having served as a vital link between the executive
and judicial branches of the government since 1789. The Marshals Service performs tasks that are essential to the operation of virtually every
aspect of the federal justice system. The service is responsible for providing support and protection for the federal courts, including security
for over 700 judicial facilities and nearly 2,000 judges and magistrates,
as well as countless other trial participants such as jurors and attor-
neys. In addition, Deputy U.S. Marshals apprehend federal fugitives; operate the federal witness security program that ensures the safety of
endangered government witnesses; maintain the custody of and trans-
porting of thousands of federal prisoners annually; execute court orders and arrest warrants; seize, manage, and sell property forfeited to
the government from drug traffickers and other criminals, and assist the
Justice Department's seizure and forfeiture program; respond to emer-

gency circumstances, including civil disturbances, terrorist incidents, and other crisis situations, through its Special Operations Group; and restore order in riot and mob violence situations.

Anticipated Positions	✪ Over 100 nationwide
Profile of Agency	
Law Enforcement Personnel:	2,600 Deputy Marshals and administrative personnel
Major States of Assignment:	427 office locations in all 94 federal judicial districts.
Qualifications	
Age:	21 to 37 years
Education:	Bachelor's Degree and/or
Experience:	Three years general (GS-5) One year specialized (GS-7)
Vision:	20/20 corrected 20/40 uncorrected

COMMENTS   *Employment Conditions:* Deputy U.S. Marshals travel frequently for extended periods of time and must be available for reassignment to other duty stations.
Training Location: Federal Law Enforcement Training Center, Glynco, GA
Retirement: 20 years/age 55

WHERE TO APPLY   Above address or FEIC (Federal Employment Information Center)

WEB   *www.marshals.gov*

DEPARTMENT OF STATE

**Department of State
Diplomatic Security Service**
2201 C Street NW
Washington, DC 20520
(202) 647-7284

◯ Special Agent (FS-6)

MISSION   Department of State Special Agents work both overseas and within the United States. They are responsible for personnel security investigations, special protection of dignitaries, and handling sensitive information. Diplomatic Security Service staff conduct special investigations and provide protection to embassy personnel and facilities. In addition, DSS enforces the laws pertaining to the issuance, use, or manufacture of passports and visas.

Anticipated Positions	Under 100
Qualifications	
Age:	21 to 35 years
Education:	Bachelor's Degree and/or
Experience:	Three years general
	One year specialized

COMMENTS   *Employment Conditions:* The Foreign Service requires international assignment. Candidates with language skills have an edge.
Training Location: Federal Law Enforcement Training Center, Glynco, GA
Retirement: 20 years/age 55
Separate Pay Scale: FS-6 = $25,670

**WHERE TO
APPLY**   Civil Service Personnel Office
24-hour job phone line (202) 647-7284

Department of State
Civil Service
2201 C Street NW
Washington, DC 20520

Foreign Service
P.O. Box 9317
Arlington, VA 22210
(703) 875-7490

Security Officer
Recruitment Division
P.O. Box 9317
Rosslyn Station
Arlington, VA 22219

U.S. TREASURY DEPARTMENT

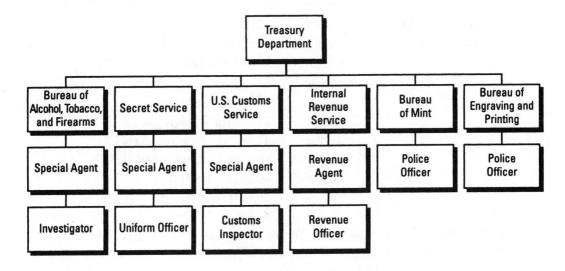

Bureau of Alcohol, Tobacco, and Firearms
650 Massachusetts Avenue
Washington, DC 20226
(202) 566-7321

⬡ **Special Agent GS (5/7)**
⬡ **Investigator (GS-5/7)**

MISSION The Bureau of Alcohol, Tobacco, and Firearms (ATF) is the primary federal agency that investigates the criminal use of firearms and explosives and enforces federal alcohol and tobacco regulations. ATF's mission is to reduce the criminal use of firearms and to assist other federal, state, local, and foreign law enforcement agencies in reducing crime and violence by effective enforcement of the federal firearms laws; to provide for the public safety by reducing the criminal misuse of explosives, combating arson-for-profit schemes, and removing safety hazards caused by improper and unsafe storage of explosive materials; to ensure the collection of all alcohol, tobacco, and firearms tax revenues and obtain a high level of compliance with the alcohol, tobacco, and firearms tax statutes; to suppress the commercial bribery, consumer deception, and other prohibited trade practices in the alcoholic beverage industry by effective enforcement and administration of the Federal Alcohol Administration Act; to assist the states in their efforts to eliminate interstate trafficking in the sale and distribution of contraband cigarettes; to actively target and investigate those individuals who possess or use firearms in furtherance of their illegal narcotics/drug-related activities; and to suppress illicit manufacture and sale of untaxed alcoholic beverages.

Anticipated Positions ✪ Over 100 nationwide

Profile

Law Enforcement Personnel: 1,850

Major States of Assignment: California, D.C., Florida, Georgia, Illinois, Michigan, New York, Texas

Qualifications

Age: 21 to 37 years

Education: Bachelor's Degree and/or

Experience: Three years general (GS-5)
One year specialized (GS-7)

Vision: 20/20 corrected
20/40 uncorrected

COMMENTS *Preferred Degree Fields:* Accounting, Criminal Justice, Law
Training Location: Federal Law Enforcement Training Center, Glynco, GA
Retirement: 20 years/age 55

WHERE TO APPLY Nearest Regional Office or OEM FDIC

WEB *www.ustreas.gov*

REGIONAL OFFICES

Alcohol, Tobacco, and Firearms
2121 8th Avenue North
Room 725
Birmingham, AL 35203

Alcohol, Tobacco, and Firearms
3003 North Central Avenue
Suite 1010
Phoenix, AZ 85012

Alcohol, Tobacco, and Firearms
350 South Figueroa Street
Suite 800
Los Angeles, CA 90071

Alcohol, Tobacco, and Firearms
221 Main Street
Suite 1250
San Francisco, CA 94105

Alcohol, Tobacco, and Firearms
607 14th Street NW
Suite 620
Washington, DC 20005

Alcohol, Tobacco, and Firearms
8420 NW 52nd Street
Suite 120
Miami, FL 33166

Alcohol, Tobacco, and Firearms
Suite 406
101 Marietta Street NW
Atlanta, GA 30303

Alcohol, Tobacco, and Firearms
300 South Riverside Plaza
Suite 350 South
Chicago, IL 60606

Alcohol, Tobacco, and Firearms
510 West Broadway
Suite 807
Louisville, KY 40202

Alcohol, Tobacco, and Firearms
111 Veterans Memorial Highway
Heritage Plaza Building
Suite 1050
New Orleans, LA 70005

Alcohol, Tobacco, and Firearms
Suite 210
103 South Gray Street
Baltimore, MD 21202

Alcohol, Tobacco, and Firearms
10 Causeway Street
Room 701
Boston, MA 02222

Alcohol, Tobacco, and Firearms
1155 Brewery Park Blvd.
Suite 300
Detroit, MI 48207

Alcohol, Tobacco, and Firearms
1870 Minnesota World Trade
Center
30 East 7th Street
St. Paul, MN 66202

Alcohol, Tobacco, and Firearms
2600 Grand Avenue
Suite 200
Kansas City, MO 64108

Alcohol, Tobacco, and Firearms
100 South 4th Street
Suite 550
St. Louis, MO 63102

Alcohol, Tobacco, and Firearms
90 Church Street
Room 1016
New York, NY 10007

Alcohol, Tobacco, and Firearms
4530 Park Road
Suite 400
Charlotte, NC 28209

Alcohol, Tobacco, and Firearms
7251 Engle Road
Middleburg Heights, OH 44130

Alcohol, Tobacco, and Firearms
2nd and Chestnut Streets
Room 504
Philadelphia, PA 19106

Alcohol, Tobacco, and Firearms
215 Centerview Drive
Suite 215
Brentwood, TN 37027

Alcohol, Tobacco, and Firearms
P.O. Box 50906
Dallas, TX 50906

Alcohol, Tobacco, and Firearms
15355 Vantage Parkway West
Suite 210
Houston, TX 77032

Alcohol, Tobacco, and Firearms
915 2nd Avenue
Room 806
Seattle, WA 98174

U.S. Customs Service
1301 Constitution Avenue NW
Washington, DC 20229
(202) 927-2095

- ⬡ **Special Agent (GS-9)**
- ⬡ **Criminal Investigator (GS-5/7)**
- ⬡ **Customs Inspector (GS-5/7)**
- ⬡ **Canine Enforcement Officer (GS-5/7)**
- ⬡ **Customs Pilot (GS-5/7)**

MISSION As the nation's principal border agency, the United States Customs Service has the mission to ensure that all goods entering and exiting the United States do so in accordance with all United States laws and regulations. This mission includes enforcing U.S. laws intended to prevent illegal trade practices; protecting the American public and environment from the introduction of prohibited hazardous and noxious products; assessing and collecting revenues in the form of duties, taxes, and fees on imported merchandise; regulating the movement of persons, carriers, merchandise, and commodities between the United States and other nations while facilitating the movement of all legitimate cargo, carriers, travelers, and mail; interdicting narcotics and other contraband; and, enforcing certain provisions of the export control laws of the United States. Special Agents investigate organized crime groups for a wide variety of customs crimes. Customs Inspectors enforce the laws governing the importation or exportation of merchandise, including the inspection of persons and carriers entering or leaving the United States. Pilots perform flight duties in support of a program involving air surveillance of illegal traffic crossing U.S. borders. Canine Enforcement Officers train and use dogs to enforce customs laws and regulations.

Anticipated Positions	✪ Over 1,000 nationwide
Profile of Agency	
Law Enforcement Personnel:	10,000
Major States of Assignment:	Arizona, California, Florida, New Jersey, New York, Texas
Qualifications	
Age:	21 to 37 years
Education:	Bachelor's Degree and/or
Experience:	Three years general (GS-5)
	One year specialized (GS-7)
Vision:	20/20 corrected
	20/200 uncorrected

COMMENTS   ✪ *Special Opportunity:* U.S. Customs hires a large number of "Summer" Customs Inspectors in key border crossings/certain areas. The hiring takes place mainly in the summer months due to the influx of tourism and the regular staff taking vacations. While the employment usually lasts only for the summer, it is an ideal opportunity for experience.

Preferred Degree Fields: Accounting, Aviation, Criminal Justice, Law

Pilot Requirements: Must have a current FAA Commercial Pilot's License and Class 1 Physical Examination; must meet the required hours for Fixed-Wing/Dual-Rated operation.

Training Location: Federal Law Enforcement Training Center, Glynco, GA

Retirement: 20 years/age 55

WHERE TO APPLY   Directly to Agency or Regional Office nearest you

WEB   *www.customs.treas.com*

REGIONAL OFFICES

U.S. Customs Service
150 North Royal
Mobile, AL 36602
(334) 441-6061

U.S. Customs Service
605 West 4th Avenue
Anchorage, AK 99501
(907) 271-2675

U.S. Customs Service
International and Terrace Streets
Nogales, AZ 85621
(520) 287-1410

U.S. Customs Service
Suite 705
1 World Trade Center
Long Beach, CA 90831
(310) 980-3100

U.S. Customs Service
880 Front Street
San Diego, CA 92188
(619) 557-5455

U.S. Customs Service
555 Battery Street
San Francisco, CA 94718
(415) 744-7700

U.S. Customs Service
300 South Ferry Street
San Pedro, CA 90731
(310) 514-6001

U.S. Customs Service
1301 Constitution Avenue NW
Washington, DC 20229
(202) 927-1000

U.S. Customs Service
P.O. Box 17423
Washington, DC 20041
(703) 318-5900

U.S. Customs Service
909 SE 1st Avenue
Miami, FL 33131
(305) 536-5952

U.S. Customs Service
77 SE 5th Street
Miami, FL 33131
(305) 869-2800

U.S. Customs Service
4430 East Adams Drive
Tampa, FL 33605
(813) 228-2381

U.S. Customs Service
1 East Bay Street
Savannah, GA 31401
(912) 652-4256

U.S. Customs Service
335 Merchant Street
Honolulu, HI 96806
(808) 522-8060

U.S. Customs Service
55 East Monroe Street
Chicago, IL 60603
(312) 353-4733

U.S. Customs Service
610 S. Canal Street
Chicago, IL 60607
(312) 353-6100

U.S. Customs Service
423 Canal Street
New Orleans, LA 70130
(504) 589-6324

U.S. Customs Service
312 Fore Street
Portland, ME 04112
(207) 780-3326

U.S. Customs Service
40 South Gray Street
Baltimore, MD 21202
(410) 962-2666

U.S. Customs Service
10 Causeway Street
Boston, MA 02222
(617) 898-6210

U.S. Customs Service
477 Michigan Avenue
Detroit, MI 48226
(313) 226-3177

U.S. Customs Service
209 Federal Building
Duluth, MN 55802
(218) 720-5201

U.S. Customs Service
110 South 4th Street
Minneapolis, MN 55401
(612) 348-1690

U.S. Customs Service
7911 Forsyth Building
St. Louis, MO 63105
(314) 428-2662

U.S. Customs Service
300 2nd Avenue South
Great Falls, MT 59401
(406) 453-7631

U.S. Customs Service
111 West Huron Street
Buffalo, NY 14202
(716) 846-4373

U.S. Customs Service
6 World Trade Center
New York, NY 10048
(212) 466-5550

U.S. Customs Service
Kennedy Airport
New York, NY 11430
(718) 553-1542

U.S. Customs Service
127 North Water Street
Ogdensburg, NY 13669
(315) 393-0660

U.S. Customs Service
1801-R Crossbeam Drive
Charlotte, NC 28217
(704) 329-6100

U.S. Customs Service
Post Office Building
Pembina, ND 58271
(701) 825-6201

U.S. Customs Service
55 Erie View
Cleveland, OH 44114
(216) 891-3800

U.S. Customs Service
511 NW Broadway
Columbia Snake, OR 97209
(503) 326-2865

U.S. Customs Service
2nd and Chestnut Streets
Philadelphia, PA 19106
(215) 597-4606

U.S. Customhouse
P.O. Box 2112
San Juan, PR 00903
(809) 729-6950

U.S. Customs Service
49 Pavillon Avenue
Providence, RI 02905
(401) 528-5081

U.S. Customs Service
200 East Bay Street
Charleston, SC 29401
(803) 727-4312

U.S. Customs Service
1205 Royal Lane
Dallas/Fort Worth Airport
Dallas/Fort Worth, TX 75261
(214) 574-2170

U.S. Customs Service
Bridge of the Americas
P.O. Box 9516
El Paso, TX 79985
(915) 540-5800

U.S. Customs Service
5850 San Felipe Street
Houston, TX 77057
(713) 942-6843

U.S. Customs Service
1717 East Loep
Houston, TX 77019
(713) 671-1000

U.S. Customs Service
Lincoln-Juarez Bridge
Laredo, TX 78044
(210) 726-2267

U.S. Customs Service
4550 75th Avenue
Port Arthur, TX 77642
(409) 724-0087

U.S. Customs Service
Main and Stebbins Streets
St. Albans, VT 05478
(802) 524-7352

U.S. Customs Service
U.S. Federal Building
Veterans Drive
St. Thomas, VI 60801
(809) 774-2510

U.S. Customs Service
101 East Main Street
Norfolk, VA 23510
(804) 441-3400

U.S. Customs Service
1000 2nd Avenue
Seattle, WA 97104
(206) 553-0554

U.S. Customs Service
6269 Ace Industrial Drive
Milwaukee, WI 53237
(414) 571-2860

Internal Revenue Service
Criminal Investigation Division
1111 Constitution Avenue, NW
Washington, DC 20224
(202) 622-5000

○ **Revenue Agent (GS-5/7)**
○ **Revenue Officer (GS-5/7)**

MISSION   The Internal Revenue Service (IRS) is responsible for administrating and enforcing the internal revenue of the country. The IRS determines, collects, and assesses internal revenue taxes. It determines noncompliance and enforces the tax laws. There are 62 IRS districts that conduct the mission programs of taxpayer service, examination, collection, and criminal investigation. Revenue Agents conduct criminal investigations involving U.S. tax laws. Revenue Officers collect delinquent taxes and take enforcement actions to protect the U.S. government's interests.

Profile

Law Enforcement Personnel:	3,700
Major States of Assignment:	California, D.C., Florida, Illinois, New York, Ohio, Pennsylvania, Texas

Qualifications

Age:	21 to 37 years
Education:	Bachelor's Degree and/or
Experience:	Three years general (GS-5)
	One year specialized (GS-7)
Vision:	20/20 corrected
	20/200 uncorrected

COMMENTS   *Preferred Degree Fields:* Accounting, Criminal Justice, Law
Training Location: Federal Law Enforcement Training Center, Glynco, GA
Retirement: 20 years/age 55

WHERE TO APPLY   Above address, Regional Office, or FEIC

WEB   *www.irs.treas.gov*

REGIONAL
OFFICES

Internal Revenue Service
1650 Mission Street
San Francisco, CA 94103

Internal Revenue Service
550 Main Street
Cincinnati, OH 45202

Internal Revenue Service
401 West Peachtree Street NE
Atlanta, GA 30365

Internal Revenue Service
841 Chestnut Street
Philadelphia, PA 19107

Internal Revenue Service
Gateway IV Building
300 South Riverside Plaza
Chicago, IL 60606

Internal Revenue Service
4050 Alpha Road
Dallas, TX 75244

Internal Revenue Service
90 Church Street
New York, NY 10007

U.S. Secret Service
Personnel Division
1800 G Street NW
Washington, DC 20223
(202) 435-5708

○ **Secret Service Agent (GS-5/7)**
○ **Secret Service Uniform Officer (GS-5/7)**

MISSION   The Secret Service is charged with protecting the life of the president
and vice president of the United States and their immediate families,
the president-elect and vice president-elect and their immediate families, former presidents and their wives, the widows of former presidents until death or remarriage, minor children of a former president
until they reach 16 years of age, heads of a foreign state or foreign
government, and, at the direction of the president, official representatives of the United States performing special missions abroad. Fur-
thermore, the Secret Service provides security at the White House
complex, the Treasury Building, and Treasury Annex, buildings that
house presidential offices, the vice president's residence, and various
foreign diplomatic missions in the Washington, DC metropolitan area
or in other areas as designated by the president. The mission of the
Secret Service includes investigations related to certain criminal violations of the Federal Deposit Insurance Act, the Federal Land Bank
Act, and the Government Losses in Shipment Act. The Secret Service
is also charged with the detection and arrest of any person committing any offense against the laws of the United States relating to coins,

currency, stamps, government bonds, checks, credit/debit card fraud, computer fraud, false identification crime, and other obligations or securities of the United States. It protects dignitaries and investigates threats against them; investigates counterfeiting and computer fraud to include mobile phone cloning; and provides physical security for Treasury buildings in Washington, DC.

Anticipated Positions	✪ Over 200 nationwide
Profile	
Law Enforcement Personnel:	3,100
Major States of Assignment:	California, D.C., New York, Texas
Qualifications	
Age:	21 to 37 years
Education:	Bachelor's Degree and/or
Experience:	Three years general (GS-5)
	One year specialized (GS-7)
Vision:	20/20 corrected
	20/40 uncorrected

COMMENTS *Preferred Degree Fields:* Accounting, Criminal Justice, Law
Training Location: Federal Law Enforcement Training Center, Glynco, GA
Retirement: 20 years/age 55

WHERE TO APPLY Above address or at any local Secret Service District Office listed below.

WEB *www.ustreas.gov*

SECRET SERVICE DISTRICT OFFICES

Albany, GA	Cheyenne, WY
Albany, NY	Chicago, IL
Albuquerque, NM	Cincinnati, OH
Anchorage, AK	Cleveland, OH
Atlanta, GA	Colorado Springs, CO
Austin, TX	Columbus, OH
Baltimore, MD	Columbia, SC
Baton Rouge, LA	Dallas, TX
Birmingham, AL	Dayton, OH
Bismarck, ND	Denver, CO
Boise, ID	Des Moines, IA
Boston, MA	Detroit, MI
Buffalo, NY	El Paso, TX
Canton, OH	Fresno, CA
Charleston, SC	Grand Rapids, MI
Charlotte, NC	Great Falls, MT
Chattanooga, TN	Harrisburg, PA

Honolulu, HI
Houston, TX
Indianapolis, IN
Jackson, MS
Jacksonville, FL
Jamaica, NY
Kansas City, MO
Knoxville, TN
Las Vegas, NV
Lexington, KY
Little Rock, AR
Los Angeles, CA
Louisville, KY
Lubbock, TX
Madison, WI
McAllen, TX
Memphis, TN
Miami, FL
Milwaukee, WI
Minneapolis, MN
Mobile, AL
Montgomery, AL
Morristown, NJ
Nashville, TN
New Haven, CT
New Orleans, LA
New York, NY
Norfolk, VA
Oklahoma City, OK
Omaha, NE
Orlando, FL
Philadelphia, PA
Phoenix, AZ
Pittsburgh, PA

Portland, ME
Portland, OR
Providence, RI
Reno, NV
Richmond, VA
Rochester, NY
Riverside, CA
Roanoke, VA
Saginaw, MI
Salisbury, NC
Salt Lake City, UT
San Antonio, TX
San Diego, CA
San Francisco, CA
San Jose, CA
San Juan, PR
Seattle, WA
Shreveport, LA
Sioux Falls, SD
Spokane, WA
St. Louis, MO
Syracuse, NY
Tampa, FL
Toledo, OH
Tucson, AZ
Tulsa, OK
Tyler, TX
Ventura, CA
Washington, DC
West Palm Beach, FL
White Plains, NY
Wichita, KS
Wilmington, DE

OVERSEAS SECRET SERVICE DISTRICT OFFICES

London, England
Paris, France
Bonn, Germany
Rome, Italy
Manilla, Philippines
Bangkok, Thailand

U.S. Mint
Office of Police
633 Third Street NW
Washington, DC 20220
(202) 874-6000

⬡ U.S. Mint Police Officer (GS-5)

MISSION The U.S. Mint produces circulating coinage for the country to conduct its trade and commerce. It maintains a police staff to protect the employees, federal property, and valuable coinage.

Anticipated Positions	Under 50
Profile	
Law Enforcement Personnel:	234
Qualifications	
Age:	21 to 37 years
Education:	High school and/or
Experience:	Three years general (TR-6)
	One year specialized (TR-7)

COMMENTS *Training Location:* Federal Law Enforcement Training Center, Glynco, GA
Retirement: 20 years/age 60

WHERE TO APPLY Above address

WEB *www.ustreas.gov*

U.S. MINT OFFICES

U.S. Mint
San Francisco, CA 94102

U.S. Mint
Denver, CO 80204

U.S. Bullion Depository
Fort Knox, KY 40121

U.S. Mint
West Point, NY 10996

U.S. Mint
Philadelphia, PA 19106

Federal Law Enforcement Training Center
Glynco Facility
Glynco, GA 31524
(912) 267-2100

◌ **Criminal Investigator Instructor (GS-5/7/9)**
◌ **Training Instructor/Law Enforcement (GS-5/7/9)**
◌ **Law Enforcement Special/Instructor (GS-5/7/9)**

MISSION The Center is an interagency training facility serving over 70 federal law enforcement organizations. It specializes in teaching law enforcement skills to police and investigative personnel. It also conducts advanced programs in areas of white collar crime, computers as an investigative tool, international money laundering, marine law enforcement, and several instructor courses.

Qualifications

Education:	Bachelor's Degree and/or
Experience:	Three years general (GS-5)
	One year specialized (GS-7)

COMMENTS *Employment Conditions:* All positions are located at Federal Law Enforcement Training Center, Glynco, GA

WHERE TO APPLY Directly to Agency or FEIC (Federal Employment Information Center) (912) 267-2447

WEB *www.fletc.gov*

DEPARTMENT OF VETERANS AFFAIRS

Department of Veterans Affairs
Office of Security and Law Enforcement
810 Vermont Avenue NW
Washington, DC 20420
(202) 273-4900

◯ VA Police Officer (GS-4/5)

MISSION   Department of Veterans Affairs (DOVA) Police Officers provide law enforcement and security services for the Department of Veterans Affairs facilities and property. DOVA Police work in both urban and rural settings depending on the location of the facility assigned. The DOVA Law Enforcement system is largely decentralized. Each DOVA Police Unit operates independently from the central office.

Anticipated Positions	✪ Over 100 nationwide
Profile of Agency	
Law Enforcement Personnel:	2,300 VA Police Officers
Major Assignment Locations:	172 VA facilities nationwide
Qualifications	
Age:	21 minimum
Education:	Bachelor's Degree and/or
Experience:	Three years general (GS-5)
	One year specialized (GS-7)
Vision:	20/20 corrected

COMMENTS *Employment Conditions:* Officers work with disabled or impaired veterans and must respect their unique situation. Veterans receive special preference for employment.
Training Location: Department of Veterans Affairs Police Academy, Little Rock, AR

WHERE TO APPLY Apply to the FEIC (Federal Employment Information Center) in the region in which you are interested or directly to the DOVA facilities located in the areas in which you are willing to work

WEB *www.va.gov*

DOVA POLICE LOCATIONS

Albany, NY	Chillicothe, OH
Albuquerque, NM	Cincinnati, OH
Alexandria, VA	Clarksburg, WV
Allen Park, MI	Cleveland, OH
Altoona, PA	Coatsville, PA
Amarillo, TX	Columbia, MO
American Lake, WA	Columbia, SC
Ann Arbor, MI	Dallas, TX
Asheville, NC	Danville, IL
Atlanta, GA	Dayton, OH
Augusta, GA	Denver, CO
Baltimore, MD	Des Moines, IA
Batavia, NY	Dublin, GA
Bath, NY	Durham, NC
Battle Creek, MI	East Orange, NJ
Bay Pines, FL	Erie, PA
Beckley, WV	Fargo, ND
Bedford, MA	Fayetteville, AR
Big Spring, TX	Fayetteville, NC
Biloxi, MS	Fort Harrison, MT
Birmingham, AL	Fort Howard, MD
Boise, ID	Fort Lyon, CO
Bonham, TX	Fort Meade, SD
Boston, MA	Fort Wayne, IN
Brockton, MA	Fresno, CA
Bronx, NY	Gainesville, FL
Brooklyn, NY	Grand Island, NE
Buffalo, NY	Grand Junction, CO
Butler, PA	Hampton, VA
Canandaiga, NY	Hines, IL
Castle Point, NY	Hot Springs, SD
Charleston, SC	Houston, TX
Cheyenne, WY	Huntington, WV
Chicago, IL	Indianapolis, IN

Iowa City, IA
Iron Mountain, MI
Jackson, MS
Kansas City, MO
Kerrville, TX
Knoxville, IA
Lake City, FL
Leavenworth, KS
Las Vegas, NV
Lebanon, PA
Lexington, KY
Lincoln, NE
Little Rock, AR
Loma Linda, CA
Long Beach, CA
Los Angeles, CA
Louisville, KY
Lyons, NJ
Madison, WI
Manchester, NH
Marion, IL
Marion, IN
Marlin, TX
Martinsburgh, WV
Memphis, TN
Miami, FL
Miles City, MT
Milwaukee, WI
Minneapolis, MN
Montgomery, AL
Montrose, NY
Mountain Home, TN
Murfreesboro, TN
Muskogee, OK
Nashville, TN
New Orleans, LA
New York, NY
Newington, CT
North Chicago, IL
Northampton, MA
Northport, NY
Oklahoma City, OK
Omaha, NE
Palo Alto, CA
Perry Point, MD

Philadelphia, PA
Phoenix, AZ
Pittsburgh, PA
Poplar Bluff, MO
Portland, OR
Prescott, AZ
Providence, RI
Reno, NV
Richmond, VA
Roseburgh, OR
Saginaw, MI
Salem, VA
Salisbury, NC
Salt Lake City, UT
San Antonio, TX
San Diego, CA
San Francisco, CA
San Juan, PR
Seattle, WA
Sepulveda, CA
Sheridan, WY
Shreveport, LA
Sioux Falls, SD
Spokane, WA
St. Cloud, MN
St. Louis, MO
Syracuse, NY
Tampa, FL
Temple, TX
Togus, ME
Tomah, WI
Topeka, KS
Tucson, AZ
Tuscaloosa, AL
Tuskegee, AL
Waco, TX
Walla Walla, WA
Washington, DC
West Haven, CT
West Palm Beach, FL
White City, OR
White River Junction, VT
Witchita, KS
Wilkes-Barre, PA
Wilmington, DE

INDEPENDENT FEDERAL AGENCIES

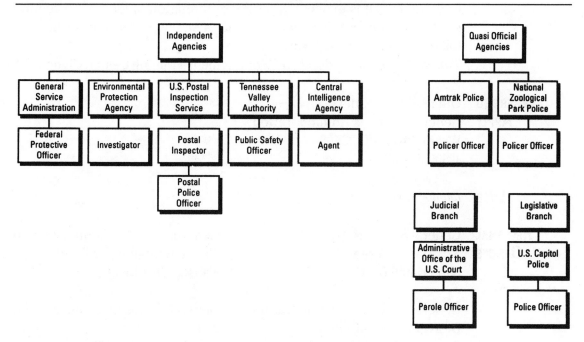

General Services Administration
Federal Protective Service
18th Street NW
U.S. Capitol Building
Washington, DC 20510
(202) 708-5082

○ Federal Protective Officer (GS-5)

MISSION   Federal Protective Officers (FPOs) provide police services and security for federal buildings and property nationwide. FPOs protect federal employees, investigate crime, and maintain special security devices to protect federal buildings.

Anticipated Positions   Over 50

Profile of Agency

Law Enforcement Personnel: 640

Major States of Assignment: California, D.C., Illinois, Massachusetts, Missouri, New York, Texas

Qualifications

Age: 21 to 37 years

Education: Bachelor's Degree and/or

Experience: Three years general (GS-5)
One year specialized (GS-7)

COMMENTS   *Employment Outlook:* In the wake of the bombing of the Oklahoma Federal Building, it is expected that a reexamination of federal protection staffing may occur. It is possible that a sharp increase in hiring will take place in the near future.
Training Location: Federal Law Enforcement Training Center, Glynco, GA

WHERE TO APPLY   Office of Personnel
General Services Administration
Washington, DC 20405
1-800-347-3378

WEB   *www.gsa.gov*

REGIONAL OFFICES

General Services Administration
525 Market Street
San Francisco, CA 94105

General Services Administration
Denver Federal Center
Denver, CO 80225

General Services Administration
7th and D Streets SW
Washington, DC 20407

General Services Administration
401 West Peachtree Street NW
Suite 2800
Atlanta, GA 30365

General Services Administration
230 South Dearborn Street
Chicago, IL 60604

General Services Administration
10 Causeway Street
Boston, MA 02222

General Services Administration
1500 East Bannister Road
Kansas City, MO 64131

General Services Administration
26 Federal Plaza
New York, NY 10278

General Services Administration
100 Penn Square East
Philadelphia, PA 19107

General Services Administration
819 Taylor Street
Fort Worth, TX 76102

General Services Administration
CSA Center
Auburn, WA 98002

Environmental Protection Agency
401 M Street SW
Washington, DC 20460
(202) 260-2090

☐ Criminal Investigator (GS-5/7)

MISSION The overall mission of the Environmental Protection Agency (EPA) is to protect and enhance our national environment today and for future generations to the fullest extent possible under the laws enacted by Congress. EPA controls and abates pollution in the areas of air, water, solid waste, pesticides, radiation, and toxic substances. Its mandate is to mount an integrated, coordinated attack on environmental pollution in cooperation with state and local governments.

Anticipated Positions	Undetermined
Qualifications	
Age:	21 to 37 years
Education:	Bachelor's Degree and/or
Experience:	Three years general (GS-5)
	One year specialized (GS-7)

COMMENTS *Training Location:* Federal Law Enforcement Training Center, Glynco, GA

WHERE TO APPLY Above address or Regional Office

WEB *www.epa.gov*

REGIONAL OFFICES

Environmental Protection Agency
215 Fremont Street
San Francisco, CA 94105

Environmental Protection Agency
John F. Kennedy Federal Building
Boston, MA 02203

Environmental Protection Agency
999 18th Street
Denver, CO 80202

Environmental Protection Agency
26 Federal Plaza
New York, NY 10278

Environmental Protection Agency
345 Courtland Street NE
Atlanta, GA 30365

Environmental Protection Agency
841 Chestnut Street
Philadelphia, PA 19107

Environmental Protection Agency
230 South Dearborn Street
Chicago, IL 60604

Environmental Protection Agency
1445 Ross Avenue
Dallas, TX 75202

Environmental Protection Agency
726 Minnesota Avenue
Kansas City, KS 66101

Environmental Protection Agency
1200 6th Avenue
Seattle, WA 98101

U.S. Postal Inspection Service
475 L'Enfant Plaza SW
Washington, DC 20260
(202) 268-4267

◌ **U.S. Postal Inspector (EAS-17)**
◌ **U.S. Postal Police Officer**

MISSION   The Postal Inspection Service is the law enforcement and audit arm of the Postal Service, which has jurisdiction in criminal matters affecting the integrity and security of the mail. It acts as the Inspector General for the Postal Service. The U.S. Postal Inspection Service investigates and seeks to prevent criminal assaults against the Postal Service or its employees, misuse of the nation's postal system, and offenses such as armed robberies, murder of, or assault upon postal employees, burglaries, theft of mail, mailing of obscene matter, child pornography, bombs and drugs, and use of the mails to swindle the public. In addition, the U.S. Postal Police Force provides police and security service at U.S. post office properties nationwide.

Anticipated Positions	Under 50 (Postal Inspector)
	✪ Over 50 (Postal Police Officer)
Profile	
Law Enforcement Personnel:	3,587
Qualifications	
Age:	21 to 37 years
Education:	Bachelor's Degree and/or
Experience:	Three years general (GS-5)
	One year specialized (GS-7)
Vision:	20/20 corrected

COMMENTS   *Preferred Degree Fields:* Accounting, Criminal Justice, Law
Training Location: U.S. Postal Inspector Course, Potomac, MD
Retirement: 20 years/age 50

WHERE TO APPLY   Above address or at nearest Regional Offices

WEB   *www.uspo.gov*

REGIONAL OFFICES

U.S. Postal Inspection Service
P.O. Box 20666
Phoenix, AZ 85036
(602) 223-3660

U.S. Postal Inspection Service
P.O. Box 2000
Pasadena, CA 91102
(818) 405-1200

U.S. Postal Inspection Service
P.O. Box 2110
San Diego, CA 92112
(619) 233-0610

U.S. Postal Inspection Service
P.O. Box 882000
San Francisco, CA 94188
(415) 550-5700

U.S. Postal Inspection Service
P.O. Box 329
Denver, CO 80201
(303) 295-5320

U.S. Postal Inspection Service
P.O. Box 96096
Washington, DC 20066
(202) 636-2300

U.S. Postal Inspection Service
3400 Lakeside Drive
6th Floor
Miramar, FL 33027
(305) 436-7200

U.S. Postal Inspection Service
P.O. Box 22526
Tampa, FL 33622
(813) 281-5200

U.S. Postal Inspection Service
P.O. Box 16489
Atlanta, GA 30321
(404) 765-7369

U.S. Postal Inspection Service
433 West Van Buren Street MPO
Chicago, IL 60669
(312) 765-4500

U.S. Postal Inspection Service
P.O. Box 51690
New Orleans, LA 70151
(504) 589-1200

U.S. Postal Inspection Service
P.O. Box 2217
Boston, MA 02205
(617) 654-5825

U.S. Postal Inspection Service
P.O. Box 330119
Detroit, MI 48232
(313) 226-8184

U.S. Postal Inspection Service
P.O. Box 64558
St. Paul, MN 55164
(612) 293-3200

U.S. Postal Inspection Service
Suite 850
3101 Broadway
Kansas City, MO 64111
(816) 932-0400

U.S. Postal Inspection Service
1106 Walnut Street
St. Louis, MO 63199
(314) 539-9300

U.S. Postal Inspection Service
P.O. Box 509
Newark, NJ 07101
(210) 596-5400

U.S. Postal Inspection Service
1200 Main Place Tower
Buffalo, NY 14202
(716) 853-5300

U.S. Postal Inspection Service
P.O. Box 555
James Farley Building
New York, NY 10116
(212) 330-3844

U.S. Postal Inspection Service
2901 I-85 South GMF
Charlotte, NC 28228
(704) 329-9120

U.S. Postal Inspection Service
P.O. Box 14487
Cincinnati, OH 45250
(513) 684-5700

U.S. Postal Inspection Service
P.O. Box 5726
Cleveland, OH 44101
(216) 443-4000

U.S. Postal Inspection Service
P.O. Box 7500
Philadelphia, PA 19101
(215) 895-8450

U.S. Postal Inspection Service
1001 California Avenue
Pittsburgh, PA 15290
(412) 359-7900

U.S. Postal Inspection Service
P.O. Box 363667
San Juan, PR 00936
(809) 749-7600

U.S. Postal Inspection Service
P.O. Box 3180
Memphis, TN 38173
(901) 576-2077

U.S. Postal Inspection Service
P.O. Box 162929
Fort Worth, TX 76161
(817) 625-3400

U.S. Postal Inspection Service
P.O. Box 1276
Houston, TX 77251
(713) 238-4400

U.S. Postal Inspection Service
P.O. Box 25009
Richmond, VA 23260
(804) 775-6267

U.S. Postal Inspection Service
P.O. Box 400
Seattle, WA 98111
(206) 442-6300

Tennessee Valley Authority
400 West Summit Hill Drive
Knoxville, TN 37902
(615) 632-2101

◯ **TVA Public Safety Officer**

MISSION The Tennessee Valley Authority (TVA) is a U.S. Government corporation that conducts a unified program of resource development for the advancement of economic growth in the Tennessee Valley Region. The Authority's program of activities include flood control, navigation development, electric power production, fertilizer development, recreation improvement and forestry and wildlife development. The TVA maintains its own federal police and security service for facilities and lands to include security and protection at the nuclear and fossil fuel plants.

Anticipated Positions	Over 50
Profile of Agency	
Law Enforcement Personnel:	740 Officers
Major States of Assignment:	Alabama, Tennessee
Qualifications	
Age:	21 to 37 years
Education:	Bachelor's Degree and/or
Experience:	Three years general (GS-5)
	One year specialized (GS-7)

COMMENTS *Training Location:* Federal Law Enforcement Training Center, Glynco, GA

WHERE TO APPLY Tennessee Valley Authority
Human Resources Services
400 West Summit Hill Drive
Knoxville, TN 37902
(615) 632-3341

WEB *www.tva.gov*

Central Intelligence Agency
P.O. Box 1925
Washington, DC 20013
(703) 482-1100

⬡ **Intelligence Agent**
⬡ **Security Specialist**

MISSION The overall mission of the Central Intelligence Agency is not law enforcement, however, the CIA has a venue of related duties and plays a critical part in the nation's security. For the most part, the CIA correlates and evaluates intelligence relating to the national security. It collects, produces, and disseminates vital information relating to political, military, economic, and scientific matters. Intelligence Agents conduct counterintelligence activities outside the United States. Security Specialists protect its installations, activities, information, and property.

Anticipated Positions	Numerous
Profile of Agency:	The CIA does not provide the number of employees
Qualifications	
Age:	21 to 37 years
Education:	Bachelor's Degree

COMMENTS *Preferred Degree Programs:* The CIA maintains numerous internships and programs
Employment Conditions: Worldwide Assignment

WHERE TO APPLY Above address

WEB *www.cia.gov*

JUDICIAL BRANCH AGENCY

Administrative Office of the Court
Human Resources Division
Washington, DC 20544
(202) 273-1270

⌣ United States Probation Officer

MISSION   U.S. Probation Officers conduct pre-sentence investigations for the court on defendants pending sentence. They perform other investigative functions at the request of the U.S. Bureau of Prisons and the U.S. Parole Commission. U.S. Probation Officers supervise federal offenders on probation or parole and the arrest of violations.

Anticipated Positions	✪ Over 100
Profile	
Law Enforcement Personnel:	3,763
Major States of Assignment:	Arizona, California, Florida, New York, Texas
Qualifications	
Age:	21 to 37 years
Education:	Bachelor's Degree and/or
Experience:	Three years general (GS-5) One year specialized (GS-7)

COMMENTS   *Employment Outlook:* Applicants with college and specialized law enforcement experience fare better.
Training Location: Federal Law Enforcement Training Center, Glynco, GA

WHERE TO APPLY   Apply directly to the district office in which you are interested in working.

LEGISLATIVE BRANCH AGENCY

United States Capitol Police
119 D Street NW
U.S. Capitol Building
Washington, DC 20510
(202) 224-9819

○ United States Capitol Police Officer

MISSION   U.S. Capitol Police Officers provide police services for U.S. Capitol Building and property. In addition, they provide special protection to members of Congress and officers of Congress and their families. U.S. Capitol Police have several specialty units such as drug enforcement, emergency response, K-9, and bicycle patrol, to name few.

Anticipated Positions	Over 50
Profile of Agency	
Police Officers:	1,000
Qualifications	
Age:	21 to 37 years
Education:	High school
Vision:	20/20 corrected
	20/100 uncorrected

COMMENTS   *Training Location:* Federal Law Enforcement Training Center, Glynco, GA
Starting Salary: $32,337

WHERE TO APPLY   Above address

QUASI-OFFICIAL AGENCIES

Amtrak Police Department
(National Railroad Passenger Corporation)
30th Street Station
Philadelphia, PA 19104
(215) 349-2812

○ Amtrak Police Officer

MISSION Amtrak Police provide law enforcement services to the nation's passenger railroad system. They conduct criminal investigations and provide protection to employees, passengers, and Amtrak property.

Anticipated Positions	Under 50
Profile	
Officers:	340
Qualifications	
Age:	21 minimum
Education:	Two-year college degree
Vision:	20/40 corrected

COMMENTS *Employment Conditions:* Amtrak Police Officers may be required to travel frequently. Officers are commissioned by both the state and federal statutes.
Starting Salary: $29,618
Retirement: 30 years/age 65

WHERE TO APPLY Above address or at Regional Office

WEB *www.amtrak.com*

REGIONAL OFFICES
Los Angeles, CA
San Jose, CA
Washington, DC
Chicago, IL

Boston, MA
New York, NY
Philadelphia, PA

Smithsonian Institution
National Zoological Park Police
3001 Connecticut Avenue NW
Washington, DC 20008
(202) 673-4721

○ **Park Police Officer (GS-5)**

MISSION   National Zoological Park Police patrol 165 acres of parkland in Washington, D.C. and the 3,000-acre conservation and research center at Fort Royal, VA.

Anticipated Positions	Over 50
Qualifications	
Age:	21 to 37 years
Education:	High school
Vision:	20/20 corrected
	20/100 uncorrected

COMMENTS   *Training Location:* Federal Law Enforcement Training Center, Glynco, GA

WHERE TO   Above address
APPLY

WEB   *www.si.edu.*

UNITED STATES INSPECTOR GENERAL AGENCIES

INSPECTOR
GENERAL
OFFICES

Department of Agriculture
Department of Commerce
Department of Defense
Department of Education
Department of Energy
Department of Health and Human Services
Department of Housing and Urban Renewal
Department of Interior
Department of Justice
Department of Labor
Department of State
Department of Transportation
Department of Treasury
Department of Veterans Affairs
Agency for International Development
Amtrak
Environmental Protection Agency
General Service Administration
NASA
Office of Personnel Management
Railroad Retirement Board
Small Business Administration
Tennessee Valley Authority

◯ **Criminal Investigator (GS-5/7/9)**
◯ **Auditor (GS-5/7/9)**

MISSION   A large number of federal agencies maintain Inspector General offices to provide policy direction and conduct and supervise investigations of alleged fraud, waste, and abuse of government resources. Inspector General offices serve to keep the Agency administration and Congress informed of program problems and abuses. The Inspector General offices are mandated to maintain both audit and investigative staff. Inspector General personnel conduct complex investigations and audits of white collar crimes. They work closely with other law enforcement agencies. Investigative findings that establish criminal or civil violations are presented for prosecution or appropriate action. Inspector General cases are routinely published by the General Accounting Office as public documents.

Anticipated Positions	Over 100 nationwide
Profile	
Law Enforcement Officers:	Over 4,000 agencies nationwide
Qualifications	
Age:	21 to 37 years
Education:	Bachelor's Degree and/or
Experience:	Three years general (GS-7)
	One year specialized (GS-7)
Location:	Federal Law Enforcement Training Center, Glynco, GA

COMMENTS   *Employment Outlook:* There are a limited number of positions. Most agencies maintain an applicant supply file, which is purged every year. When a vacancy occurs, the applications in that file are forwarded for review and selection. Candidates with law enforcement or auditing experience have an advantage.
Preferred Degree Fields: Accounting, Criminal Justice, Law
Employment Conditions: Investigators spend over half their time traveling the country during investigations
Retirement: 20 years/age 50

WHERE TO APPLY   Apply directly to the Inspector General offices

Opportunities

U.S. Department of Agriculture
Office of Inspector General
1400 Independence Avenue
Washington, DC 20250
(202) 205-3674

Anticipated Positions	Under 50
Profile of Agency	Law Enforcement Officers: 240
Where to Apply	Above address or Regional Office
Major Regional Offices	San Francisco, CA
	Washington, DC
	Atlanta, GA
	Chicago, IL
	Hyattsville, MD
	Kansas City, MO
	New York, NY
	Temple, TX
Web	*www.usda.gov*

U.S. Department of Commerce
Office of Inspector General
14th Street and Constitution Avenue NW
Washington, DC 20230
(202) 377-4661

Anticipated Positions	Under 50
Profile of Agency	Law Enforcement Officers: 140
Where to Apply	Above address or Regional Office
Major Regional Offices	San Francisco, CA
	Denver, CO
	Washington, DC
	Atlanta, GA
	New York, NY
	Seattle, WA
Web	*www.doc.gov*

U.S. Department of Defense
Office of Inspector General
400 Army/Navy Drive
Arlington, VA 22202
(202) 695-4249

Web   *www.dod.gov*

U.S. Department of Education
Office of Inspector General
400 Maryland SW
Washington, DC 20202
(202) 453-3550

Major Regional Offices   San Francisco, CA
Denver, CO
Washington, DC
Atlanta, GA
Chicago, IL
Boston, MA
Kansas City, MO
New York, NY
Philadelphia, PA
Dallas, TX
Seattle, WA

Web   *www.ed.gov*

U.S. Department of Energy
Office of Inspector General
1000 Independence Avenue SW
Washington, DC 20585
(202) 586-2488

Anticipated Positions	Undetermined
Profile of Agency	Law Enforcement Officers: 40
Where to Apply	Above address or Regional Office
Major Regional Offices	San Francisco, CA
	Denver, CO
	Washington, DC
	Chicago, IL
	New Orleans, LA
	Princeton, NJ
	Albuquerque, NM
	Las Vegas, NV
	Aiken, SC
	Oak Ridge, TN
	Richland, WA
Web	*www.doe.gov*

U.S. Department of Health and Human Services
Office of Inspector General
330 Independence Avenue SW
Washington, DC 20201
(202) 619-3148

Anticipated Positions	Under 50
Profile of Agency	Law Enforcement Officers: 1,300
Where to Apply	Above address or Regional Office
Major Regional Offices	San Francisco, CA
	Denver, CO
	Washington, DC
	Atlanta, GA
	Chicago, IL
	Boston, MA
	Kansas City, MO
	New York, NY
	Philadelphia, PA
	Dallas, TX
	Seattle, WA
Web	*www.os.dhhs.gov*

U.S. Department of Housing and Urban Development (HUD)
Office of Inspector General
451 7th Street SW
Washington, DC 20410
(202) 708-0430

Major Regional Offices	San Francisco, CA
	Denver, CO
	Washington, DC
	Atlanta, GA
	Chicago, IL
	Boston, MA
	Kansas City, MO
	New York, NY
	Philadelphia, PA
	Fort Worth, TX
	Seattle, WA
Web	*www.hud.gov*

U.S. Department of Interior
Office of Inspector General
1849 C Street NW
Washington, DC 20240
(202) 208-6752

Anticipated Positions	Under 10
Profile of Agency	Law Enforcement Officers: 36
Where to Apply	Above address or Regional Office (202) 208-6459
Major Regional Offices	Sacramento, CA
	Lakewood, CO
	Washington, DC
	Agana, Guam
	Albuquerque, NM
	Portland, OR
	Arlington, VA
	St. Thomas, U.S. Virgin Islands
Web	*www.doi.gov*

U.S. Department of Justice
Office of Inspector General
1425 New York Avenue, NW
Washington, DC 20530
(202) 616-4501

Anticipated Positions	Under 50
Profile of Agency	Law Enforcement Officers: 125
Where to Apply	Above address

U.S. Department of Labor
Office of Inspector General
200 Constitution Avenue NW
Washington, DC 20210
(202) 523-7296

Anticipated Positions	Undetermined
Profile of Agency	Law Enforcement Officers: 154
Where to Apply	Above address or Regional Office
Regional Offices	Los Angeles, CA
	San Francisco, CA
	Denver, CO
	Washington, DC
	Miami, FL
	Atlanta, GA
	Chicago, IL
	New Orleans, LA
	Boston, MA
	Detroit, MI
	Kansas City, MO
	Buffalo, NY
	New York, NY
	Cleveland, OH
	Philadelphia, PA
	Dallas, TX
	Seattle, WA
Web	*www.dol.gov*

Department of State
Office of Inspector General
2201 C Street NW
Washington, DC 20520
(202) 647-8890

Anticipated Positions	Under 10
Profile of Agency	Law Enforcement Officers: 37
Where to Apply	Above address
Web	*www.dos.gov*

Department of Transportation
Office of Inspector General
400 7th Street SW
Washington, DC 20590
(202) 426-8584

Anticipated Positions	Under 50
Profile of Agency	Law Enforcement Officers: 470
Where to Apply	Above address or Regional Office
Major Regional Offices	San Francisco, CA
	Atlanta, GA
	Chicago, IL
	Baltimore, MD
	Cambridge, MA
	Kansas City, MO
	New York, NY
	Fort Worth, TX
	Seattle, WA
Web	*www.dot.gov*

Department of Treasury
Office of Inspector General
740 15th Street NW
Washington, DC 20220
(202) 927-5260

Anticipated Positions	Under 10
Profile of Agency	Law Enforcement Officers: 40
Where to Apply	Above address or Regional Office
Major Regional Offices	San Francisco, CA
	Denver, CO
	Washington, DC
	Glynco, GA
	Philadelphia, PA
	Parkersburg, WV
Web	*www.ustreas.gov*

U.S. Department of Veterans Affairs
Office of Inspector General
810 Vermont Avenue NW
Washington, DC 20420
(202) 565-5357

Anticipated Positions	Under 20
Profile of Agency	Law Enforcement Officers: 69
Where to Apply	Above address or Regional Office
Major Regional Offices	Los Angeles, CA
	Hartford, CT
	Washington, DC
	Atlanta, GA
	Chicago, IL
	Hyattsville, MD
	Kansas City, MO
	New York, NY
	Dallas, TX
	Seattle, WA
Web	*www.va.gov*

Agency for International Development
Office of Inspector General
320 21st Street NW
Washington, DC 20523
(202) 632-7844

Web   *www.ida.gov*

Amtrak
Office of Inspector General
400 North Capital Street
Washington, DC 20001
(202) 906-4600

Web   *www.amtrak.gov*

Environmental Protection Agency
Office of Inspector General
401 M Street SW
Washington, DC 20460
(202) 260-4912

Major Regional Offices   Sacramento, CA
San Francisco, CA
Washington, DC
Atlanta, GA
Chicago, IL
Boston, MA
Kansas City, MO
New York, NY
Durham, NC
Cincinnati, OH
Philadelphia, PA
Dallas, TX
Seattle, WA

Web   *www.epa.gov*

U.S. General Services Administration
Office of Inspector General
18th and F Street NW
Washington, DC 20405
(202) 501-0360

Major Regional Offices   San Francisco, CA
Denver, CO
Washington, DC
Atlanta, GA
Chicago, IL
Boston, MA
Kansas City, MO
New York, NY
Philadelphia, PA
Fort Worth, TX
Auburn, WA

Web   *www.gsa.gov*

National Aeronautics and Space Administration (NASA)
Two Independence Square
Washington, DC 20546
(202) 358-1238

Major Regional Offices   Huntsville, AL
Moffett Field, CA
Pasadena, CA
Washington, DC
Cape Canaveral, FL
Greenbelt, MD
Cleveland, OH
Houston, TX
Hampton, VA

Web   *www.nasa.gov*

Office of Personnel Management
Office of Inspector General
1900 East Street NW
Washington, DC 20415
(202) 606-1200

Web   *www.opm.gov*

Railroad Retirement Board
Office of Inspector General
884 Rush Street
Chicago, IL 60611
(312) 751-4690

Web   *www.rrb.gov*

Small Business Administration
Office of Inspector General
409 Third Street SW
Washington, DC 20416
(202) 205-6580

Anticipated Positions	Under 10
Profile of Agency	Law Enforcement Officers: 40
Where to Apply	Above address or Regional Office
Major Regional Offices	San Francisco, CA
	Denver, CO
	Washington, DC
	Atlanta, GA
	Chicago, IL
	Boston, MA
	New York, NY
	Philadelphia, PA
	Dallas, TX
Web	*www.sba.gov*

Tennessee Valley Authority
Office of Inspector General
400 West Summit Hill Drive
Knoxville, TN 37902
(615) 632-7718

Web   *www.tva.gov*

Chapter 9

FEDERAL APPLICATION PROCESS

THE GENERAL PROCESS

1. Call or write to ask for position announcements and required applications.
2. Read the announcements carefully, then fill out the applications.
3. Submit the applications (SF171/OF612 or Federal Résumé).
4. Take the required tests; wait for results and next steps.
5. If at first you don't succeed, examine what went wrong and TRY . . . TRY . . . AGAIN!

OVERVIEW   In recent years there have been extensive cuts in federal jobs and opportunities, however, federal law enforcement agencies continue to hire and increase their ranks. The key to obtaining a position in federal law enforcement is the willingness to start out at a low rate of pay and to relocate for opportunities and advancement. Remember, in the federal system, once your foot is in the door, you can then apply to transfer to a position or area you wish to work in.

FEDERAL LAW ENFORCEMENT REQUIREMENTS

Federal law enforcement positions have specific requirements for each of the following:

- U.S. citizenship
- Age range
- Education level
- Experience level
- Vision standard
- Physical condition
- Driver's license
- Polygraph
- Psychological assessment
- Intense background investigation
- Urinalysis

BASIC QUALIFICATION REQUIREMENTS FOR FEDERAL LAW ENFORCEMENT POSITIONS

The federal application process allows candidates to combine education with experience in order to qualify.

Grade	Education or Experience (or Equivalent Combination)
GS-5	Four-year course of study above high school leading to a bachelor's degree (or) Three years of general experience, one year of which was at least equivalent to GS-4
GS-7	One full academic year of graduate level education or law school or superior academic achievement (or) One year of specialized experience at least equivalent to GS-5
GS-9	Two full academic years of graduate level education or master's or equivalent graduate degree of a J.D. (or) One year of specialized experience at least equivalent to GS-7
GS-11	Three full academic years of graduate level education or PhD or equivalent doctoral degree (or) One year of specialized experience at least equivalent to GS-9

GENERAL EXPERIENCE Work in administrative, law enforcement, or other work that showed ability to:

- Deal with interpersonal relationships
- Learn and interpret facts
- Seek cooperation of others in following procedures and regulations

SPECIALIZED EXPERIENCE
- Work that demonstrated specific knowledge, skills, and abilities (KSA) in relationship to the law enforcement position.

- Ability to collect, develop, and evaluate facts, evidence, and other data in compliance with laws, rules, or regulations.

SAMPLE FEDERAL ANNOUNCEMENT

UNITED STATES
DEPARTMENT OF INTERIOR
NATIONAL PARK SERVICE

VACANCY ANNOUNCEMENT

The National Park Service is an Equal Opportunity Employer. Selection for this position will be made solely on the basis of merit, fitness, and qualifications without regard to race, sex, color, creed, age, marital status, national origin, sexual orientation, nondisqualifying handicap conditions, or any other nonmerit factors.

POSITION: Park Ranger—Law Enforcement
Three Positions to Be Filled

ANNOUNCEMENT NUMBER: XXXX-97-13

GS SERIES: GS-0025-05/07/09

FULL LEVEL: GS-0025-09

OPENING DATE: January 25, 2001

CLOSING DATE: June 14, 2001

REGION/AREA: Nationwide

LOCATION: Yellowstone Historical Park, Division of Protection

ADDRESS OF PERSONNEL OFFICE: National Park Service
Division of Human Resources
Yellowstone National Park

STATEMENT OF DUTIES

Park Rangers contribute to resource protection through the use of law enforcement authorities, methods, and techniques designed to fit the nature of the offenses committed or suspected. Offenses may range from homicides, rapes, assaults, burglaries, car theft, use of alcoholic beverages to excess, and use of and trafficking in illegal drugs. Rangers participate with federal, state, and local authorities in preparation for prosecutions and appear as arresting officials or witnesses in court or magistrate proceedings. They perform intelligence gathering and undercover or surveillance work in connection with known or suspected illegal activities. Rangers perform duties educating the public about the park's resources and requirements pertaining to their use, and specialized duties directed toward protection of the park's natural and cultural resources. They also provide safety and security of park visitors, park employees, contractor and concessionaire employees, and other members of the public, as well as protection of public and private property.

POSITION INFORMATION

The position is subject to shift rotation, night and/or weekend work. It may be eligible for a 20-year retirement program. Currently, there is no cost-of-living allowance for this position. Those in this position will be required to wear uniforms. This position has promotion potential to the next level without further competition, once all legal and regulatory requirements are met; however, promotion is not automatic. Selectees of this position must be able to secure and maintain a Level I Authority NPS Law Enforcement Commission. This position requires a law enforcement commission and is critical-sensitive. Applicants who do not hold commissions will be considered; however, if selected, they must be able to obtain the commission and will be subject to a full-field background investigation for suitability determination. They must be able to operate a government vehicle. A valid state driver's license is required.

Applications will not be returned. It is the applicant's responsibility to provide documentation or proof of claimed qualifications, education, veterans' preference, status, and/or verification of eligibility for a noncompetitive appointment. Applicants will not be solicited for further data if that provided is found to be inadequate or incomplete. Unless the selectee has received acceptable prior training and has been granted a Level I commission by the Regional Law Enforcement Specialist, the agency, at its convenience, will send the selectee to a law enforcement and managers training course at the Federal Law Enforcement Training Center (FLETC). Barring documented, debilitating physical injury or circumstances out of the selectee's control, he/she will be given only *one* opportunity to successfully complete all segments of the approved training course. Failure to graduate from the program will result in termination of the employee. The employee may be subject to strenuous or unusual physical requirements and may be required to work weekends, holidays, evenings, and during special events or snow emergencies. This is a required-occupancy position; selectee will be required to live in government quarters, if available. Prolonged walking, standing, and occasional running are required. The selectee may be required to work frequent overtime with little or no notice. Relocation costs will not be authorized.

The maximum entry age for this position is 37.

Candidates will be rated on knowledge, abilities, skills, and other characteristics (KASOCS), such as:

1. Knowledge of and ability to perform law enforcement.
2. Ability to communicate in writing.
3. Ability to communicate orally.
4. Knowledge of physical security techniques and practices (with specific regard to fire and intrusion alarm systems).
5. Knowledge of emergency first aid procedures.
6. Skill in customer service.

All applicants tentatively selected for this position will be required to submit to urinalysis to screen for illegal drug use prior to appointment.

THE FEDERAL PROCESS CHANGES

In the last several years, significant changes have occurred in the federal employment process. The Office of Personnel Management has:

- Introduced new formats of applying. In addition to the Standard Form 171, OPM now allows candidates the choice of a new form or submitting their own Federal Style Résumé.

- Changed the law enforcement testing procedures. Many agencies no longer have OPM administer the exam on their behalf. Several agencies allow the candidate to apply directly to them for consideration.

- Renamed the OPM field offices the Federal Employment Information Center (FEIC).

- Introduced new technology to their information services. Special phone systems, web sites, and information kiosks are now being employed to bring information to candidates exploring the federal opportunities.

THE NEW FEDERAL APPLICATION PROCESS

Until January 1, 1995, the federal government only had one form available to apply for a federal position: the Standard Form 171 (SF171). The SF171, the Standard Application form for federal employment, is a complex application form. Now the government allows candidates to choose the written format. They are now offered the choice of applying by submitting the new Optional Form 612 (OF612)—Optional Application for Federal Employment—or by a federal-style résumé of the old SF171. While the change has made applying for most federal positions easier, it leaves law enforcement candidates with an unusual dilemma: the Federal Law Enforcement Agency needs background information on candidates and the rule of thumb is to call and ask the agency directly what form they prefer. Some may still want the SF171 submitted but, to further add to the confusion, different regions of the same organization may want a different form. Again, ask first and have a copy of both prepared.

FEDERAL APPLICATION FORM OF612

You may apply for most federal jobs with a résumé, the SF171, or OF612. If your résumé or application does not provide all the information requested on this form and in the job vacancy announcement, you may lose consideration for a position. Type or print clearly in dark ink. Help speed the selection process by keeping your application brief and sending only the requested information. It is essential to attach additional pages and include your name and Social Security number on each page. Include the following:

JOB INFORMATION Announcement number, and title and grade(s) of the job you are applying for.

PERSONNEL INFORMATION Full name, mailing address (with zip code), day and evening phone numbers (with area code)

Social Security number

Country of citizenship (most federal jobs require U.S. citizenship)

Veterans' preference

Reinstatement eligibility

Highest federal civilian grade held

EDUCATION High school

Colleges or universities attended (send a copy of your college transcript only if the job vacancy announcement requests it)

WORK EXPERIENCE Provide the following information from your paid and nonpaid work experience related to the job for which you are applying.

1. Job title
2. Duties and accomplishments
3. Employers' names and addresses
4. Supervisors' names and phone numbers
5. Starting and ending dates
6. Hours worked per week
7. Salary earned
8. Indicate if we may contact your current supervisor.

OTHER QUALIFICATIONS Job-related training courses

Job-related skills, for example, other languages, computer software/hardware

Job-related certificates and licenses

Job-related honors, awards, and special accomplishments, for example, anything published, memberships in professional or honor societies, leadership activities, public speaking and performance awards.

Hints for Filling Out Your Application

Make master copies of your SF171/OF612 before you sign them to be sure you will have a clear legal signature on the copy you send to various agencies. Leave several questions blank on your master copy to allow you to apply for positions with different titles and announcement numbers. Also, sign the copy that is being submitted, never send a photocopy of your signature.

Questions to leave blank on Master Copy

SF171/OF612:   #1 Job Title:
OF612:   #2 Grade
   #3 Announcement Number

Standard Form 171
Application for Federal Employment

Read The Following Instructions Carefully Before You Complete This Application

- DO NOT SUBMIT A RESUME INSTEAD OF THIS APPLICATION.

- TYPE OR PRINT CLEARLY IN DARK INK.

- IF YOU NEED MORE SPACE for an answer, use a sheet of paper the same size as this page. On each sheet write your name, Social Security Number, the announcement number or job title, and the item number. Attach all additional forms and sheets to this application at the top of page 3.

- If you do not answer all questions fully and correctly, you may delay the review of your application and lose job opportunities.

- Unless you are asked for additional material in the announcement or qualification information, do not attach any materials, such as: official position descriptions, performance evaluations, letters of recommendation, certificates of training, publications, etc. Any materials you attach which were not asked for may be removed from your application and will not be returned to you.

- We suggest that you keep a copy of this application for your use. if you plan to make copies of your application, we suggest you leave items 1, 48 and 49 blank. Complete these blank items each time you apply. YOU MUST SIGN AND DATE, IN INK, EACH COPY YOU SUBMIT.

- To apply for a specific Federal civil service examination (whether or not a written test is required) or a specific vacancy in a Federal agency:

  -- Read the announcement and other materials provided.

  -- Make sure that your work experience and/or education meet the qualification requirements described.

  -- Make sure the announcement is open for the job and location you are interested in. Announcements may be closed to receipt of applications for some types of jobs, grades, or geographic locations.

  -- Make sure that you are allowed to apply. Some jobs are limited to veterans, or to people who work for the Federal Government or have worked for the Federal Government in the past.

  -- Follow any directions on "How to Apply". If a written test is required, bring any material you are instructed to bring to the test session. For example, you may be instructed to "Bring a completed SF 171 to the test." If a written test is not required, mail this application and all other forms required by the announcement to the address specified in the announcement.

Work Experience *(Item 24)*

- Carefully complete each experience block you need to describe your work experience. Unless you qualify based on education alone, your rating will depend on your description of previous jobs. Do not leave out any jobs you held during the last ten years.

- Under Description of Work, write a clear and brief, but complete description of your major duties and responsibilities for each job. Include any supervisory duties, special assignments, and your accomplishments in the job. We may verify your description with your former employers.

- If you had a major change of duties or responsibilities while you worked for the same employer, describe each major change as a separate job.

Veteran Preference in Hiring *(Item 22)*

- DO NOT LEAVE Item 22 BLANK. If you do not claim veteran preference place an "X" in the box next to "NO PREFERENCE".

- You cannot receive veteran preference if you are retired or plan to retire at or above the rank of major or lieutenant commander, unless you are disabled or retired from the active military Reserve.

- To receive veteran preference your separation from active duty must have been under honorable conditions. This includes honorable and general discharges. A clemency discharge does not meet the requirements of the Veteran Preference Act.

- Active duty for training in the military Reserve and National Guard programs is not considered active duty for purposes of veteran preference.

- To qualify for preference you must meet ONE of the following conditions:

  1. Served on active duty anytime between December 7, 1941, and July 1, 1955; (If you were a Reservist called to active duty between February 1, 1955 and July 1, 1955, you must meet condition 2, below.)
  or
  2. Served on active duty any part of which was between July 2, 1955 and October 14, 1976 or a Reservist called to active duty between February 1, 1955 and October 14, 1976 and who served for more than 180 days;
  or
  3. Entered on active duty between October 15, 1976 and September 7, 1980 or a Reservist who entered on active duty between October 15, 1976 and October 13, 1982 and received a Campaign Badge or Expeditionary Medal or are a disabled veteran;
  or
  4. Enlisted in the Armed Forces after September 7, 1980 or entered active duty other than by enlistment on or after October 14, 1982 and:

     a. completed 24 months of continuous active duty or the full period called or ordered to active duty, or were discharged under 10 U.S.C. 1171 or for hardship under 10 U.S.C. 1173 and received or were entitled to receive a Campaign Badge or Expeditionary Medal; or

     b. are a disabled veteran.

- If you meet one of the four conditions above, you qualify for 5-point preference. If you want to claim 5-point preference and do not meet the requirements for 10-point preference, discussed below, place an "X" in the box next to "5-POINT PREFERENCE".

- If you think you qualify for 10-Point Preference, review the requirements described in the Standard Form (SF) 15, Application for 10-Point Veteran Preference. The SF 15 is available from any Federal Job Information Center. The 10-point preference groups are:

  -- Non-Compensably Disabled or Purple Heart Recipient.

  -- Compensably Disabled (less than 30%).

  -- Compensably Disabled (30% or more).

  -- Spouse, Widow(er) or Mother of a deceased or disabled veteran.

  If you claim 10-point preference, place an "X" in the box next to the group that applies to you. To receive 10-point preference you must attach a completed SF 15 to this application together with the proof requested in the SF 15.

Privacy Act Statement

The Office of Personnel Management is authorized to rate applicants for Federal jobs under sections 1302, 3301, and 3304 of title 5 of the U.S. Code. Section 1104 of title 5 allows the Office of Personnel Management to authorize other Federal agencies to rate applicants for Federal jobs. We need the information you put on this form and associated application forms to see how well your education and work skills qualify you for a Federal job. We also need information on matters such as citizenship and military service to see whether you are affected by laws we must follow in deciding who may be employed by the Federal Government.

We must have your Social Security Number (SSN) to keep your records straight because other people may have the same name and birth date. The SSN has been used to keep records since 1943, when Executive Order 9397 asked agencies to do so. The Office of Personnel Management may also use your SSN to make requests for information about you from employers, schools, banks, and others who know you, but only as allowed

by law or Presidential directive. The information we collect by using your SSN will be used for employment purposes and also may be used for studies, statistics, and computer matching to benefit and payment files.

Information we have about you may also be given to Federal, State and local agencies for checking on law violations or for other lawful purposes. We may send your name and address to State and local Government agencies, Congressional and other public offices, and public international organizations, if they request names of people to consider for employment. We may also notify your school placement office if you are selected for a Federal job.

Giving us your SSN or any of the other information is voluntary. However, we cannot process your application, which is the first step toward getting a job, if you do not give us the information we request. Incomplete addresses and ZIP Codes will also slow processing.

Standard Form 171-A— *Continuation Sheet for SF 171*

Form Approved:
OMB No. 3206-0012

● *Attach all SF 171-A's to your application at the top of page 3.*

1. Name *(Last, First, Middle Initial)*	2. Social Security Number

3. Job Title or Announcement Number You Are Applying For	4. Date Completed

ADDITIONAL WORK EXPERIENCE BLOCKS

Name and address of employer's organization *(include ZIP Code, if known)*	Dates employed *(give month, day and year)* From: To: Salary or earnings Starting $ per Ending $ per	Average number of hours per week	Number of employees you supervised
		Your reason for leaving	

Your immediate supervisor Name	Area Code	Telephone No.	Exact title of your job	If Federal employment *(civilian or military)* list series, grade or rank, and, if promoted in this job, the date of your last promotion

Description of work: Describe your specific duties, responsibilities and accomplishments in this job, **including the job title(s) of any employees you supervised.** *If you describe more than one type of work (for example, carpentry and painting, or personnel and budget), write the approximate percentage of time you spent doing each.*

For Agency Use (skill codes, etc.)

Name and address of employer's organization *(include ZIP Code, if known)*	Dates employed *(give month, day and year)* From: To: Salary or earnings Starting $ per Ending $ per	Average number of hours per week	Number of employees you supervised
		Your reason for leaving	

Your immediate supervisor Name	Area Code	Telephone No.	Exact title of your job	If Federal employment *(civilian or military)* list series, grade or rank, and, if promoted in this job, the date of your last promotion

Description of work: Describe your specific duties, responsibilities and accomplishments in this job, **including the job title(s) of any employees you supervised.** *If you describe more than one type of work (for example, carpentry and painting, or personnel and budget), write the approximate percentage of time you spent doing each.*

For Agency Use (skill codes, etc.)

THE FEDERAL GOVERNMENT IS AN EQUAL OPPORTUNITY EMPLOYER

PREVIOUS EDITION USABLE

Standard Form 171-A (Rev. 6-88)
U.S. Office of Personnel Management
FPM Chapter 295

SAMPLE

Application for Federal Employment—SF 171

Read the instructions before you complete this application. *Type or print clearly in dark ink.*

Form Approved:
OMB No. 3206-0012

GENERAL INFORMATION

1 What kind of job are you applying for? *Give title and announcement no. (if any)*

2 Social Security Number

3 Sex
☐ Male ☐ Female

4 Birth date *(Month, Day, Year)*

5 Birthplace *(City and State or Country)*

6 Name *(Last, First, Middle)*

Mailing address *(include apartment number, if any)*

City   State   ZIP Code

7 Other names ever used *(e.g., maiden name, nickname, etc.)*

8 Home Phone
Area Code | Number

9 Work Phone
Area Code | Number | Extension

10 Were you ever employed as a civilian by the Federal Government? If "NO", go to item 11. If "YES", mark each type of job you held with an
☐ Temporary ☐ Career-Conditional ☐ Career ☐ Excepted
What is your highest grade, classification series and job title?

Dates at highest grade: FROM   TO

DO NOT WRITE IN THIS AREA

FOR USE OF EXAMINING OFFICE ONLY

Date entered register

Form reviewed:
Form approved:

Option	Grade	Earned Rating	Veteran Preference	Augmented Rating
			☐ No Preference Claimed	
			☐ 5 Points (Tentative)	
			☐ 10 Pts. (30% Or More Comp. Dis.)	
			☐ 10 Pts. (Less Than 30% Comp. Dis.)	
			☐ Other 10 Points	

Initials and Date

☐ Disallowed ☐ Being Investigated

FOR USE OF APPOINTING OFFICE ONLY

Preference has been verified through proof that the separation was under honorable conditions, and other proof as required.

☐ 5-Point ☐ 10-Point—30% or More Compensable Disability ☐ 10-Point—Less Than 30% Compensable Disability ☐ 10-Point—Other

Signature and Title

Agency   Date

AVAILABILITY

11 When can you start work? *(Month and Year)*

12 What is the lowest pay you will accept? (You will not be considered for jobs which pay less than you indicate.)
Pay $ _____ per _____ OR Grade _____

13 In what geographic area(s) are you willing to work?

14 Are you willing to work:	YES	NO
A. 40 hours per week *(full-time)*?		
B. 25-32 hours per week *(part-time)*?		
C. 17-24 hours per week *(part-time)*?		
D. 16 or fewer hours per week *(part-time)*?		
E. An intermittent job *(on-call/seasonal)*?		
F. Weekends, shifts, or rotating shifts?		
15 Are you willing to take a temporary job lasting:		
A. 5 to 12 months *(sometimes longer)*?		
B. 1 to 4 months?		
C. Less than 1 month?		
16 Are you willing to travel away from home for:		
A. 1 to 5 nights each month?		
B. 6 to 10 nights each month?		
C. 11 or more nights each month?		

MILITARY SERVICE AND VETERAN PREFERENCE

	YES	NO
17 Have you served in the United States Military Service? *If your only active duty was training in the Reserves or National Guard, answer "NO". If "NO", go to item 22.*		
18 Did you or will you retire at or above the rank of major or lieutenant commander?		

MILITARY SERVICE AND VETERAN PREFERENCE

	YES	NO
19 Were you discharged from the military service under honorable conditions? *(If your discharge was changed to "honorable" or "general" by a Discharge Review Board, answer "YES". If you received a clemency discharge, answer "NO".) If "NO", provide below the date and type of discharge you received.*		

Discharge Date *(Month, Day, Year)*   Type of Discharge

20 List the dates *(Month, Day, Year)*, and branch for all active duty military service.
From   To   Branch of Service

21 If your active military duty was after October 14, 1976, list the full names and dates of all campaign badges or expeditionary medals you received or were entitled to receive.

22 Read the instructions that came with this form before completing this item. When you have determined your eligibility for veteran preference from the instructions, place an "X" in the box next to your veteran preference claim.

☐ NO PREFERENCE

☐ 5-POINT PREFERENCE -- You must show proof when you are hired.

☐ 10-POINT PREFERENCE -- If you claim 10-point preference, place an "X" in the box below next to the basis for your claim. To receive 10-point preference you must also complete a Standard Form 15, Application for 10-Point Veteran Preference, which is available from any Federal Job Information Center. ATTACH THE COMPLETED SF 15 AND REQUESTED PROOF TO THIS APPLICATION.

☐ Non-compensably disabled or Purple Heart recipient.
☐ Compensably disabled, less than 30 percent.
☐ Spouse, widow(er), or mother of a deceased or disabled veteran.
☐ Compensably disabled, 30 percent or more.

THE FEDERAL GOVERNMENT IS AN EQUAL OPPORTUNITY EMPLOYER

PREVIOUS EDITION USABLE UNTIL 12-31-90

NSN 7540-00-935-7150   171-109

Standard Form 171 (Rev. 6-88)
U.S. Office of Personnel Management
FPM Chapter 295

Page 1

WORK EXPERIENCE *If you have no work experience, write "NONE" in A below and go to 25 on page 3.*

23 May we ask your present employer about your character, qualifications, and work record? *A "NO" will not affect our review of your* **YES** **NO**
qualifications. If you answer "NO" and we need to contact your present employer before we can offer you a job, we will contact you first. . . . .

24 READ WORK EXPERIENCE IN THE INSTRUCTIONS BEFORE YOU BEGIN.

- Describe your current or most recent job in Block A and work backwards, describing each job you held during the past 10 years. If you were unemployed for longer than 3 months within the past 10 years, list the dates and your address(es) in an experience block.

- You may sum up in one block work that you did more than 10 years ago. But if that work is related to the type of job you are applying for, describe each related job in a separate block.

- INCLUDE VOLUNTEER WORK *(non-paid work)--if the work (or a part of the work) is like the job you are applying for*, complete all parts of the experience block just as you would for a paying job. You may receive credit for work experience with religious, community, welfare, service, and other organizations.

- INCLUDE MILITARY SERVICE--You should complete all parts of the experience block just as you would for a non-military job, including all supervisory experience. Describe each major change of duties or responsibilities in a separate experience block.

- IF YOU NEED MORE SPACE TO DESCRIBE A JOB--Use sheets of paper the same size as this page (be sure to include all information we ask for in A and B below). On each sheet show your name, Social Security Number, and the announcement number or job title.

- IF YOU NEED MORE EXPERIENCE BLOCKS, use the SF 171-A or a sheet of paper.

- IF YOU NEED TO UPDATE (ADD MORE RECENT JOBS), use the SF 172 or a sheet of paper as described above.

A | Name and address of employer's organization *(include ZIP Code, if known)* | Dates employed *(give month, day and year)* | Average number if hours per week | Number of employees you supervise
From: To:
Salary or earnings | Your reason for wanting to leave
Starting $ per
Ending $ per

Your immediate supervisor
Name | Area Code | Telephone No. | Exact title of your job | If Federal employment *(civilian or military)* list series, grade or rank, and, if promoted in this job, the date of your last promotion

Description of work: Describe your specific duties, responsibilities and accomplishments in this job, including the job title(s) of any employees you supervise. *If you describe more than one type of work (for example, carpentry and painting or personnel and budget), write the approximate percentage of time you spent doing each.*

For Agency Use (skill codes, etc.)

B | Name and address of employer's organization *(include ZIP Code, if known)* | Dates employed *(give month, day and year)* | Average number of hours per week | Number of employees you supervised
From: To:
Salary or earnings | Your reason for leaving
Starting $ per
Ending $ per

Your immediate supervisor
Name | Area Code | Telephone No. | Exact title of your job | If Federal employment *(civilian or military)* list series, grade or rank, and, if promoted in this job, the date of your last promotion

Description of work: Describe your specific duties, responsibilities and accomplishments in this job, including the job title(s) of any employees you supervised. *If you describe more than one type of work (for example, carpentry and painting, or personnel and budget), write the approximate percentage of time you spent doing each.*

For Agency Use (skill codes, etc.)

Page 2 IF YOU NEED MORE EXPERIENCE BLOCKS, USE SF 171-A *(SEE BACK OF INSTRUCTION PAGE).*

← **ATTACH ANY ADDITIONAL FORMS AND SHEETS HERE**

EDUCATION

25 Did you graduate from high school? *If you have a GED high school equivalency or will graduate within the next nine months, answer "YES".*

26 Write the name and location *(city and state)* of the last high school you attended or where you obtained your GED high school equivalency.

YES ▶ If "YES", give month and year graduated or received GED equivalency: . . . .

NO ▶ If "NO", give the highest grade you completed:

27 Have you ever attended college or graduate school?   YES ▶ If "YES", continue with 28.   NO ▶ If "NO", go to 31.

28 NAME AND LOCATION *(city, state and ZIP Code)* OF COLLEGE OR UNIVERSITY.. *If you expect to graduate within nine months, give the month and year you expect to receive your degree:*

	Name	City	State	ZIP Code	MONTH AND YEAR ATTENDED From	To	NUMBER OF CREDIT HOURS COMPLETED Semester	Quarter	TYPE OF DEGREE *(e.g. B.A., M.A.)*	MONTH AND YEAR OF DEGREE
1)										
2)										
3)										

29 CHIEF UNDERGRADUATE SUBJECTS *Show major on the first line* — NUMBER OF CREDIT HOURS COMPLETED Semester | Quarter

		Semester	Quarter
1)			
2)			
3)			

30 CHIEF GRADUATE SUBJECTS *Show major on the first line* — NUMBER OF CREDIT HOURS COMPLETED Semester | Quarter

		Semester	Quarter
1)			
2)			
3)			

31 If you have completed any other courses or training related to the kind of jobs you are applying for *(trade, vocational, Armed Forces, business)* give information below.

NAME AND LOCATION *(city, state and ZIP Code)* OF SCHOOL.	MONTH AND YEAR ATTENDED From	To	CLASS-ROOM HOURS	SUBJECT(S)	TRAINING COMPLETED YES	NO
School Name 1)						
City State ZIP Code						
School Name 2)						
City State ZIP Code						

SPECIAL SKILLS, ACCOMPLISHMENTS AND AWARDS

32 Give the title and year of any honors, awards or fellowships you have received. List your special qualifications, skills or accomplishments that may help you get a job. *Some examples are: skills with computers or other machines; most important publications (do not submit copies); public speaking and writing experience; membership in professional or scientific societies; patents or inventions; etc.*

33 How many words per minute can you:
TYPE?   TAKE DICTATION?
Agencies may test your skills before hiring you.

34 List job-related licenses or certificates that you have, such as: registered nurse; lawyer; radio operator; driver's; pilot's; etc.

	LICENSE OR CERTIFICATE	DATE OF LATEST LICENSE OR CERTIFICATE	STATE OR OTHER LICENSING AGENCY
1)			
2)			

35 Do you speak or read a language other than English *(include sign language)*? *Applicants for jobs that require a language other than English may be given an interview conducted solely in that language.*   YES   NO

If "YES", list each language and place an "X" in each column that applies to you. If "NO", go to 36.

LANGUAGE(S)	CAN PREPARE AND GIVE LECTURES Fluently	With Difficulty	CAN SPEAK AND UNDERSTAND Fluently	Passably	CAN TRANSLATE ARTICLES Into English	From English	CAN READ ARTICLES FOR OWN USE Easily	With Difficulty
1)								
2)								

REFERENCES

36 List three people who are not related to you and are not supervisors you listed under 24 who know your qualifications and fitness for the kind of job for which you are applying. At least one should know you well on a personal basis.

FULL NAME OF REFERENCE	TELEPHONE NUMBER(S) *(Include Area Code)*	PRESENT BUSINESS OR HOME ADDRESS *(Number, street and city)*	STATE	ZIP CODE
1)				
2)				
3)				

Page 3

BACKGROUND INFORMATION-- *You must answer each question in this section before we can process your application*

37 Are you a citizen of the United States? *(In most cases you must be a U.S. citizen to be hired. You will be required to submit proof of identity and citizenship at the time you are hired.)* If **"NO"**, give the country or countries you are a citizen of: _____

	YES	NO

NOTE: It is important that you give complete and truthful answers to questions 38 through 44. If you answer **"YES"** to any of them, provide your explanation(s) in **Item 45. Include** convictions resulting from a plea of nolo contendere *(no contest)*. **Omit:** 1) traffic fines of $100.00 or less; 2) any violation of law committed before your 16th birthday; 3) any violation of law committed before your 18th birthday, if finally decided in juvenile court or under a Youth Offender law; 4) any conviction set aside under the Federal Youth Corrections Act or similar State law; 5) any conviction whose record was expunged under Federal or State law. We will consider the date, facts, and circumstances of each event you list. In most cases you can still be considered for Federal jobs. However, **if you fail to tell the truth or fail to list all relevant** events or circumstances, this may be grounds for not hiring you, for firing you after you begin work, or for criminal prosecution (18 USC 1001).

		YES	NO
38	During the last **10 years**, were you **fired from any job** for any reason, did you **quit** after being told that you would be fired, or did you leave by mutual agreement because of specific problems?		
39	Have you **ever** been convicted of, or forfeited collateral for **any felony violation?** *(Generally, a felony is defined as any violation of law punishable by imprisonment of longer than one year, except for violations called misdemeanors under State law which are punishable by imprisonment of two years or less.)*		
40	Have you **ever** been convicted of, or forfeited collateral for **any firearms or explosives violation?**		
41	Are you **now** under charges for **any violation of law?**		
42	During the **last 10 years** have you forfeited collateral, been convicted, been imprisoned, been on probation, or been on parole? Do **not** include violations reported in 39, 40, or 41, above.		
43	Have you **ever** been convicted by a military **court-martial?** If no military service, answer **"NO".**		
44	Are you **delinquent** on any Federal debt? *(Include delinquencies arising from Federal taxes, loans, overpayment of benefits, and other debts to the U.S. Government plus defaults on Federally guaranteed or insured loans such as student and home mortgage loans.)*		

45 If **"YES"** in: 38 - Explain for each job the problem(s) and your reason(s) for leaving. Give the employer's name and address.
  39 through 43 - Explain each violation. Give place of occurrence and name/address of police or court involved.
  44 - Explain the type, length and amount of the delinquency or default, and steps you are taking to correct errors or repay the debt. Give any identification number associated with the debt and the address of the Federal agency involved.
  NOTE: If you need more space, use a sheet of paper, and include the item number.

Item No.	Date (Mo./Yr.)	Explanation	Mailing Address
			Name of Employer, Police, Court, or Federal Agency
			City State ZIP Code
			Name of Employer, Police, Court, or Federal Agency
			City State ZIP Code

		YES	NO
46	Do you receive, or have you ever applied for retirement pay, pension, or other pay based on military, Federal civilian, or District of Columbia Government service?		
47	Do any of your relatives work for the United States Government or the United States Armed Forces? Include: *father; mother; husband; wife; son; daughter; brother; sister; uncle; aunt; first cousin; nephew; niece; father-in-law; mother-in-law; son-in-law; daughter-in-law; brother-in-law; sister-in-law; stepfather; stepmother; stepson; stepdaughter; stepbrother; stepsister; half brother; and half sister.* . . . . If **"YES"**, provide details below. If you need more space, use a sheet of paper.		

Name	Relationship	Department, Agency or Branch of Armed Forces

SIGNATURE, CERTIFICATION, AND RELEASE OF INFORMATION

YOU MUST SIGN THIS APPLICATION.   Read the following carefully before you sign.

- A false statement on any part of your application may be grounds for not hiring you, or for firing you after you begin work. Also, you may be punished by fine or imprisonment (U.S. Code, title 18, section 1001).
- If you are a male born after December 31, 1959 you must be registered with the Selective Service System or have a valid exemption in order to be eligible for Federal employment. You will be required to certify as to your status at the time of appointment.
- I understand that any information I give may be investigated as allowed by law or Presidential order.
- I consent to the release of information about my ability and fitness for Federal employment by *employers, schools, law enforcement agencies and other individuals and organizations, to investigators, personnel staffing specialists, and other authorized employees of the Federal Government.*
- I certify that, to the best of my knowledge and belief, all of my statements are true, correct, complete, and made in good faith.

48 SIGNATURE *(Sign each application in dark ink)*	**49** DATE SIGNED *(Month, day, year)*

Page 4

☆ U.S. Government Printing Office: 1999–201-700/80137

Form Approved
OMB No. 3206-0219

OPTIONAL APPLICATION FOR FEDERAL EMPLOYMENT - OF 612

You may apply for most jobs with a resume, this form, or other written format. If your resume or application does not provide all the information requested on this form and in the job vacancy announcement, you may lose consideration for a job.

1 Job title in announcement	2 Grade(s) applying for	3 Announcement number

4 Last name	First and middle names	5 Social Security Number

6 Mailing address		7 Phone numbers (include area code)
		Daytime ( )
City	State ZIP Code	Evening ( )

WORK EXPERIENCE

8 Describe your paid and nonpaid work experience related to the job for which you are applying. Do **not** attach job descriptions.

1) Job title (if Federal, include series and grade)

From (MM/YY)	To (MM/YY)	Salary $	per	Hours per week

Employer's name and address	Supervisor's name and phone number ( )

Describe your duties and accomplishments

2) Job title (if Federal, include series and grade)

From (MM/YY)	To (MM/YY)	Salary $	per	Hours per week

Employer's name and address	Supervisor's name and phone number ( )

Describe your duties and accomplishments

50612-101   NSN 7540-01-351-9178   Optional Form 612 (September 1994)
U.S. Office of Personnel Management

9 May we contact your current supervisor? ‒

YES [   ]   NO [   ] ▶ If we need to contact your current supervisor before making an offer, we will contact you first.

EDUCATION

10 Mark highest level completed. **Some HS** [   ]   **HS/GED** [   ]   **Associate** [   ]   **Bachelor** [   ]   **Master** [   ]   **Doctoral** [   ]

11 Last high school (HS) or GED school. Give the school's name, city, State, ZIP Code (if known), and year diploma or GED received.

12 Colleges and universities attended. Do **not** attach a copy of your transcript unless requested.

Name			Total Credits Earned		Major(s)	Degree - Year
			Semester	Quarter		(if any) Received
1) City		State ZIP Code				
2)						
3)						

OTHER QUALIFICATIONS

13 **Job-related** training courses (give title and year). **Job-related skills** (other languages, computer software/hardware, tools, machinery, typing speed, etc.). **Job-related** certificates and licenses (current only). **Job-related** honors, awards, and special accomplishments (publications, memberships in professional/honor societies, leadership activities, public speaking, and performance awards). Give dates, but do **not** send documents unless requested.

GENERAL

14 Are you a U.S. citizen?   YES [   ]   NO [   ] ▶ Give the country of your citizenship. _____

15 Do you claim veterans' preference? **NO** [   ]   **YES** [   ] ▶ Mark your claim of 5 or 10 points below.
   5 points [   ] ▶ Attach your DD 214 or other proof. **10 points** [   ] ▶ Attach an *Application for 10-Point Veterans' Preference* (SF 15) and proof required.

16 Were you ever a Federal civilian employee?

			Series	Grade	From (MM/YY)	To (MM/YY)

   NO [   ]   **YES** [   ] ▶ For highest civilian grade give:

17 Are you eligible for reinstatement based on career or career-conditional Federal status?
   NO [   ]   **YES** [   ] ▶ If requested, attach SF 50 proof.

APPLICANT CERTIFICATION

18 **I certify** that, to the best of my knowledge and belief, all of the information on and attached to this application is true, correct, complete and made in good faith. **I understand** that false or fraudulent information on or attached to this application may be grounds for not hiring me or for firing me after I begin work, and may be punishable by fine or imprisonment. **I understand** that any information I give may be investigated.

SIGNATURE   **DATE SIGNED**

*U.S. Government Printing Office: 1995 — 387-722/20002

Standard Form 15 (Rev. 2/90)
U.S. Office of Personnel Management
FPM Supplement 296-33
FPM Chapter 211

APPLICATION FOR 10-POINT VETERAN PREFERENCE
(TO BE USED BY VETERANS & RELATIVES OF VETERANS)

Form Approved:
O.M.B. No. 3206-0001

PERSON APPLYING FOR PREFERENCE

1. Name (Last, First, Middle)

2. Name and Announcement Number of Civil Service or Postal Service Exam You Have Applied For or Position Which You Currently Occupy

3. Home Address (Street Number, City, State and ZIP Code)

4. Social Security Number

5. Date Exam Was Held or Application Submitted

VETERAN INFORMATION (to be provided by person applying for preference)

6. Veteran's Name (Last, First, Middle) Exactly As It Appears on Service Records

7. Veteran's Periods of Service

Branch of Service	From	To	Service Number

8. Veteran's Social Security Number

9. VA Claim Number, If Any

TYPE OF 10-POINT PREFERENCE CLAIMED

INSTRUCTIONS: Check the block which indicates the type of preference you are claiming. Answer all questions associated with that block. The "DOCUMENTATION REQUIRED" column refers you to the back of this form for the documents you must submit to support your application. [PLEASE NOTE: Eligibility for veterans' preference is governed by 5 U.S.C. § 2108, 5 CFR Part 211, and FPM chapter 211. All conditions are not fully described in this form because of space restrictions. The office to which you apply can provide additional information. Instructions on how to apply for five point preference are on SF 171, Application for Federal Employment, or PS Form 2591, Application for Employment (U.S. Postal Service Application).]

DOCUMENTATION REQUIRED
(See reverse of this form.)

10. VETERAN'S CLAIM FOR PREFERENCE based on non-compensable service-connected disability; award of the Purple Heart; or receipt of disability pension under public laws administered by the VA. ➤ A and B

11. VETERAN'S CLAIM FOR PREFERENCE based on eligibility for or receipt of compensation from the VA or disability retirement from a Service Department for a service-connected disability. ➤ A and C

		YES	NO	
12. PREFERENCE FOR A SPOUSE of a living veteran based on the fact that the veteran, because of a service-connected disability, has been unable to qualify for a Federal or D.C. Government job, or any other position along the lines of his/her usual occupation. (If your answer to item "a" is "NO", you are ineligible for preference and need not submit this form.)	a. Are you presently married to the veteran?			C and H
13. PREFERENCE FOR WIDOW OR WIDOWER of a veteran. (If your answer is "NO" to item "a" or "YES" to item "b", you are ineligible for preference and need not submit this form.)	a. Were you married to the veteran when he or she died?			A, D, E, and G (Submit G when applicable.)
	b. Have you remarried? (Do not count marriages that were annulled.)			
14. PREFERENCE FOR (NATURAL) MOTHER of a service-connected permanently and totally disabled, or deceased veteran provided you are or were married to the father of the veteran, and —your husband (either the veteran's father or the husband of a remarriage) is totally and permanently disabled, or —you are now widowed, divorced, or separated from the veteran's father and have not remarried, or —you are widowed or divorced from the veteran's father and have remarried, but are now widowed, divorced, or separated from the husband of your remarriage. (if your answer is "NO" to item "c" or "d", you are ineligible for preference and need not submit this form.)	a. Are you married?			DISABLED VETERAN: C, F, and H (Submit F when applicable.)
	b. Are you separated? If "YES", do not complete "c". Go to "d".			
	c. If married now is your husband totally and permanently disabled?			DECEASED VETERAN: A,D,E, and F (Submit F when applicable.)
	d. If the veteran is dead, did he/she die in active service?			

PRIVACY ACT AND PUBLIC BURDEN STATEMENT.

The Veterans' Preference Act of 1944 authorizes the collection of this information. The information will be used, along with any accompanying documentation, to determine whether you are entitled to 10-point veterans' preference. This information may be disclosed to: (1) the Department of Veterans Affairs, or the appropriate branch of the Armed Forces to verify your claim; (2) a court, or a Federal, State, or local agency for checking on law violations or for other related authorized purposes; (3) a Federal, State, or local government agency, if you are participating in a special employment assistance program; or (4) other Federal, State, or local government agencies, congressional offices, and international organizations for purposes of employment consideration, e.g., if you are on an Office of Personnel Management list of eligibles. Executive order 9397 authorizes Federal agencies to use the Social Security Number (SSN) to identify individual persons in Federal personnel records systems. Your SSN will be used to ensure accurate retention of records pertaining to you and may also be used to identify you to others from

whom information about you is sought. Furnishing your SSN and the other information sought is voluntary. However, failure to provide any part of the information may result in a ruling that you are not eligible for 10-point veterans' preference or in delaying the processing of your application for employment.

Public burden reporting for this collection of information is estimated to take approximately 10 minutes per response, including time for reviewing instructions, searching existing data sources, gathering and maintaining the data needed, and completing and reviewing the collection of information. Send comments regarding the burden estimate or any other aspect of this collection of information, including suggestions for reducing this burden to Reports and Forms Management Officer, U.S. Office of Personnel Management, 1900 E Street, N.W., Room 6410, Washington, D.C. 20415; and to the Office of Management and Budget, Paperwork Reduction Project (3206-0001), Washington, D.C. 20503.

I certify that all of the statements made in this claim are true, complete, and correct to the best of my knowledge and belief and are made in good faith. [A false answer to any question may be grounds for not employing you, or for dismissing you after you begin work, and may be punishable by fine or imprisonment (U.S. Code, Title 18, Section 1001).]

This Form Must Be Signed By All Persons Claiming 10-Point Preference

Signature of Person Claiming Preference

Date Signed (Month, Day, Year)

FOR USE BY APPOINTING OFFICER ONLY
Signature and Title of Appointing Officer

Preference Entitlement Was Verified
Name of Agency

Date Signed (Month, Day, Year)

PREVIOUS 7-83 EDITION USABLE

15-110

NSN: 7540-00-634-3972

DOCUMENTATION REQUIRED—READ CAREFULLY
(PLEASE SUBMIT PHOTOCOPIES OF DOCUMENTS BECAUSE THEY WILL **NOT** BE RETURNED)

A. DOCUMENTATION OF SERVICE AND SEPARATION UNDER HONORABLE CONDITIONS

Submit any of the documents listed below as documentation, provided they are dated on or after the day of separation from active duty military service:

1. Honorable or general discharge certificate.
2. Certificate of transfer to Navy Fleet Reserve, Marine Corps Fleet Reserve, or enlisted Reserve Corps.
3. Orders of Transfer to Retired List.
4. Report of Separation from a branch of the Armed Forces.
5. Certificate of Service or release from active duty, provided honorable separation is shown.
6. Official Statement from a branch of the Armed Forces showing that honorable separation took place.
7. Notation by the Department of Veterans Affairs or a branch of the Armed Forces on an official statement, described in B or C below, that the veteran was honorably separated from military service.
8. Official statement from the Military Personnel Records Center that official service records show that honorable separation took place.

B. DOCUMENTATION OF SERVICE-CONNECTED DISABILITY (NON-COMPENSABLE, I.E., LESS THAN 10%); PURPLE HEART; AND NONSERVICE-CONNECTED DISABILITY PENSION

Submit one of the following documents:

1. An official statement, *dated within the last 12 months,* from the Department of Veterans Affairs or from a branch of the Armed Forces, certifying to the present existence of the veteran's service-connected disability of less than 10%.
2. An official citation, document, or discharge certificate, issued by a branch of the Armed Forces, showing the award to the veteran of the Purple Heart for wound or injuries received in action.
3. An official statement, *dated within the last 12 months,* from the Department of Veterans Affairs, certifying that the veteran is receiving a nonservice-connected disability pension.

C. DOCUMENTATION OF SERVICE-CONNECTED DISABILITY (COMPENSABLE, I.E., 10% OR MORE)

Submit one of the following documents, if you checked Item 11 on the front of this form:

1. An official statement, *dated within the last 12 months,* from the Department of Veterans Affairs or from a branch of the Armed Forces, certifying to the veteran's present receipt of compensation for service-connected disability or disability retired pay.
2. An official statement, *dated within the last 12 months,* from the Department of Veterans Affairs or from a branch of the Armed Forces, certifying that the veteran has a service-connected disability of 10% or more.

3. An official statement or retirement orders from a branch of the Armed Forces, showing that the retired serviceman was retired because of permanent service-connected disability or was transferred to the permanent disability retirement list. The statement or retirement orders must indicate that the disability is 10% or more.

For spouses and mothers of disabled veterans checking Items 12 or 14, submit the following:

An official statement, *dated within the last 12 months,* from the Department of Veterans Affairs or from a branch of the Armed Forces, certifying: 1) the present existence of the veterans service-connected disability, 2) the percentage and nature of the service-connected disability or disabilities (including the combined percentage), 3) a notation as to whether or not the veteran is currently rated as "unemployable" due to the service-connected disability, and 4) a notation as to whether or not the service-connected disability is rated as permanent and total.

D. DOCUMENTATION OF VETERAN'S DEATH

1. If on active military duty at time of death, *submit* official notice, from a branch of the Armed Forces, of death occurring under honorable conditions.
2. If death occurred while not on active military duty, *submit* death certificate.

E. DOCUMENTATION OF SERVICE OR DEATH DURING A WAR, IN A CAMPAIGN OR EXPEDITION FOR WHICH A CAMPAIGN BADGE IS AUTHORIZED, OR DURING THE PERIOD OF APRIL 28, 1952, THROUGH JULY 1, 1955

Submit documentation of service or death during a war or during the period April 28, 1952, through July 1, 1955, or during a campaign or expedition for which a campaign badge is authorized.

F. DOCUMENTATION OF DECEASED OR DISABLED VETERAN'S MOTHER'S CLAIM FOR PREFERENCE BECAUSE OF HER HUSBAND'S TOTAL AND PERMANENT DISABILITY

Submit a statement from husband's physician showing the prognosis of his disease and percentage of his disability.

G. DOCUMENTATION OF ANNULMENT OF REMARRIAGE BY WIDOW OR WIDOWER OF VETERAN

Submit either:

1. Certification from the Department of Veterans Affairs that entitlement to pension or compensation was restored due to annulment.
2. A certified copy of the court decree of annulment.

H. DOCUMENTATION OF VETERAN'S INABILITY TO WORK BECAUSE OF A SERVICE-CONNECTED DISABILITY

Answer questions 1-7 below:

1. Is the veteran currently working? . . . . ☐ YES ☐ NO If "NO", go to Item 3.	2. If currently working, what is the veteran's present occupation?
3. What was the veteran's occupation, if any, before military service?	4. What was the veteran's military occupation at the time of separation?

5. Has the veteran been employed, or is he/she now employed, by the Federal civil service or D.C. Government? . . . . ☐ YES ☐ NO

A. Title and Grade of Position Most Recently, or Currently, Held	B. Name and Address of Agency	C. Dates of Employment
		From To

6. Has the veteran resigned from, been disqualified for, or separated from a position in the Federal civil service or D. C. Government along the lines of his/her usual occupation because of service-connected disability? . . . . ☐ YES ☐ NO
If "YES", submit documentation of the resignation, disqualification, or separation.

7. Is the veteran receiving a civil service retirement pension? . ☐ YES ☐ NO
If "YES", give the Civil Service or Federal Employee retirement annuity number ——————→ **CSA** _____

STANDARD FORM 15 (REV. 2/90) BACK

*U.S. Government Printing Office: 1992 — 342-199/50163

U.S. OFFICE OF PERSONNEL MANAGEMENT
QUALIFICATIONS & AVAILABILITY FORM

FORM APPROVED
OMB No. 3206-0040

FORM C

PRINT YOUR RESPONSE IN THE BOXES AND BLACKEN IN THE APPROPRIATE OVALS.

USE A NO. 2 PENCIL

DO NOT FOLD, STAPLE, TEAR OR PAPER CLIP THIS FORM.
DO NOT SUBMIT PHOTOCOPIES OF THIS FORM.
We can process this form only if you:
- Use a number 2 lead pencil.
- Completely blacken each oval you choose.
- Completely erase any mistakes or stray marks.

1 YOUR NAME: _____

2 JOB APPLYING FOR: _____

3 ANNOUNCEMENT NUMBER: _____

EXAMPLES

012-34

YES NO

CORRECT MARK   INCORRECT MARKS

FOLLOW THE DIRECTIONS ON THE
"FORM C INSTRUCTION SHEET"

4 OCCUPATION (OCC)

5 CASE NO. (CNO)

6 LOWEST GRADE (LAG)

7 **EMPLOYMENT AVAILABILITY**

ARE YOU AVAILABLE FOR:

	YES	NO			YES	NO
A) full-time employment -40 hours per week?	Y	N (FTE)	D) jobs requiring travel away from home for			(TRV)
			-1 to 5 nights/month?		Y	N
B) part-time employment of		(PTE)	-6 to 10 nights/month?		Y	N
-16 or fewer hrs/week?	Y	N	-11 plus nights/month?		Y	N
-17 to 24 hrs/week?	Y	N				
-25 to 32 hrs/week?	Y	N	E) other employment questions (see directions)			(OEM)
C) temporary employment lasting		(TMP)	Question 1?		Y	N
-less than 1 month?	Y	N	Question 2?		Y	N
-1 to 4 months?	Y	N	Question 3?		Y	N
-5 to 12 months?	Y	N	Question 4?		Y	N

8 (OSP) **OCCUPATIONAL SPECIALTIES**

1 2 3 4 5

6 7 8 9 10

9 (GAV) **GEOGRAPHIC AVAILABILITY**

1 2 3 4 5

6 7 8 9

2056251

OPM FORM 1203-AW (7-92)

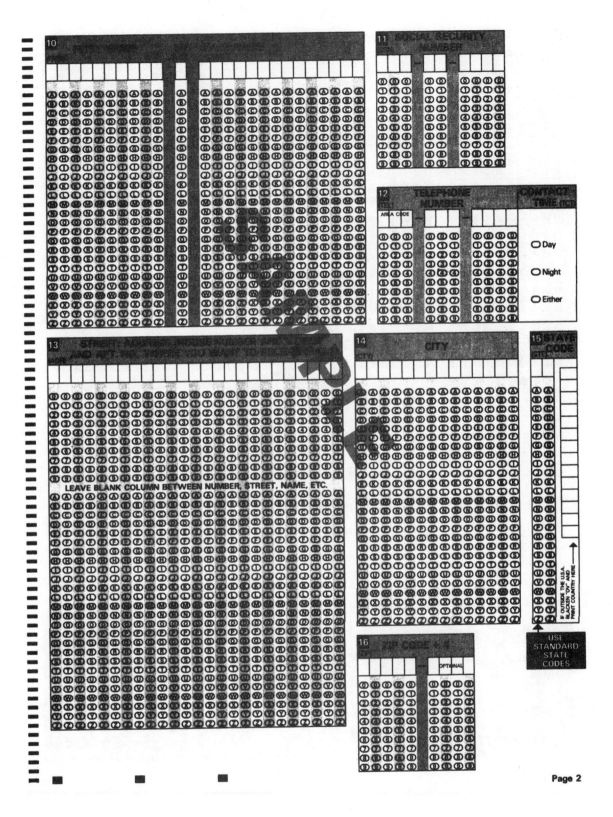

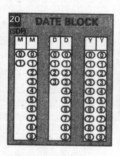

23 (VET) VETERAN PREFERENCE CLAIM

○ No preference claimed

○ 5 points preference claimed

10 POINT PREFERENCE- You must enclose a completed Standard Form 15.

○ 10 points preference claimed (award of a Purple Heart or noncompensable service-connected disability)

○ 10 points compensable disability preference claimed (disability rating of less than 30%)

○ 10 points other (wife, widow, husband, widower, mother preference claimed)

○ 10 points compensable disability preference claimed (disability rating of 30% or more)

24 (SB1) BACKGROUND INFORMATION

	YES	NO
1. Are you a citizen of the United States?	Ⓨ	Ⓝ
2. During the last 10 years, were you fired from any job for any reason or did you quit after being told that you would be fired?	Ⓨ	Ⓝ
3. Are you now or have you ever been: (Answer the following questions.)		
a) convicted of or forfeited collateral for any felony?	Ⓨ	Ⓝ
b) convicted of or forfeited collateral for any firearms or explosive violation?	Ⓨ	Ⓝ
c) convicted, forfeited collateral, imprisoned, on probation, or on parole, during the last 10 years?	Ⓨ	Ⓝ
d) convicted by a court martial?	Ⓨ	Ⓝ
4. Are you currently under charges for any violation of law?	Ⓨ	Ⓝ

25 DATES OF ACTIVE DUTY - MILITARY SERVICE

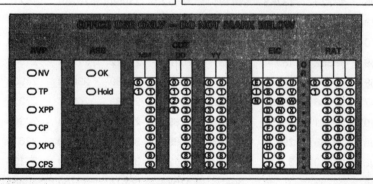

26 SIGNATURE/DATE

I certify that the information on this form is true and correct to the best of my knowledge. **NOTE:** A false statement on any part of your application may be grounds for not hiring you, or for firing you after you begin work. Also, you may be punished by fine or imprisonment (U.S. Code, title 18, section 1001).

Signature _____

Date signed _____

PRIVACY ACT

The Office of Personnel Management is authorized to rate applicants for Federal jobs under sections 1302, 3301, and 3304 of title 5 of the U.S. Code. Section 1104 of title 5 allows the Office of Personnel Management to authorize other Federal agencies to rate applicants for Federal jobs. We need the information you put on this form to see how well your education and work skills qualify you for a Federal job. We also need information on matters such as citizenship and military service to see whether you are affected by laws we must follow in deciding who may be employed by the Federal Government.

We must have your Social Security (SSN) to identify your records because other people may have the same name and birthdate. The Office of Personnel Management may also use your SSN to make requests for information about you from employers, schools, banks, and others who know you, but only as allowed by law or Presidential directive. The information we collect by using your SSN will be used for employment purposes and also for studies and statistics that will not identify you.

Information we have about you may also be given to Federal, State and local agencies for checking on law violations or for other lawful purposes. We may send your name and address to State and local Government agencies, Congressional and other public offices, and public international organizations, if they request names of people to consider for employment. We may also notify your school placement office if you are selected for a Federal job.

Giving us your SSN or any of the other information is voluntary. However, we cannot process your application, which is the first step toward getting a job, if you do not give us the information we request.

PUBLIC REPORTING BURDEN

The public reporting burden of information is estimated to vary from 20 minutes to 45 minutes to complete this form, including time for reviewing instructions, gathering the data needed, and completing and reviewing entries. The average time to complete this form is 30 minutes. Send comments regarding the burden estimate or any other aspect of this collection of information, including suggestions for reducing this burden to: US Office of Personnel Management, Office of Information Management, 1900 E Street, NW, CHP 500, Washington, DC 20415; and to the Office of Information and Regulatory Affairs, Office of Management and Budget, Paperwork Reduction Project 3206-0040, Washington, DC 20503.

2056251

Remember

- The more applications you submit, the greater your chances of obtaining a position.

- Use a computer or have the SF171, OF612, or Federal Résumé typed.

- Do not sign the original; use the original as a master and sign each copy.

- Make clear copies.

VETERAN PREFERENCE In hiring, the federal government gives preference to qualified veterans. Veterans must fill out the Standard Form 15 (SF15), a blue form, and attach a copy of their DD214 as proof of their service.

MAIN FEDERAL LAW ENFORCEMENT BENEFITS

FEDERAL PAY SCALE For the most part, federal law enforcement officers are paid on the general schedule of pay known as the GS system. Most agencies start entry level officers at the GS-5 level.

FEDERAL PAY SCALE
ANNUAL RATES (IN DOLLARS)

BASE GENERAL SCHEDULE PAY SCALE

STEP	1	2	3	4	5	6	7	8	9	10
GS-01	12895	13326	13753	14181	14612	14864	15285	15712	15731	16129
GS-02	14498	14844	15325	15731	15905	16372	16840	17307	17775	18243
GS-03	15820	16347	16874	17401	17928	18455	18982	19509	20036	20563
GS-04	17759	18352	18944	19537	20129	20722	21314	21907	22499	23092
GS-05	19869	20531	21194	21856	22518	23180	23843	24505	25167	25829
GS-06	22147	22686	23624	24362	25101	25839	26577	27315	28054	28792
GS-07	24510	25431	26251	27072	27892	28713	29533	30364	31174	31995
GS-08	27256	28165	29074	29983	30892	31801	32710	33619	34528	35438
GS-09	30106	31110	32114	33118	34121	35125	36129	37133	38137	39140
GS-10	33154	34259	35384	36468	37573	38678	39783	40888	41995	43097
GS-11	36425	37640	38854	40068	41282	42496	43711	44925	46139	47353
GS-12	43658	45113	46569	48025	49480	50936	52392	53848	55303	56759
GS-13	51915	53646	55376	57107	58838	60568	62299	64030	65760	67491
GS-14	61348	63393	65438	67484	69529	71574	73619	75664	77709	79754
GS-15	72162	74567	76973	79378	81784	84189	86595	89000	91405	93811

BASE PAY RATES FOR LAW ENFORCEMENT OFFICERS

STEP	1	2	3	4	5	6	7	8	9	10
GS-03	18299	18735	19241	19747	20253	20759	21265	21771	22277	22783
GS-04	20469	21083	21067	22176	22745	23314	23883	24452	25021	25590
GS-05	23533	24169	24805	25441	26077	26713	27349	27985	28621	29257
GS-06	24814	25523	26232	26941	27650	28359	29568	29777	30486	31195
GS-07	26786	27574	28362	29150	29938	30726	31514	32302	33090	33878
GS-08	27921	28794	29667	30540	31413	32286	33159	34032	34905	35778
GS-09	29876	30840	31804	32768	33732	34696	35660	36624	37588	38552
GS-10	32900	33961	35022	36083	37144	38205	39205	40327	41388	42449

LEAVE Federal employees receive sick and vacation leave credits that increase with time.

HEALTH Federal employees have a variety of health insurance plans available.

RETIREMENTS Federal law enforcement employees are eligible to retire at age 50 or with 20 years of service. Employees with 25 years of service are eligible to retire at any age.

TRANSFERS It is possible for federal employees to transfer from one position to another agency or position; usually, employees must have at least six months of service.

FEDERAL PROMOTIONS Federal law enforcement agencies maintain a steady advancement track for employees who demonstrate their suitability for their position.

INFORMATION SOURCES OF FEDERAL LAW ENFORCEMENT POSITIONS

OPM's Career America Connection

This automated phone system provides information 24 hours a day, seven days a week about current employment opportunities (nation-wide and worldwide), special programs for students, veterans, and people with disabilities, the Presidential Management Intern Program, salaries and benefits, and application request services. Call the main nationwide number of the location nearest.

Nationwide	**(912) 757-3000**
Huntsville, AL	(205) 937-0894
San Francisco, CA	(415) 744-5627
Denver, CO	(303) 969-7050
Washington, DC	(202) 606-2700
Atlanta, GA	(404) 331-4315
Honolulu, HI	(808) 541-2791
Chicago, IL	(312) 353-6192
Detroit, MI	(313) 226-6950
Twin Cities, MN	(612) 725-3430
Kansas City, MO	(816) 426-5702
Raleigh, NC	(919) 790-2822
Dayton, OH	(513) 225-2720
Philadelphia, PA	(215) 597-7440
San Antonio, TX	(210) 805-2402
Norfolk, VA	(804) 441-3355
Seattle, WA	(206) 553-0888

FEDERAL JOB OPPORTUNITIES BOARD Call this computer bulletin board at (912) 757-3100. To use the system you need a personal computer equipped with a modem and communications software, as well as a telephone line. You may access current job opportunities, obtain information about the federal employment process, or request employment applications and forms.

The Federal Job Opportunities Board can be accessed through the Internet:

www.usajobs.opm.gov

FEDERAL EMPLOYMENT INFORMATION CENTERS (FEIC) The best place to obtain information and locate openings are at the Office of Personnel Management's Federal Employment Information Centers (FEIC) found throughout the country. Bring the necessary material in order to take notes, write information, and fill out forms.

Locations

The Office of Personnel Management has installed Federal Job Information Touch Screen at several locations to provide current worldwide federal job opportunities on-line information, and the ability to request application packages. Location of these offices are noted below.

ALABAMA

Federal Employment
Information Center
3322 Memorial Parkway South
Huntsville, AL 35801
(205) 544-5803

ALASKA

Federal Employment
Information Center
222 West 7th Avenue
Anchorage, AK 99513
(907) 271-5821
Kiosk Location

ARIZONA

Federal Employment
Information Center
Century Plaza Building,
Room 1415
3225 North Central Avenue
Phoenix, AZ 85012
(602) 640-4800

ARKANSAS

(Contact San Antonio, TX FEIC)

CALIFORNIA

Federal Employment
Information Center
Los Angeles Area
9650 Flair Drive
El Monte, CA 91731
(818) 575-6510

Federal Employment
Information Center
Federal Building
1029 J Street
Sacramento, CA 95814
(916) 551-1464
Kiosk Location

Federal Employment
Information Center
211 Main Street
2nd Floor Room 235
San Francisco, CA 94120
(415) 744-5627

COLORADO

Federal Employment
Information Center
P.O. Box 25167
Denver, CO 80225
(303) 969-7050

CONNECTICUT

Federal Building
450 Main Street
Hartford, CT
Kiosk Location
(Contact Massachusetts FEIC)

DELAWARE

(Contact Philadelphia, PA FEIC)

DISTRICT OF COLUMBIA

Federal Employment
Information Center
1900 E Street NW
Washington, DC 20415
(202) 606-2700
Kiosk Location

FLORIDA

Federal Employment
Information Center
3444 McCrory Place
Orlando, FL 32803
(407) 648-6148

GEORGIA

Federal Employment
Information Center
Richard B. Russell
Federal Building
75 Spring Street SW
Atlanta, GA 30303
(404) 331-4315
Kiosk Location

GUAM

Federal Employment
Information Center
Pacific Daily News Building
Agana, Guam 96910
(671) 472-7451

HAWAII

Federal Employment
Information Center
Federal Building
300 Ala Moana Blvd.
Honolulu, HI 96850
(808) 541-2791
Overseas jobs (808) 541-2784
Kiosk Location

IDAHO

(Contact Washington FEIC Listing)

ILLINOIS

Information Center
175 West Jackson
Chicago, IL 60604
(313) 353-6192
Kiosk Location

INDIANA

Federal Employment
Information Center
Minton Capehart Federal Building
575 North Pennsylvania Street
Indianapolis, IN 46204
(317) 226-7161
Kiosk Location

IOWA

(Contact Kansas City, MO FEIC)

KANSAS

Federal Employment
Information Center
One-Twenty Building
120 South Market Street
Wichita, KS 67202
(316) 269-0552

KENTUCKY

(Contact Ohio FEIC)

LOUISIANA

Federal Employment
Information Center
1515 Poydras Street
New Orleans, LA 70112
(504) 589-2764

MAINE

Federal Building
40 Western Avenue
Augusta, ME 04333
Kiosk Location
(Contact Massachusetts FEIC)

MARYLAND

Federal Employment
Information Center
300 West Pratt Street
Baltimore, MD 21201
(410) 962-3822

MASSACHUSETTS

Federal Employment
Information Center
Federal Building
10 Causeway Street
Boston, MA 02222
(617) 565-5900
Kiosk Location

MICHIGAN

Federal Employment
Information Center
477 Michigan Avenue
Detroit, MI 48226
(313) 226-6950

MINNESOTA

Federal Employment
Information Center
Federal Building
1 Federal Drive
Twin Cities, MN 55111
(612) 725-3430
Kiosk Location

MISSISSIPPI

(Contact Alabama FEIC listing)

MISSOURI

Federal Employment
Information Center
Federal Building
601 East 12th Street
Kansas, MO 64106
(816) 426-5702
Kiosk Location

Federal Employment
Information Center
Old Post Office Building
815 Olive Street
St. Louis, MO 63101
(314) 539-2285

MONTANA

(Contact Colorado FEIC Listing)

NEBRASKA

(Contact Kansas FEIC Listing)

NEVADA

(Contact Sacramento or Los Angeles
FEIC listings)

NEW HAMPSHIRE

(Contact Massachusetts FEIC Listing)

NEW JERSEY

Federal Building
970 Broad Street
Newark, NJ
Kiosk Location
(Northern NJ: Contact New York City
FEIC Listing)
(Southern NJ: Contact Philadelphia
FEIC Listing)

NEW MEXICO

Federal Employment
Information Center
Federal Building
505 Marquette Avenue
Albuquerque, NM 87102
(505) 766-2906

NEW YORK

Federal Employment
Information Center
Jacob B. Javits Federal Building
26 Federal Plaza
New York, NY 10278
(212) 264-0422
Kiosk Location

Federal Employment
Information Center
James M. Hanley Federal Building
100 South Clinton Street
Syracuse, NY 13260
(315) 423-5660
Kiosk Location

NORTH CAROLINA

Federal Employment
Information Center
4407 Bland Road
Raleigh, NC 27609
(919) 790-2822
Kiosk Location

NORTH DAKOTA

(Contact Minnesota FEIC Listing)

OHIO

Federal Employment
Information Center
Federal Building
200 West 2nd Street
Dayton, OH 45402
(513) 225-2720
Kiosk Location

OKLAHOMA

(Contact San Antonio FEIC Listing)

OREGON

Federal Employment
Information Center
Federal Building
1220 SW 3rd Avenue
Portland, OR 97204
(503) 326-4141

PENNSYLVANIA

Federal Employment
Information Center
Federal Building
228 Walnut Street
Harrisburg, PA 17108
(717) 782-4494
Kiosk Location

Federal Employment
Information Center
Federal Building
600 Arch Street
Philadelphia, PA 19106
(215) 597-7440
Kiosk Location

Federal Employment
Information Center
Federal Building
1000 Liberty Avenue
Pittsburgh, PA 15222

PUERTO RICO

Federal Employment
Information Center
Federal Building
150 Carlos Chardon Avenue
Hato Rey, San Juan, PR 00918
(809) 766-5242
Kiosk Location

RHODE ISLAND

380 Westminster
Providence, RI 02903
Kiosk Location
(Contact Massachusetts FEIC Listing)

SOUTH CAROLINA

(Contact Raleigh FEIC Listing)

SOUTH DAKOTA

(Contact Minnesota FEIC Listing)

TENNESSEE

Federal Employment
Information Center
200 Jefferson Avenue
Memphis, TN 38103

TEXAS

Federal Employment
Information Center
1100 Commerce Street
Dallas, TX 75242
(214) 767-8035
Kiosk Location

Federal Employment
Information Center
8610 Broadway
San Antonio, TX 78217
(210) 229-6611

UTAH

(Contact Colorado FEIC Listing)

VERMONT

Federal Building
11 Elmwood Avenue
Burlington, VT 05401
Kiosk Location
(Contact Massachusetts FEIC Listing)

VIRGIN ISLANDS

(Contact Puerto Rico FEIC Listing)

VIRGINIA

Federal Employment
Information Center
Federal Building
220 Granby Mall
Norfolk, VA 23510-1886
(804) 441-3355
Kiosk Location

WASHINGTON

Federal Employment
Information Center
Federal Building
915 Second Avenue
Seattle, WA 98174
(206) 220-6400
Kiosk Location

WEST VIRGINIA

(Contact Ohio FEIC Listing)

WISCONSIN

(Contact Minnesota FEIC Listing)

WYOMING

(Contact Colorado FEIC Listing)

SECTION

SPECIAL LAW ENFORCEMENT AGENCIES

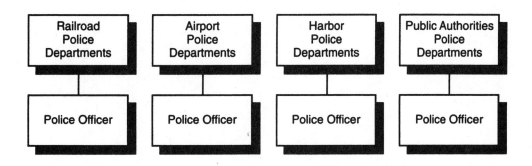

RAILROAD POLICE DEPARTMENTS

⬡ Railroad Police Officer

MISSION Railroad Police Departments have a historical background. Some Railroad Police Departments are maintained by private companies, others are public agencies.

COMMENTS *Employment Outlook:* Hiring by Railroad Police Departments is sporadic and quick, if at all, so the need for an active pool of qualified candidates that already have law enforcement experience is critical. Candidates with prior law enforcement experience fare best over education.

Employment Conditions: Railroad Police Officers work alone in large urban areas and in deserted territories. Railroad Police are required to be certified police officers in the state in which they are commissioned and are required to meet the state's law enforcement academy standards for training.

Retirement: For the most part, Railroad Police Officers are covered by the Federal Railroad Board's retirement for railroad employees, which is 30 years/age 62. Some Railroad Police are covered by state law enforcement officer retirement programs, but they are usually passenger services.

WHERE TO APPLY   Send a narrative style résumé and cover letter directly to the Railroad Police Agency in which you are interested.

Listings

Alaska Railroad
Police Department
P.O. Box 107500
Anchorage, AK 99510-7500
www.akrr.com

Southern Pacific Lines
   Denver & Rio Grande
   Western Railroad
   St. Louis/Southwestern
     Railway
   Southern Pacific
     Transportation Co.
Police Department
One Market Plaza
Room 401
San Francisco, CA 94105

CSX Transportation Company
Police Department
6737 Southport Drive
Jacksonville, FL 32216
www.csx.com

Florida East Coast Railway
Police Department
7300 NW 69th Street
Miami Springs, FL 33266

METRA
(Northeast Illinois Railroad
   Corp)
Police Department
547 West Jackson Blvd.
Chicago, IL 60661
www.metrarail.com

Illinois Central Railroad
Police Department
17641 South Ashland Avenue
Homeward, IL 60430

Elgin Joliet & Eastern Railway
Police Department
1141 Maple Road
Joliet, IL 60434

Northern Indiana
Commuter Transportation
   District
Police Department
33 East U.S. Highway 12
Chesterton, IN 46304

Indiana Harbor Belt Railroad
Police Department
2721 161st Street
Hammond, IN 46323

Iowa Interstate Railroad
Police Department
2920 Industrial Park Road
Iowa City, IA 52240

Guilford Transportation Inc. (GTI)
   Boston and Maine Railroad
   Maine Central Railroad
   Springfield Terminal
Police Departments
Iron Horse Park High Street
North Billerica, MA 08162
www.guilfordrail.com

Providence & Worcester
   Railroad
Police Department
382 Southbridge Street
Worcester, MA 01601

(CP Rail System)
Soo Line Railroad Co.
Police Department
105 South 5th Street
Minneapolis, MN 55402

Kansas City Southern Railway
Police Department
111 East Capital Street
Jackson, MS 39215

Alton & Southern Railway
Police Department
1000 South 22nd Street
East St. Louis, MO 62207

Terminal Railroad Association
of St. Louis Police Department
700 North Second Street
St. Louis, MO 63102

Union Pacific Railroad
Police Department
1416 Dodge Street
Omaha, NE 68179
www.uprr.com

New Jersey Transit
Police Department
25 University Avenue
Newark, NJ 07104

(CP Rail System)
Delaware and Hudson Railway
Police Department
200 Clifton Corporate Parkway
Clifton Park, NY 12065

New York Susquehanna &
Western Railway
Police Department
One Railroad Avenue
Cooperstown, NY 13326

Long Island Railroad
Police Department
93-59 183rd Street
Hollis, NY 11423

Bessemer & Lake Erie Railroad
Pittsburgh & Conneaut Dock
Company Union Railroad
Police Departments
135 Jamison Lane
Monroeville, PA 15146

Burlington Northern Railroad
Police Department
3017 Lou Menk Drive Building B
Fort Worth, TX 76131
www.bnsf.com

Houston Belt and Terminal
Railway
Police Department
501 Crawford Street
Houston, TX 77002

Norfolk & Southern
Corporation
Police Department
110 Franklin Road SE
Roanoke, VA 24042

AIRPORT/HARBOR/PUBLIC AUTHORITIES SPECIAL LAW ENFORCEMENT

☐ **Airport Police Officer**
☐ **Harbor Police Officer**
☐ **Public Authority Police Officer**

COMMENTS These are situational law enforcement agencies that have a unique jurisdiction or venue of operation. For the most part, these agencies are smaller than municipal police departments and hire sporadically. Send a narrative style résumé and cover letter directly to the agency.

Listings

ALASKA

Anchorage International Airport Police
Anchorage, AK 99519

CALIFORNIA

Los Angeles International Airport Police
6320 West 96th Street
Los Angeles, CA 90017

Los Angeles Port Police
425 South Palos Verdes Street
San Pedro, CA 90731
www.portla.com

San Diego Harbor Police
1401 Shelter Island Drive
San Diego, CA 92106
www.portofsandiego.com

San Francisco Airport Police
P.O. Box 8097
San Francisco, CA 94128

DELAWARE

Delaware River Bay Authority
Police Department
P.O. Box 71
New Castle, DE 19720

DISTRICT OF COLUMBIA

Washington Metro Airports Authority Police Department
MOIA Police Department
44 Canal Center Plaza
Alexandria, VA 22314

LOUISIANA

Port of New Orleans Harbor Police
1 Third Street
New Orleans, LA 70112

MARYLAND

Maryland Port Administration
Police Department
401 East Pratt Street
Baltimore, MD 21202

MINNESOTA

Minneapolis-St. Paul
International Airport Police
Lindbergh Terminal
St. Paul, MN 55111

NEW JERSEY

Delaware River Port Authority
Police Department
Ben Franklin Bridge
Camden, NJ 08101

NEW YORK

Port Authority of NY and NJ
Police Department
One Path Plaza
Jersey City, NJ 07306
www.panynj.gov

Niagara Frontier
Transportation Authority
Police Department
1404 Main Street
Buffalo, NY 14209

Waterfront Commission of
New York/New Jersey
Police Department
42 Broadway
New York, NY 10004

OREGON

Port of Portland
Police Department
7000 NE Airport Way
Portland, OR 97218
www.portofportlandor.com

TENNESSEE

Nashville International
Airport Police
921 Airport Service Road
Nashville, TN 37201

TEXAS

Dallas-Fort Worth
International Airport
Police Department
Dallas, TX 75261

WASHINGTON

Port of Seattle
Police Department
P.O. Box 68727
Seattle, WA 98168
www.portseattle.org

APPENDICES

APPENDICES

LAW ENFORCEMENT RESOURCES

LAW ENFORCEMENT PUBLICATIONS, ASSOCIATIONS, AND RESEARCH ORGANIZATIONS

The following publications, associations and research organizations are provided to serve as possible sources of law enforcement opportunities. The information these items give can lead a researcher to which agencies are hiring. Most of these organizations provide current up-to-date information on law enforcement trends for specific agencies that can give a candidate a tactical edge during the process.

Law Enforcement Publications

DPSOA Magazine
Department of Public Safety
Officer Association
(512) 451-0571

Chief of Police
National Association of
Chiefs of Police
(305) 573-0070

Law and Order Magazine
Hendon Inc.
(708) 256-8555
www.lawandordermag.com

Law Enforcement News
John Jay College of Criminal
Justice
(212) 237-8442

Federal Probation
Administrative Office
of the United States Courts
(202) 273-1627

FBI Law Enforcement Bulletin
Federal Bureau of Investigation
(703) 640-1193
www.fbi.gov

Police Magazine
Hare Publications
(619) 438-2511

Police Chief
International Association of
Chiefs of Police
(703) 836-6767
www.policechief.com

Sheriff
National Sheriff Association
(703) 836-7827

Law Enforcement Associations

Association of American
Railroad Police
50 F Street NW
Washington, DC 20001
(202) 639-2384

National Association of
Chiefs of Police
1000 Connecticut Avenue NW
Washington, DC 20036
(202) 293-9088

International Association
of Women Police
Route 2, Box 30
Elkhart, IA 50073
(515) 229-8739
www.iawp.org

Federal Law Enforcement
Officers Association
192 Oak Street
Amityville, NY 11701
(631) 264-0260
www.fleoa.org

(Affiliate)
Women of Law Enforcement
of Western New York
P.O. Box 1152
West Seneca, NY 14224
www.iawp.org

Fraternal Order of Police
1410 Donelson Park
Nashville, TN 37217
(615) 399-0900
www.fop.net

International Association of
Chiefs of Police
515 North Washington Street
Alexandria, VA 22314
(703) 836-6767
www.theiacp.org

Park Law Enforcement
Association
2775 South Quincey Street
Arlington, VA 22206
(703) 820-4940
www.parkranger.com

Law Enforcement Research Organizations

National Criminal
Justice Reference Service
P.O. Box 6000
Rockville, MD 20850
(800) 851-3420

Police Executive
Research Forum
2300 M Street N
Washington, DC 20037
(202) 466-7820

Police Foundation
1001 22nd Street
Washington, DC 20037
(202) 833-1460

National Sheriffs Association
1450 Duke Street
Alexandria, VA 22314
(703) 836-7827

GLOSSARY*

> The following words may appear on various law enforcement examinations. The use of the glossary may help you to become familiar with words and their meanings.

A

Abduct To restrain a person with intent to prevent that person's liberation by either secreting or holding that person in a place where he/she is not likely to be found, or using or threatening to use deadly physical force.

Abusive Using harsh words or inflicting bodily harm.

Accomplice One who knowingly, voluntarily, and with common intent with the principal offender unites in the commission of a crime; equally concerned in the commission of a crime.

Acquit To set free, release, or discharge as from an accusation of crime; the opposite in meaning from convict.

Addict One who has acquired the habit of using drugs or alcohol to such an extent as to be deprived of reasonable self-control.

Adjourn To put off; to postpone.

Admissible Pertinent and proper to be considered in reaching a decision. As applied to evidence, the term means that it is of such character that the court is bound to receive it, that is, allow it to be introduced.

Admission In a criminal prosecution, any act or declaration of the accused that is inconsistent with a claim of innocence. If a defendant makes a statement not amounting to a confession, but constituting an admission of acts in issue against that defendant, or of facts relevant to the issue, such a statement is admissible.

Admonish To caution or to advise.

---

*Reprinted from *Veterans Administration Police Training Manual.*

Admonition A reprimand from a judge to an accused person upon being discharged, warning that person of the consequences of his/her conduct, and intimating to him/her that a repetition of the offense will bring more severe punishment. Also, any authoritative oral communication or statement by way of advice or caution by the court.

Affadavit A sworn written statement. The affidavit is divided into three parts: The location is entered at the upper left corner—this is called the *venue*. Below this is the statement itself—the *body* of the affidavit. At the bottom, the officer who administers the oath certifies that the statement was sworn to before him/her—this is the *jurat*.

Affirmant A person who testifies on affirmation, or one who affirms instead of taking an oath.

Affirmation An oath that may be defined as a pledge given by the person taking it "that his/her attestation or promise is made under an immediate sense of responsibility to God."

Aforethought In criminal law, deliberate, planned, premeditated.

Aggression The act of making attacks.

Aggressor One who first employs hostile force; the party who first offers violence or offense.

Agitator One who stirs up, excites, ruffles, perturbs. One who incessantly advocates a social change.

Alias Any name by which one is known other than one's true name. *Alias dictus* is more technically correct, but is not commonly used.

Alibi A claim that one was in a place different from that charged.

Apprehend To seize, take, or arrest a person on a criminal charge.

Arraign To bring an arrested person before the court, where the charge against that person is explained and the plea is taken. The procedure is called an *arraignment*. If the person is later indicted, the same process is repeated in a higher court.

Arrest To take a person into custody to be held to answer for a crime. To be binding, an arrest does not require physical seizure of the person. If the person voluntarily submits to the custody of the officer, he/she is as much arrested as if he/she were handcuffed.

Arson An intentional damaging of property by fire or explosion.

Assault Unlawful offer or attempt to do injury to another with force or violence.

Authorize Give legal power to.

Autopsy The dissection of a dead body for the purpose of inquiring into the cause of death.

B

Bail Refers to the release of a prisoner from custody on the written guarantee that the person will appear in court at a specified time, or forfeit money or property.

Bail Bond The agreement signed by the released prisoner and the surety guaranteeing that the prisoner will appear at the specified time and place or will forfeit money or property.

Barricade An obstruction or block to prevent passage or access.

Blackmail The obtaining of something of value from a person by threatening to expose that person to injury, disgrace, libel, etc.

Bodily Harm Any touching of a person by another against his/her will with physical force, in an intentional, hostile, and aggressive manner.

Bribery The offering, giving, receiving, or soliciting of anything of value to influence the action of an officer or in discharge of legal or public duty.

Burden of Proof The obligation to prove the fact in issue. In a criminal case, the prosecutor has the duty of proving the guilt of the person charged beyond a reasonable doubt.

Burglary Entering or remaining unlawfully in a location with intent to commit a crime therein.

Bystander One who stands near; a chance spectator; hence, one who has no concern with the business being transacted; one present but not taking part.

C

Cadaver A dead human body; a corpse.

Capacity Function or position.

Coercion The act of compelling a person to do something that he/she does not have or want to do, or to conceal what he/she may legally do, by some illegal means (threat, force, etc.).

Collision An impact or sudden contact of a moving body with an obstruction in its line of motion, whether both bodies are in motion or one stationary and the other in motion.

Collusion An agreement between two or more persons for fraudulent or deceitful purposes.

Commitment The written order by which a court or magistrate directs an officer to take a person to prison; authority for holding in jail someone accused of a crime.

Common Knowledge Matters that the court may declare applicable to action without necessity of proof; knowledge that every intelligent person has.

Common Law As distinguished from law created by the enactment of legislatures, the common law comprises principles and rules of action relating to the government and security of persons and property that derive their authority solely from usage and customs, or from the judgments and decrees of the courts recognizing, affirming, and enforcing such usage and customs.

Competency In the law of evidence, the presence of those characteristics or the absence of those disabilities that render a witness legally fit and qualified to give testimony in a court of justice; applied, in the same sense, to documents or other written evidence.

Complainant One who instigates prosecution or who makes accusation against a suspected person.

Complaint A sworn written allegation that a specified person committed a crime. Also known as *information*.

Compulsion Forcible impulse to commit an act; an impulse or feeling of being irresistibly driven toward the performance of some act.

Concur To agree; to be in accord; to act together.

Conduct Personal behavior; deportment.

Confess To admit as true; to admit the truth of a charge or accusation.

Confession A voluntary statement made by a person charged with crime, wherein the person acknowledges guilt in the offense charged.

Confrontation The act of putting a witness face to face with a prisoner, in order that the latter may make any objections to the witness, or that the witness may identify the accused.

Consent A concurrence of wills; agreement; voluntarily yielding the will to the proposition of another.

Conspiracy In criminal law, a combination of two or more persons formed for the purpose of committing, by their joint efforts, some unlawful or criminal act.

Constitutional Right A right guaranteed to the citizens by the Constitution and thus guaranteed to prevent legislative interference.

Contempt of Court Any act that is calculated to embarrass, hinder, or obstruct the court in the administration of justice, or that is calculated to lessen its authority or dignity.

Convict To find a person guilty of a criminal charge.

Corporal Punishment Physical punishment as distinguished from pecuniary punishment or a fine; any kind of punishment of, or inflicted on the body.

Corpus Delicti The body of a crime; the substance or foundation of a crime; the substantial fact that a crime has been committed.

Corroborate To strengthen; to add weight or credibility to a thing by additional and confirming facts or evidence.

Corruption The act of an official who unlawfully and wrongfully uses his/her position to procure some benefit for that official or for another person, contrary to duty and the rights of others.

Counterfeit In criminal law, to forge; to copy, or imitate, without authority or right, and with intent to deceive or defraud, by passing off the copy or thing forged as original or genuine.

Credibility Worthiness of belief; that quality of a witness that renders the witness's evidence worthy of belief.

Crime An act or omission, forbidden by law, and punishable upon conviction as the law may prescribe.

Crimes Mala in Se Acts that are immoral or wrong in themselves, such as burglary, larceny, arson, rape, murder; those acts that are wrong by their very nature.

Criminal One who has committed a crime; one who has been legally convicted of a crime. Also, anything pertaining to or connected with the law of crimes, or the administration of penal justice, or relating to or with the character of crime.

Cross Examination The examination of a witness in a trial or hearing, or when taking a deposition, by the party opposed to the one who produced the witness, upon evidence to test its truth, to further develop it, or for other purposes.

Culpable Blamable; censurable, involving the breach of a legal duty or the commission of a fault.

Custody The charge and keeping by officers of the law.

D

Deadly Weapon A weapon or instrument made and designed for offensive or defensive purposes, or for the destruction of life or the infliction of injury.

Death The cessation of life; the ceasing to exist; defined by physicians as a total stoppage of the circulation of the blood, and a cessation of vital functions, such as respiration and pulsation.

Defendant In a criminal action, the party charged with a crime.

Defraud To practice fraud; to cheat or trick; to deprive a person of property by fraud, deceit, or artifice.

Degree In criminal law, the term denotes a division or classification of one specific crime into several grades of guilt, according to the circumstances attending its commission.

Delinquency Failure, omission, violation of duty; state or condition of one who fails to perform his/her duty; synonymous with misconduct and offense.

Demeanor One who deposes to the truth of certain facts; one who gives testimony under oath that is reduced to writing; also, outward appearance or behavior.

Deposition The testimony of a witness not taken in open court, in writing and duly authenticated, and intended to be used at the trial of an action in court; subject to cross-examination.

Detain To keep in custody.

Direct Evidence A means of proof that tends to show the existence of a fact in question, without the intervention of the proof of any other fact; distinguished from circumstantial evidence, which is often called "indirect."

Disorderly Conduct A term of loose and indefinite meaning (except as occasionally defined in statutes), but generally signifying any behavior that is contrary to law, and more particularly, that tends to disturb the public peace or decorum, scandalize the community, or shock the public sense of morality.

Double Jeopardy The act of being subjected to a second prosecution for a crime for which the defendant has once been prosecuted and duly convicted or acquitted. This is barred by the Constitution of the United States, Fifth Amendment.

Doubt Uncertainty of mind; the absence of a settled conviction or opinion.

Due Process of Law The regular course of administration of law through courts of justice.

Duress Unlawful constraint exercised upon a person whereby that person is forced to perform some act that he/she otherwise would not have done. Duress may also include the same injuries, threats, or restraint exercised upon the person's family.

E

Entrapment The act of officers or agents of the government inducing a person to commit a crime not contemplated by that person, for the purpose of instituting a criminal prosecution against him/her.

Ethical Of or relating to moral action, motive, or character, as ethical emotion; also, pertaining to moral feelings, duties, or conduct; professionally right or befitting; conforming to professional standards of conduct.

Evidence The means by which any alleged fact, the truth of which is submitted to investigation, is established or disproved.

Expert Evidence Testimony given pertaining to some scientific, technical, or professional matter by experts, such as those persons qualified to speak authoritatively due to their special training, skill, familiarity with a subject.

Extortion The obtaining of property from another, with his/her consent, induced by a wrongful use of force or fear, or considered an official right.

Extradition The surrender by one state to another of an individual accused or convicted of an offense outside that individual's own territory and within the territorial jurisdiction of the other, which, being competent to try and punish the individual, demands the surrender.

F

Fabricate To invent; to devise falsely.

False Pretenses Deliberate misrepresentation of existing facts or conditions whereby a person obtains another's money, goods, or property.

Felon A person who commits a felony.

Felony A crime of a graver or more serious nature than one designated as a misdemeanor; generally, an offense punishable by death or imprisonment in a state prison.

Forensic Medicine Medical jurisprudence, as it is also called, the science that teaches the application of every branch of medical knowledge to the purposes of the law; its limits are, on the one hand, the requirements of the law, and, on the other, the whole range of medicine.

Forgery The act or crime of false making or material altering, with intent to defraud.

Fraud A generic term embracing all multifarious means that human ingenuity can devise, and that are resorted to by one individual to gain advantage over another by false suggestions or by suppression of truth; includes all surprise, trick, cunning, dissembling, and any unfair means by which another is cheated.

Frisk The running of hands rapidly over another's person, as distinguished from search, which is to strip and examine one more thoroughly.

Fruits of Crime In the law of evidence, material objects acquired by means and in consequence of the commission of crime, and sometimes constituting the subject matter of the crime.

Fugitive One who flees; always used in law with the implication of flight, evasion, or escape from some duty or penalty or from the consequences of a misdeed.

G

Graft The popular meaning is the fraudulent obtaining of money, position, etc., by dishonest or questionable means, as by taking advantage of one's official position; also, anything thus gained.

Guilty Having committed a crime; the word used by a prisoner in pleading to the indictment when the prisoner confesses the crime of which he/she is charged, and by the jury in convicting.

H

Hearing In criminal law, the examination of a prisoner charged with a crime, and of the witnesses for the accused.

Hearsay Evidence not derived from the personal knowledge of the witness, but from the mere repetition of what the witness has heard others say; generally inadmissible except in certain specified circumstances.

Homicide The killing of one human being by the act, procurement, or omission of another. Homicide is not necessarily a crime. It is a necessary ingredient of the crimes of murder and manslaughter, but there are other cases (such as an accident) where homicide may be committed without criminal intent and without criminal consequences. The term *homicide* is neutral; while it describes the act, it pronounces no judgment on its moral or legal quality.

Hung Jury A jury so irreconcilably divided in opinion that it cannot agree on any verdict.

I

Identification Proof of identity; the proving that a person, subject, or article before the court is the very same that he/she or it is alleged, charged, or reputed to be.

Illegal Not authorized by law, unlawful.

Immoral Contrary to good morals; inconsistent with the rules and principles of morality; inimical to public welfare according to the standards of a given community, as expressed in law or otherwise.

Immunity A particular privilege; freedom from duty or penalty.

Imprison To put in a prison; to put in a place of confinement; to confine a person, or restrain that person's liberty in any way.

Inadmissible That which, under the established rules of law, cannot be admitted or received.

Incriminate To charge with a crime; to expose to an accusation or charge of a crime; to involve oneself or another in a criminal prosecution or the danger thereof, as in the rule that a witness is not bound to give testimony that would tend to incriminate that witness.

Indictment An accusation in writing, presented by a grand jury to a competent court, charging a person named therein with a crime.

Insane Of unsound mind; deranged, disordered, or diseased in mind.

Insubordination Disobedience to constituted authority; refusal to obey lawful order of a superior officer.

Integrity As occasionally used in statutes prescribing the qualifications of public officers, etc., this term means soundness of moral character and principle, as shown by one person dealing with others, and fidelity and honesty in discharge of trusts; synonymous with *probity, honesty,* and *uprightness.*

Intent Design, resolve, or determination with which a person acts; being a state of mind, it is rarely susceptible of direct proof, but must ordinarily be inferred from the facts. Intent shows the presence of will in the act that consummates a crime.

Intoxicated Drunk.

Investigation The following up, step by step, by patient inquiry or observation; the tracing or tracking mentally; the examining and inquiring into with care and accuracy; the taking of evidence; a legal inquiry.

Involuntary Without will or power of choice; opposed to volition or desire; an act is involuntary when performed under duress.

J

Jail A building designated by law, or regularly used, for the confinement of persons held in lawful custody.

Jurisdiction Sphere of authority; area of legal operation.

Justifiable Rightful; warranted or sanctioned by law.

K

Knowingly With knowledge; consciously, intelligently, willfully, intentionally. The word signifies a perception of facts necessary to make a crime.

L

Larceny Illegally taking away the possessions of someone else.

Latent Hidden; concealed; not apparent; dormant, as a *latent* fingerprint.

Law That which is laid down, ordained, or established; that which must be obeyed and followed by citizens, subject to sanctions or legal consequences; rule of conduct prescribed by the lawmaking body of state.

Legal Evidence A broad general term indicating all admissible evidence, including oral and documentary, but with a further implication that it must tend reasonably and substantially to prove the point, not to raise a mere suspicion or conjecture.

Lie Detector A machine that records by a needle on a graph varying emotional disturbances when the subject answers questions truthfully or falsely, as indicated by fluctuations in blood pressure, respiration, or perspiration; polygraph.

M

Magistrate An officer with the power to issue a warrant of arrest for a person charged with a crime.

Mala Bad; evil; wrongful.

Mala in Se Acts that are wrong in themselves; acts that are morally wrong; offenses against one's conscience.

Mala Prohibita Prohibited wrongs or offenses; acts that are made offenses by positive laws and prohibited as such.

Malfeasance Evildoing; bad conduct; the commission of some act that is positively unlawful; the doing of an act that is completely wrongful and unlawful; a comprehensive term including any wrongful conduct that affects, interrupts, or interferes with the performance of official duties.

Mandatory Containing a command; imperative.

Marshal An officer in the organization of the federal judicial system whose duties are similar to those of a sheriff. The officer must execute the process of the United States courts within the district for which that officer is appointed.

Material Evidence That which is relevant and goes to the substantial matters in dispute, or has a legitimate and effective influence or bearing on the decision of a case.

Mens Rea A guilty mind; a guilty or wrongful purpose; a criminal intent.

Misconduct A transgression of some established and definite rule of action; a forbidden act; a dereliction from duty; unlawful behavior; that which is willful in character.

Misdemeanor An offense less serious than a felony and generally punishable by fine or imprisonment in a penitentiary.

Mistrial An erroneous, invalid, or worthless trial; a trial of an action that cannot stand in law because of lack of jurisdiction, or a wrong drawing of jurors, or disregard of some other fundamental requisite.

Mitigating Circumstances Those circumstances that do not constitute a justification or excuse of the offense in question, but that, in fairness and mercy, may be considered as extenuating or reducing the degree of moral culpability.

Morgue A place where the bodies of persons found dead are kept for a limited time and exposed to view so that they may be identified.

Murder The unlawful killing of a human being by another with malice aforethought, either expressed or implied.

N

Naturalize To confer citizenship upon an alien; to give to a foreigner the same rights and privileges of a native citizen or subject.

Negligence The omission to do something that a reasonable person, guided by those ordinary considerations that ordinarily regulate human affairs, would do, or the doing of something that a reasonable or prudent person would not do.

Not Guilty A plea of general issue in criminal prosecutions; verdict in criminal cases where the jury acquits the defendant.

O

Obstruct To hinder or prevent from progress; to check; to stop; also to retard the progress of; to make the accomplishment of an act difficult and slow; to interpose impediments, to the hindrance or frustration of some act or service, as to obstruct officers in the execution of their duty.

Officer The incumbent of an office; one who is charged by a superior power (and particularly by government) with the power and duty to exercise certain functions.

Overt Open; manifest; public; action that is distinguished from thought.

P

Pathology In medical jurisprudence, the science or doctrine of diseases; that part of medicine that explains the nature of diseases, their causes, and their symptoms.

Peace Officers Term that generally includes sheriffs and their deputies, constables, members of the police forces of cities, and other officers whose duty it is to enforce and preserve the public peace.

Penal Laws Those laws that specify the persons who are capable of committing crimes; laws that specify those liable to punishment therefor; laws that define the nature of the various crimes and that prescribe the kind and measure of punishment to be inflicted for each crime.

Perjury In criminal law, the willful assertion as to a matter of fact, opinion, belief, or knowledge made by a witness in a judicial proceeding as part of that witness's evidence, either upon oath or in any form allowed by law to and known by such witness to be false.

Perpetrator Someone who commits a crime.

Police That branch of the administrative machinery of government that is charged with the preservation of public order and tranquility, the promotion of the public health, safety, and morals, and the prevention and detection of crimes.

Police Power That inherent and absolute power in state over persons and property that enables the people to prohibit all things inimical to comfort, safety, health, and welfare of society.

Possess To have control of; to own.

Postmortem After death; a term usually applied to an autopsy or examination of a dead body to ascertain the cause of death.

Premeditate To think of an act beforehand; to contrive and design; to plot or lay plans for the execution of a purpose.

Premeditation The act of meditating in advance; deliberation upon a contemplated act; plotting or contriving; a design formed to do something before it is done; a prior determination to do and act, but such determination need not exist for any particular period before it is carried out.

Premises Property.

Prima Facie Case A case that will suffice until contradicted and overcome by other evidence; a case that has proceeded upon sufficient proof to that stage where it will support the verdict if evidence to the contrary is disregarded.

Prison A penal institution, run by the state, to which are sentenced those convicted of felonies.

Prisoner One who is deprived of his/her liberty; one under arrest and confined upon a charge of violating the law.

Probable Cause Reasonable cause. There is no fixed formula for the determination of probable cause. Probable cause is held to exist where the facts and circumstances within the arresting officer's knowledge and of which the officer has reasonably trustworthy information are sufficient in themselves to warrant a belief that an offense has been or is being committed. Simply stated, probable cause may be defined as reasonable grounds for the belief of guilt.

Probation Trial; test; the act of proving; in modern criminal administration, allowing a person convicted of an offense to go free, under a suspension of sentence, during good behavior, and generally under the supervision or guardianship of a probation officer.

Probation Officer An officer of the court who assists in the administration of the probation system for offenders against the criminal laws.

Prohibit To forbid by law; to prevent; not synonymous with *regulate*.

Proof The effect of evidence; the establishment of a fact by evidence.

Prosecute To follow up; to carry on an action or other judicial proceeding; to proceed against a person criminally. To prosecute an action is not merely to commence it, but includes following it to an ultimate conclusion.

Punishment In criminal law, any pain, penalty, suffering, or confinement inflicted upon a person by the authority of the law and the judgment and sentence of a court, for some crime or offense committed by that person, or for his/her omission of a duty enjoined by law. *Cruel and unusual punishment:* Such punishment that would not be known to the common law; also any punishment that would shock the moral sense of the community.

R

Real Evidence Evidence furnished by things themselves, on view or inspection, as distinguished from a description of them by the words of a witness, such as the weapons or instruments used in a crime, and other inanimate objects, and evidence of the physical appearance of a place (crime scene) as obtained by a jury when taken to view it.

Reasonable Doubt The state of the case that, after the comparison and consideration of all the evidence, leaves the minds of the jurors in a condition in which they cannot say they feel an abiding conviction to a moral certainty of the truth of the charge. If, upon proof, there is reasonable doubt remaining, the accused is entitled to an acquittal. A reasonable doubt would cause a reasonable and prudent person to pause and hesitate to act upon the truth of the matter charged.

Reckless Driving Operation of a motor vehicle manifesting reckless disregard of possible consequences and indifference to the rights of others.

Resisting an Officer In criminal law, the offense of obstructing, opposing, and endeavoring to prevent (with or without actual force) a peace officer in the execution of a writ or in the lawful discharge of the officer's duty while making an arrest or otherwise enforcing the peace.

Rigor Mortis In medical jurisprudence, a rigidity or stiffening of the muscular tissue and joints of the body that occurs at varied intervals after death, but usually within a few hours, and that is one of the recognized tests of death.

Robbery Forcible stealing.

S

Search In criminal law, an examination of someone's house or other buildings or premises, or of one's person, with a view to the discovery of contraband or illicit or stolen property, or some evidence of guilt to be used in the prosecution of a criminal action for some crime or offense with which a person is charged.

Search Warrant An order in writing in the name of the people, signed by a judge, justice, or magistrate of a court of criminal jurisdiction, directed to a peace officer, commanding the officer to search for personal property and bring it before the judge, justice, or magistrate.

Sentence The judgment formally pronounced by the court or judge upon the defendant after conviction in a criminal prosecution, awarding the punishment to be inflicted; judgment formally declaring to the accused the legal consequences of guilt to which the accused has confessed or of which the accused has been convicted.

Statute An act of the legislature declaring, commanding, or prohibiting something; a particular law enacted and established by the will of the legislative department of government.

Subordinate Placed in a lower order, class, or rank; occupying a lower position in a regular descending series.

Subpoena A document requiring a witness to appear and give testimony, commanding that the witness appear before a court or magistrate, under a penalty therein mentioned.

Subdue To overpower.

Superior One who has a right to command; one who holds a superior rank.

Suspect To have a slight or even vague idea concerning, not necessarily involving, knowledge or belief or likelihood; also used to designate the person wanted for the commission of a crime.

T

Testify To bear witness; to give evidence as a witness; to make a solemn declaration, under oath or affirmation in a judicial inquiry for the purpose of establishing or proving some fact.

Trial A judicial examination, in accordance with the law of the land, of a cause, either civil or criminal, of the issues between parties, whether of law or fact, before a court that has jurisdiction over it.

U

Unwarranted Unauthorized.

V

Venue The place or county in which an injury is declared to have been done, or in fact is declared to have happened; also, the county in which an action or prosecution is brought for trial, and that is to furnish the panel of jurors.

Verdict The formal and unanimous decision or finding by a jury, impaneled and sworn for the trial of a cause, and reported to the court, upon the matters or questions duly submitted to them at the trial.

Victimize To make someone suffer.

Violation Breaking of a law.

W

Waiver The intentional or voluntary relinquishment of a known right.

Warrant A writ or precept from a competent authority in pursuance of law, directing the performance of an act, and addressed to an officer or person competent to perform the act, and affording that person protection from damage, if he/she does it.

Witness To subscribe one's name to a document for the purpose of attesting its authenticity, and proving its execution, if required, by bearing witness thereto. In general, one who, being present, personally sees or beholds a thing; a spectator, or eyewitness; one who testifies to what he/she has seen or heard.

THE AUTHORS

DONALD B. HUTTON

Donald B. Hutton has served in a variety of law enforcement positions since 1979, has conducted field research over the years for this book by progressively working for several different law enforcement agencies: New York State Office of Inspector General, Delaware & Hudson Railroad Police Department, United States Department of Veterans Affairs Police, Coxsackie Police Department, and U.S. Customs Service. In addition, Mr. Hutton served in the U.S. Coast Guard Reserves in the capacities of Pollution Investigator and Special Agent. He has a master's degree in Criminal Justice from Buffalo State College. Mr. Hutton is also author of Barron's *Guide to Military Careers* (1998) and the novel, *A Deep Blue Sounding: Dark Voyage with the U.S. Coast Guard* (2000).

ANNA MYDLARZ

Anna Mydlarz has been a career law enforcement officer with the Buffalo Police Department since 1982. She has had experience in patrol work, the Burglary Task Force, Vice Squad, and as a detective with the Narcotics Squad. Ms. Mydlarz now serves in the Buffalo Department's Communication Crime Unit, which investigates telephone harassment, pornography, and computer crimes.